The Treacherous Imagination

The Treacherous Imagination

INTIMACY, ETHICS, AND AUTOBIOGRAPHICAL FICTION

Robert McGill

THE OHIO STATE UNIVERSITY PRESS · COLUMBUS

Copyright © 2013 by The Ohio State University.
All rights reserved.

Library of Congress Cataloging-in-Publication Data

McGill, Robert, 1976–
The treacherous imagination : intimacy, ethics, and autobiographical fiction / Robert McGill.
p. cm.
Includes bibliographical references and index.
ISBN 978-0-8142-1231-8 (cloth : alk. paper) — ISBN 978-0-8142-9333-1 (cd)
1. Autobiographical fiction—History and criticism. 2. Ethics in literature. 3. Sexual ethics in literature. I. Title.
PN3448.A8M43 2013
809.3'82—dc23
2013011171

Cover design by Mary Ann Smith
Type set in Adobe Sabon

♾ The paper used in this publication meets the minimum requirements of the American National Standard for Information Sciences—Permanence of Paper for Printed Library Materials. ANSI Z39.48-1992.

9   8   7   6   5   4   3   2   1

For Bruce, David, and Marcy McGill

Contents

Preface   ix
Acknowledgments   xiii

INTRODUCTION   1
    Infidelity, Fiction, and Desire   3
    Defining Autobiographical Fiction   5
    Treacherous Ethics   11

1   A SHORT HISTORY OF TRANSGRESSION   20
    Early Libels and Denials   22
    The Private Life of Novels   26
    Nineteenth-Century Publicity   31
    Modernism and the Confessional Age   35
    The Scandal of Confessional Poetry   41

2   BIOGRAPHICAL DESIRE   47
    Elizabeth Smart and Confessional Culture   50
    Intimacy with the Absent Author   60
    Biographical Reading as Play   66
    Philip Roth's Fictional Selves   70
    Moralizing Confessional Culture   76

3	**FICTION'S BETRAYALS, INTIMACY'S TRIALS**	**83**
	Mortification and Uncanny Doubles	86
	Family and Fantasy in A. S. Byatt's *The Game*	89
	Authorial Detachment and Impositions	95
	Metafiction's Turn of the Screw	100
	Hanif Kureishi and the Trouble with Intimacy	106
	The Problem of Rebel Privilege	112
4	**IN BED WITH AN AUTHOR**	**117**
	Alice Munro and the Hazards of Protest	120
	Claire Bloom and the Public Machine	129
	How to Use People	133
	Reshaping Intimacy, Rebelling Together	137
	An Ethics of Uncertainty	145

CONCLUSION   150

Works Cited   *155*
Index   *168*

Preface

> All writing is autobiography: everything that you write, including criticism and fiction, writes you as you write it.
>
> —J. M. Coetzee, *Doubling the Point* 18

> Giving the public details about oneself is a bourgeois temptation that I have always resisted.
>
> —Gustave Flaubert (qtd. in Barnes, *Flaubert's* 94)

A few weeks after beginning to work on this book and think more carefully than I had about the ethics of authors drawing on private life in fiction, I awoke one morning to find a single phrase scrawled on the notepad beside my bed: "*The pleasures of infidelity.*" The words were in my handwriting, although I did not remember recording them. Apparently an idea had occurred to me in the night, but I could not be entirely sure that the phrase referred to my research. Even if it did, I was not reassured by the possibility that overnight my brain had been mulling the question of fiction's treacheries. I was skeptical about the soundness of insights emerging from dreams, with their blend of fantasy and facts as well as their betrayal of unconscious desires. If this was to become my method for generating ideas, I worried, my work on autobiographical fiction might end up speaking autobiographically in unintended ways. Staring at the note, I also wondered whether my partner, arising earlier, had seen it, and if so, what she had thought. As I understood things, we were in a monogamous relationship, yet anyone who saw such a note on my bedside table could be forgiven for wondering otherwise. In

Louise DeSalvo's *Adultery*, the author warns her audience that they may find themselves having unfaithful thoughts after reading her book; she observes that people can go through a "cycle of reading about adultery, and committing adultery, and writing about adultery" (4). The phrase on my notepad similarly suggested that I was treading dangerous ground by taking an interest in fiction's betrayals. But as the following chapters show, it can also be dangerous to ignore the possibility of infidelity and avoid exploring the connections between reality and imagination. Those who insist on maintaining a strict border between the two are bound to end up confused and distraught as fantasy irrupts in their lives, not least when it is channeled through novels and short stories. Such people are also apt to become incensed when others traverse the border that they themselves adamantly defend.

As I began my exploration of this border, I had the impression that fiction offends authors' closest relations with some frequency. Nevertheless, discussions of actual cases seemed relegated to the back corner of literary studies, with brief references made to examples such as Charles Dickens's fictionalization of his friend Leigh Hunt as Harold Skimpole in *Bleak House*. When I told acquaintances what I was doing, I discovered that at the level of gossip, things were different. Everyone knew somebody in Hunt's position, and everyone was ready to tell me the story of what had transpired. If I had a predilection for real-life case studies, I would find no lack of examples from which to choose, no scarcity of people eager to describe scandalous fictional appropriations. This revelation was both exciting and worrisome. I was glad that my chosen terrain of inquiry was so fertile, but I was less than pleased at the notion that I might become a vessel for all these stories. Despite my interest in the ethical issues involved, I also held the belief that talking about authors' personal lives in relation to their texts was unseemly. This belief was not due to any particular allegiance to New Critical or poststructuralist tenets. Rather, it was paradoxically out of deference to what I took to be the preferences of authors: surely, I thought, they would want people to study their fiction, not their lives. However, the work of writers such as Alice Munro, Henry Miller, and Philip Roth suggests that the very opposition of life to fiction is unstable and that there is a vital, unavoidable relation between authors and their texts, especially in the present day. As I argue in the following pages, it is hard to imagine a literary culture in a liberal, capitalist society that does not link authors' names to their writing or their personal lives to their literature, and it is even harder to imagine how such linkages could fail to create ethical complications.

On those occasions when I disclosed my research topic, people's desire to read fiction biographically became amply evident, and not simply in virtue of the tales they offered about authors' iniquities. Rather, those who knew that I had recently published a novel, *The Mysteries,* were not afraid to ask whether my interest in fiction's ethics emerged from the experience of writing that book. In fact, I had decided to investigate the subject before conceiving of *The Mysteries,* but my lines of inquiry quickly developed in conjunction with the novel's reception. For instance, although the plot and characters of *The Mysteries* are invented, the small town described in the novel was inspired by the village of Wiarton where I had grown up, and the topographical resemblance caused problems. Some readers familiar with Wiarton took the resemblance to signal that the book was a *roman à clef,* while others were unsettled by the fact that I seemed to have denuded a Wiarton-like place of its real inhabitants and replaced them with various unsavory characters. My mother, still living in the area, worried that the book offered too negative a portrayal of the region. I responded that it was a novel about a fictive place, not a tourist brochure for Wiarton. She agreed that it was certainly not the latter.

In the end, various Wiartonians did identify parallels between *The Mysteries* and real life, but they were not parallels I could have predicted. For instance, people told me how accurately I had portrayed the new owner of a local convenience store, although in fact I had not known there *was* a new convenience store owner. There was also an argument among my extended family members about whether the blurry photograph on the novel's cover was of my mother or my cousin (in fact, it was of neither of them). My father, appreciating the humor in such referential scavenger hunting, reminded me that his childhood nickname had been "Tiger" and declared himself the model for the tiger in my book. A friend of mine who is a champion whistler—yes, there are such championships—wondered whether a short reference to a character whistling in *The Mysteries* was a nod to him. And at readings that I gave, the most common question asked of me was: "Is your novel based on real people?" There was usually an air of disappointment when I said no. In retrospect, a more interesting response on my part would have been to ask in turn: "Why do you care?" That question, posed not rhetorically but genuinely, and applied to biographical curiosity about fiction more broadly, is one of the present book's impetuses. It has often been said by authors that they write the kinds of stories they would want to read. This book sets out to be one I have wanted to read as a critic of novels and a writer of them; as someone who guards his privacy but has published fiction about private life and, for that matter, is not above reading about literary scandals involving other people. If there are tensions, if not outright contradictions, in such practices, then the necessity of such a book is clear. Among the questions that need to be asked are: To what extent has fiction always offended author's intimates? How might intimacy itself have changed over time? What strategies have been adopted to deal with conflicts arising from fiction, and why do these strategies so often fail? In addressing these questions, I aim to contextualize people's confusion and curiosity about autobiographical fiction while developing a conceptual framework and vocabulary to describe how such fiction functions in contemporary culture. I also wish to suggest various alternatives for ethical action that are open to authors and their intimates, not least in terms of revising conceptions and practices of intimacy itself.

Acknowledgments

My thanks to Fiona Coll, Julia Markovits, David McGill, and Siobhan Phillips, who were perceptive readers of this book. Thanks also to two anonymous readers at The Ohio State University Press for their feedback, to Maggie Diehl for her fine copyediting, and to Sandy Crooms for her sure editorial hand. Further help was provided along the way by Donna Bennett, Alan Bewell, Nicholas Bradley, Russell Brown, Brian Corman, John Fraser, Marlene Goldman, Elizabeth Harvey, Richard Holmes, Daniel Justice, John Kelly, George Kovacs, Andrew Lesk, Naomi Morgenstern, Nick Mount, Reecia Orzeck, William Robins, Sidonie Smith, Sam Solecki, Rosemary Sullivan, and John Thieme. Sara Salih's support was invaluable. Linda Hutcheon's generosity was boundless. Thanks to Eleanor Wachtel for permission to quote from her unpublished letter, and to Catherine Hobbs at Library and Archives Canada for her assistance with my research there.

Parts of chapters 2 and 4 have been published in different form in *English Studies in Canada* 33.3 and *University of Toronto Quarterly* 76.3, respectively. I have revisited the material with the kind permission of *ESC* and the University of Toronto Press (www.utpjournals.com, © University of Toronto Press Incorporated 2007). Meanwhile, for their financial support, thanks to the Chancellor Jackman Program in the Humanities at the University of Toronto; Massey College; the Social Sciences and Humanities Research Council of Canada; the Harvard Society of Fellows; the University of Toronto Department of English; and the University of Toronto Humanities Centre.

Introduction

> "Do you write about real people?" . . . "Did those things really happen?" . . . People go on asking these same questions because the subject really does interest and bewilder them. It would seem to be quite true that they don't know what fiction is.
>
> And how could they know, when what it is, is changing all the time, and we differ among ourselves, and we don't really try to explain because it is too difficult?
>
> —Alice Munro, "What Is Real" 223

> The imagination gets to work. It is not a pleasant sight. The imagination is pitiless, brutal and cruel. It lacks common decency, discretion, manners, loyalty—yes, it lacks even compassion. The imagination has a conscience all its own; you wouldn't want it as a friend.
>
> —Philip Roth, National Book Critics Circle Award Acceptance Speech 3

Imagine an author who agrees to a meeting with his former lover. At this meeting she tells him she recognizes herself as a character in one of his novels. She accuses him of violating their prior intimacy by appropriating private conversations that were joint property and publicizing details that she thought would remain confidential. She says mutual acquaintances who have read the novel are offended on her behalf. She tells him he has borrowed too closely from the facts in certain respects, while in others he has been unfaithful to them, distorting them cruelly and misrepresenting her. This skewed portrait suggests to her that he had a warped perception of her even during their relationship and that he has displaced his own problems onto the fictional version of her. Moreover, she suspects he wrote the novel as an act of revenge. She tells him she feels abused. In response, the author defends himself by saying that his novel had many sources of inspiration and that the character with whom she identifies was not necessarily based on her. He also claims that fiction has a transformative effect, so her putative alter ego should not be taken as a reflection of his real opinions about her. He says his purposes in writing fiction are not interpersonal, much less vindictive, and her sense of having been abused by him is really a displaced resentment of other people who have abused her in more literal ways. She fails to be convinced by these arguments, and the two of them reach a stalemate. Still, they continue to feel an intimacy with one another, and they end up sleeping together one more time. Then, as the author returns home to his family, he feels compelled to jot down notes about the day's encounter, knowing that soon he will turn them into yet another fiction, further betraying both his current wife and his ex-lover, but also managing literally to have the last word in the earlier argument.

This narrative is related in "That Was Then," a short story by the British writer Hanif Kureishi that appeared in his 1999 collection, *Midnight All Day*. The fact that Kureishi himself had been publicly rebuked by his ex-partner, Tracey Scoffield, the previous year for fictionalizing their relationship in his novel *Intimacy* does not mean one should take "That Was Then" to be autobiographical, but it does suggest that the conflict depicted in Kureishi's story is not uncommon and that the relationship between life and fiction is often contentious, especially in the case of autobiographical fiction: that is, narrative prose labeled as fiction but identified as drawing significantly on its author's life. Most people would agree that all writers of fiction make use of their lives in some way, but certain authors do so more conspicuously than others. When they do, frequently they draw on the lives of others as well, and often friends, lovers, and family members take umbrage when they find themselves transfigured, however obliquely, into literary characters without their collaboration or consent. Accordingly, the authors' fiction becomes bound up in complicated ways with intimacy, infidelity, ethics, and desire. In "That Was Then," the writer-protagonist's ex-lover believes authors are supposed to be "wise, with enough honesty, bravery and conscience for us all" (71), but they are sometimes accused of libeling their intimates and invading their privacy. Given these possible transgressions, authors must weigh their desire for self-expression against the wishes of their closest relations. However, when a published fiction causes offense, nuanced consideration of the matter is often neglected in the ensuing exchange of accusation and self-justification.

A more complex account of autobiographical fiction's production and reception is needed, one that considers the perspectives of writers and their alleged victims, as well as the reading habits of a culture that is eager to view fictional stories as the veiled confessions of their authors. Autobiographical fiction betrays much about why people read literature, how they talk about it, and how they discipline it through laws as well as informal moral codes. An investigation into why some individuals become upset when they see themselves represented in fiction also needs to examine such broader issues as the status of authors in society and the challenges facing intimacy in a confessional age. Accordingly, this book explores autobiographical fiction not to condemn or celebrate it but to consider the discourse of ethics surrounding it, a discourse that configures such fiction alternately as an injurious failure of authorial responsibility and as a heroic infidelity to stifling norms of decorum.

INFIDELITY, FICTION, AND DESIRE

In a sense, all writing is a betrayal, not least of its authors. As an act of communication, to write is to "betray" oneself in the sense of the word's root, *tradere*, meaning "to hand over." It is a surrender of words to the page and, by extension, to readers, a relinquishment of private thought into the public medium of print. Once there, writing betrays the writer again through language's proliferating meanings. What is more, from a psychoanalytic perspective, writing inevitably betrays the authorial mind, which unwittingly freights every sentence with the rumbles of the unconscious. In a culture that particularly values acts of confession, though, some texts are more traitorous than others. The "tell-all" memoir, for one, seems to traduce the intimacy of the author's closest relations by recounting experiences that were once privately shared. And when a story is labeled "fiction," frequently the sense of betrayal is only heightened: although names may be changed and details altered, in the eyes of the people who have been affronted, these transformations can be yet another infidelity—namely, to the truth. In fact, the violation is often double-edged: people are wounded by the invasion of privacy entailed in the details that are true, while they are equally hurt by what seems false, or "fictionalized." From their perspective, the very inventions that ostensibly cloak their identity also risk creating a defamatory impression of them in readers who identify them with their fictional counterparts.

For people like the ex-lover in "That Was Then," their literary doppelgängers can be equally upsetting insofar as they have been produced unilaterally in the wake of shared private experience, such that their authors appear to have been less participants in intimacy than observers of it, sufficiently detached and disloyal to depict their loved ones on the page. Given this appearance, it is not a surprise that descriptions of autobiographical fiction's betrayals often invoke the language of adultery. For many people, bonds of intimacy are predicated on exclusivity in terms of shared stories as well as shared experience; as a result, when such narrative monogamy is sacrificed for the public intimations of fiction, authors' seeming indifference to their intimates can be devastating. In fact, autobiographical fiction has also been described as a metaphorical rape. Taking that trope into account, this book considers whether there is something intrinsically sexual about the processes of reading and writing—something Roland Barthes suggests when he refers to "the reader's pleasure" as involving *jouissance*, with its connotations of orgasmic bliss (*Pleasure* 10)—as well as something intrinsically exploitative.

Central in answering this question are the role and character of desire. If intimates see authors of autobiographical fiction as unfaithful, the third party in the love triangle is the reader, and one needs to ask what kinds of intimacy and infidelity take place when authors "cheat" on their intimates with their audiences. For that reason, in the chapters that follow I develop an account of the various, sometimes conflicting desires that are expressed or disrupted by autobiographical fiction. In particular, readers of fiction often manifest what I call biographical desire: a desire to connect with authors through their texts, which are read in terms of their possible autobiographical content.[1] Authors are compelled to confront and satisfy this desire, even while they also exploit and confound it. As they do so, fiction has a tendency to turn flirtatious, proffering intimations that are both candid and coy. Along with authorial commentary in the mass media, fiction serves as a mediator in the phantasmatic relationship between authors and their audiences. A consequence is that the ethics of autobiographical fiction is closely related to its erotics, not to mention its semantics and commercial aspects. Attention to the history and mechanisms of the confessional culture in which author–reader relationships are carried out promises to facilitate a better understanding of the issues underlying instances when authors' fiction offends their intimates.

Among these issues are fiction's relationship to reality and authors' rights to use the lives of others in their work. Although both issues have

---

1. For a discussion of biographical desire that focuses on its manifestation in scholarly discourse, see McGill, "Biographical."

been considered separately by scholars—the first by philosophers, the second by critics of life writing—there are particular, compelling questions that are raised only when the issues come together in autobiographical fiction. For instance, at stake is the matter of whether authors have the right not merely to tell other people's stories, as in the case of memoirs and biographies, but also to transform them. Furthermore, while in nonfiction it is a given that the author's personal perspective has shaped the text's portraits of others, fiction can present an illusion of authorial detachment by ascribing opinions to some fictional narrator, causing the models for characters to feel frustrated by what seems to be a lack of accountability. Because authors of fiction can always claim their stories are not referential, intimates may worry further that they will be seen as tilting at windmills if they contest the narratives. There is also the risk that by identifying themselves as figures in fiction, they will only invite more extensive biographical readings of the text. Intimates may even feel frustrated or confused by the very labeling of the text as "fiction," a term sometimes associated with purely invented narratives. With an eye to such confusions, in this book I present a more rigorous vocabulary to discuss autobiographical fiction's infidelities. If the definitional and ethical issues attending such fiction are laid out more precisely, readers and writers alike will be better equipped to discuss them without talking past one another.

DEFINING AUTOBIOGRAPHICAL FICTION

The first point of vocabulary that merits attention is the term "autobiographical fiction." Above I have called autobiographical fiction "narrative prose labeled as fiction but identified as drawing significantly on its author's life," but this definition requires elaboration, not least with regard to the definition of "fiction" itself. In a certain sense, all literary texts are fictional, insofar as they are all discursive constructions—not the world but representations of it. What is more, critics have observed that nonfictional forms such as autobiography involve "fictions" in the sense that they include "lapses of memory, errors, involuntary distortions, etc." (Lejeune 22).[2] However, to call all texts "fiction" is to fail in providing an account of how the distinction between fiction and nonfiction shapes readers' approaches to texts. One needs to be able to explain why readers of

---

2. See also Timothy Dow Adams's *Telling Lies in Modern American Autobiography*, Paul John Eakin's *Fictions in Autobiography*, and Gunnthorunn Gudmundsdottir's *Borderlines: Autobiography and Fiction in Postmodern Life Writing*.

James Frey's bestselling memoir *A Million Little Pieces* were so incensed to discover in 2006 that experiences recounted in his book never actually happened, even while the same readers were no doubt perfectly content to accept that the events of Stieg Larsson's novel *The Girl with the Dragon Tattoo* were likewise invented. Therefore, rather than referring to all texts as "fictional" in virtue of their status as representation, it is more appropriate and precise to describe as "fictive" those aspects of texts that are imagined and not referential. Meanwhile, "fiction" can be reserved for a narrower use: that is, to name the category of prose texts that are granted the prerogative to be nonreferential or counterfactual in some respects, even as they may contain much factuality and truth. Generic contracts as to the limits of invention do arise between authors of fiction and their audiences—for example, most of Agatha Christie's readers would not countenance Bilbo Baggins appearing in Miss Marple's sitting room—but authors of fiction have a unique license to make things up.

Usually fiction is marked as such from the outset by some element of the apparatus accompanying the text: a publisher's blurb, for example, or a cataloging note—material that Gérard Genette calls "paratexts." In this book I will expand the application of Genette's term to refer to other kinds of authorial performance that supplement and comment upon literature, from interviews to literary readings. Like other paratexts, these performances play a crucial role in classifying a text and orienting readers toward it. This orientation is necessary because the "central" text is radically unstable, unable to adjudicate its own status as fiction or nonfiction.[3] For instance, at the intratextual level there is nothing to distinguish an autobiography by a real human being from a first-person autobiographical narrative by an imagined character.[4] As Philippe Lejeune argues, the only thing guaranteeing for readers the nonfictionality of the former is the "autobiographical pact" enacted by the correlation of the author's name with the name of the narrator (3). But as is clear from examples such as Philip Roth's novel *Operation Shylock,* in which the narrator claims to be the real Roth but has unlikely experiences that would cause any reader to question the story's authenticity, even this pact may be disrupted.[5] As a

---

3. Peter McCormick makes this point when he writes: "An identifying criterion for fictional discourse is authorial illocutionary intention. These intentions, however, are expressed in discourse about fictional works and not in fictional discourse itself. Neither textual properties nor generic notions can properly identify a discourse as fictional" (61).

4. Thomas F. Petruso calls such fictive narratives "pseudo-autobiography" (41).

5. Innumerable other books also pointedly resist a straightforward classification as fiction or nonfiction. For instance, Maxine Hong Kingston's *The Woman Warrior* and Georges Perec's *W, or the Memory of Childhood* present segments of autobiography next to nar-

result, suspicious readers inevitably rely on paratexts for confirmation of the text's referentiality. The role of paratexts in this regard indicates that they are not merely supplementary to fiction but intrinsic to the process of its signification. At the same time, the manner in which they orient readers toward texts is not always straightforward: in the case of autobiographical fiction, for instance, paratexts often encourage readers to accept the text as possibly nonreferential and also as significantly related to its author's life.

But how "significantly" autobiographical must fiction be for one to consider it autobiographical fiction? On the one hand, it is sometimes said that all fiction is autobiographical, at least insofar as it is an expression of its author's mind. On the other hand, a narrow definition might limit discussions of autobiographical fiction to *romans à clef* that are essentially memoirs with only the names changed. To broaden the definition slightly, one might point to the case of a novel such as Sylvia Plath's *The Bell Jar,* where nobody would dispute that the protagonist bears more than a passing resemblance to her author. If one considered such examples alone, it might be attractive to define autobiographical fiction as fiction that takes autobiographical form, narrating a life that resembles the author's own. Lejeune more or less follows this logic, defining the "autobiographical novel" as a fictional text "in which the reader has reason to suspect, from the resemblances that he thinks he sees, that there is identity of author and *protagonist*" (13). However, this definition does not accommodate texts that seem intriguingly autobiographical in other ways: for instance, J. M. Coetzee's book *Elizabeth Costello,* in which the South African male author's titular counterpart is an Australian female novelist and in which the strongest presumptive parallels between them are of philosophical perspective. Many writers lurk in their fiction with even greater obliquity, manifesting themselves through a line of dialogue, a scenic description, or a narrator's *aperçu*. For example, one might say that Raymond Carver's short story "Errand," about the death of Anton Chekhov, is autobiographical in a figurative rather than a literal manner and that Carver's depiction of the Russian writer is also a meditation on Carver's own literary

---

ratives that are obviously fictive. Meanwhile, a sufficient number of contemporary French authors have written referentially ambiguous autobiographical texts for critics to classify their work as a distinct genre, "autofiction." Lejeune has called such texts "phantasmatic," contending that they involve a pact in which the author declares, "This has meaning in relation to me, but is not I" (33). Often the implicit statement can be even more ambiguous, akin to saying, "This has meaning in relation to me, and it may represent some version of me." Neologism has been a popular device for inscribing the dual imaginative and referential aspects of such writing: for instance, Audre Lorde describes her autobiographical narrative *Zami* as a "biomythography."

career, influences, and mortality. To include such a story under the rubric of "autobiographical fiction" might seem to throw open the definitional doors so wide as to weaken the usefulness of the term, but, conversely, to exclude this species of text risks impoverishing the notion of what counts as autobiographical.

If a definition of autobiographical fiction in terms of its content will not suffice, it may be tempting to accord authors the right to decide whether their texts should be considered autobiographical. After all, no one is in a better position to know the extent to which a particular fiction is based in personal experience. No doubt due to such reasoning, authors are customarily granted the prerogative to categorize their texts as fiction or nonfiction, and if they do declare their fiction to be autobiographical, the texts are usually treated as such. However, even authors' authority can be contested. For instance, after Tracey Scoffield read Hanif Kureishi's *Intimacy,* she proclaimed it to be "not merely a novel. You may as well call it a fish. Nobody believes that it's just pure fiction" (qtd. in Johnston 8). When quoted in *The Observer,* this comment spurred a debate in the British press over the referential character of fiction in general and of *Intimacy* in particular. It would seem that for authors to identify their fiction as self-referential is sufficient but not necessary for the text to be considered autobiographical fiction.

Because a text's fictionality can often be established only by appeals beyond the text itself, and because authors' claims about the counterfactual character of their works can be contested, it seems appropriate to think of autobiographical fiction, like fiction in general, not as a formal quality but as a hermeneutic orientation toward a text. In other words, "autobiographical fiction" is a lens through which one reads. Peter Lamarque and Stein Haugom Olsen argue along these lines in asserting that a text's fictionality is determined by whether its readers assume a "fictional stance," consenting to the author's implicit request that they suspend their disbelief and allow the text to depart from reality (32).[6] In the case of autobiographical fiction, readers assume a similar stance, but not necessarily one that follows the author's intentions. For some readers—especially the intimates of authors who, like Tracey Scoffield, find their alter egos occupying a text—it can be impossible to view the text as

---

6. Lejeune has similarly identified a *"fictional pact"* (14), while Genette refers to "the bilateral contract" that exists between authors and readers of fiction (182), and H. Porter Abbott observes that "the difference . . . between an autobiography and a novel lies not in the factuality of one and the fictiveness of the other but in different orientations toward the text they elicit in the reader" (603).

"fiction" at all, insofar as they refuse to grant the author any imaginative license. Others may follow the model of reading supplied by Lamarque and Olsen, who argue that "the primary response to fiction *qua* fiction is concerned with internal relations of sense rather than external relations of reference" (122–23). For most people, though, to see a text as autobiographical fiction is to see it doubly, with an eye to both its participation in make-believe and its possible echoes of the author's life. Every time a work of fiction is read, there is the possibility that to some degree it will be approached in this doubled manner.

Although autobiographical fiction so conceived is an expansive category insofar as it applies potentially to all texts, in practice it is a strongly delimiting one that brings into focus particular issues, such as fiction's relationship to its authors and those authors' right to draw on the lives of people they know personally. In this respect, autobiographical fiction both parallels and differs from several other types of literature—historical fiction and documentary fiction, among them—that similarly incorporate both the factual and the imaginative. For instance, in the eyes of some, historical fiction threatens dangerously to mix facts not only with hypotheses but with outright fabrications, thereby effacing the "real" historical record, and descendants of the figures represented in such fiction may feel affronted if their forbears are rendered in ways they find exploitative or defamatory. Likewise, people may take offense if an author of documentary fiction has told their story without consulting them. And it is not uncommon for members of a particular community—for example, a religion or a nation—to be upset if a fiction portrays one of their members in a manner that seems to cast a poor light on the group as a whole. For instance, consider people's charges against Philip Roth that he was a "self-hating Jew" because they disliked his depictions of Jewish characters. Roth reflects on this phenomenon in his novel *The Counterlife*, where the author Zuckerman is told that because of his similar fictional creations, "Everyone is now prepared to listen to all kinds of zany, burlesque views of Jews" (157). An even stronger reaction greeted the French author Pierre Jourde, who in 2005 was attacked by inhabitants of the village where he summered after they encountered his fictionalization of local life in the novel *Pays Perdu*. And a year later, Monica Ali was criticized for what some Bangladeshi Londoners saw as a misrepresentation of their community in her novel *Brick Lane*. The question of what responsibility authors of fiction have to such groups is a pressing one, especially in a literary culture where authors are often construed as what Timothy Brennan calls "native informants," with their texts offering intimate, apparently authentic access to the world of a particular community (41). However, it is one thing when people believe an author has created an offensive character who shares their communal identity, and another when they think an author has misrepresented them personally by fictionalizing their experiences.

Accordingly, my focus in this book is fiction that draws on authors' intimates, the kind of people whom Paul John Eakin calls "the *proximate* other" ("Unseemly" 171). Those who experience intimacy together share an interrelational state involving a certain degree of exclusivity as well as affect, if not love, and thus are vulnerable to one another in some way.[7] However, the question of who counts as an intimate cannot be easily answered in the abstract. Instead there is a spectrum of acquaintance with no clear demarcation line between intimates and nonintimates. In the case of the contemporary Spanish writer Javier Marías, the people offended by his novel *All Souls* included his ex-colleagues at Oxford University, who felt he had appropriated their stories after the narratives were communicated to him through personal revelations as well as communal gossip. The greater detachment and indirectness associated with the latter mode of communication arguably takes the text beyond autobiographical fiction and puts it on a par with documentary fiction. However, the difficulty of distinguishing the two at such a juncture is a reminder that intimates are not the only people who can feel wounded by fiction and that autobiographical fiction's issues are rarely exclusive to it.

Similarly, autobiographical fiction is not the only art form to problematize the border between fictiveness and autobiography. But, because prose is unique in its division into fiction and nonfiction, the issues it raises are also distinct. In contrast, other art forms tend either to conflate the two categories or to offer a more complicated taxonomy. In the latter camp, film and television have embraced a proliferation of subcategories, from the "docudrama" to the use of tags such as "based on" or "inspired by." In the former camp is lyric poetry, which offers speakers who may or may not be identified with their authors. Likewise, painting and photography can blur the line between artist and subject, as well as the one between fact

---

7. A narrower, more idealistic definition of intimacy might require the relationship to involve consensual participation and a reciprocity of affection. For instance, Rochelle Gurstein defines intimacy as involving "love, affection, tenderness, fidelity, trust, gratitude, and the mutual baring of souls" (29). However, intimate relationships do not always achieve these qualities: for instance, children have little choice over the intimacy they share with their families, and after the end of a romantic relationship, neither partner may have much affection for the other. Nevertheless, both sorts of relationship often involve considerable amounts of shared experience as well as mutual vulnerability.

and fantasy, not least in the case of "disguised self-portraits" that, like the *Mona Lisa,* have been seen as representations of their creators.[8] Although each of these media engenders questions about fictiveness and self-representation, their respective formal qualities and conventions mean that each must be dealt with on its own terms.

If there are reasons to reserve the label "autobiographical fiction" for narrative prose, there are also good ones to focus on contemporary texts when considering the ethical issues involved. Every documented culture in history has accepted some distinction between factual and fantastic stories, as well as between the public and the private, but the precise nature of these distinctions has varied, and as conventions of literary fiction have evolved over time, so have the semantic and ethical debates attending these conventions. A result is that conflicts related to autobiographical fiction have never been so conspicuous as in the contemporary West, with its privileging of juridical and empiricist discourse, its collective compulsion to separate fantasy from facts, and its preoccupation with privacy and confession. The capitalist insistence on individual ownership of ideas and narratives, too, has led to changes in the relationship between authors, their texts, and their audiences. Accordingly, in this book I examine autobiographical fiction in the context of contemporary confessional culture, with its rampant production of paratexts, its manifestations of biographical desire, and its appetite for scandal. I also consider the implications of this culture for contemporary intimacy, which itself is distinctive not least in terms of the psychoanalytic vocabulary it has available to it and the dyadic exclusivity it often privileges.

TREACHEROUS ETHICS

Given the frequency with which autobiographical fiction is viewed as unethical, it might seem surprising that there has been virtually no serious study of the subject.[9] Instead, debates about the matter have occurred principally in gossip and private conversation, in angry letters, sometimes in newspaper columns, and very occasionally before judges, almost always in the context of one emotionally laden dispute or another, when the interests of the parties concerned are forefront and divert attention from the

---

8. See Bal 13.
9. To my knowledge there is only one article that treats the topic at any length: Claudia Mills's "Appropriating Others' Stories: Some Questions about the Ethics of Writing Fiction."

cultural circumstances that gave rise to the situation. A few creative writers have articulated personal rules with regard to what stories they will or will not tell, but there has been little effort to explore the possibility of a shared ethics. For some authors, the very idea of such an ethics might seem fundamentally misconceived insofar as it would require submission to a normative code, when they consider it a writer's duty to stand apart and critique such codes. As for literary scholars, they have discussed at length the ethics of autobiography and biography, but they seem reluctant to address autobiographical fiction.[10] Perhaps they think of fiction as sufficiently bound up with fantasy to stand beyond ethical reproach, or perhaps they view fiction's offenses as trivial ones blown out of proportion by bourgeois overvaluations of privacy and personal reputation. However, such a perspective fails to recognize that not only the bourgeoisie invest considerable psychosocial capital in their public image, their privacy, and their closest interpersonal relations. Intimacy and the circulation of stories about oneself are things in which virtually everyone has an interest. Indeed, there is sufficient investment in these matters that when people feel aggrieved by fiction seeming to depict them, usually they are not eager to draw attention to the problem and risk further disseminating the injurious representation. Consequently there is a relative dearth of material about intimates' reactions that is publicly available for study. There is also the problem that to scrutinize cases where privacy has been invaded risks being itself invasive, a replication of the initial transgression through the act of "publishing the deed."[11]

With an awareness of that danger, in this book I avoid the historiographical detective work of the sort one finds in volumes such as Louise DeSalvo's *Conceived with Malice,* which uncovers previously unpublished information about modernist authors and their intimates, correlates that information with the authors' fiction, and documents the sense of injury felt by the authors' intimates when they perceived those correlations themselves. In DeSalvo's defense, she is dealing with people who are no longer alive. Here, given my focus on contemporary literary culture, I limit the discussion of examples to high-profile cases that involved public state-

---

10. For discussions of life writing's ethics, see John D. Barbour, *The Conscience of the Autobiographer;* G. Thomas Couser, *Vulnerable Subjects;* Eakin, ed., *The Ethics of Life Writing;* Janet Malcolm, *The Silent Woman;* Mary Rhiel and David Suchoff, eds., *The Seductions of Biography;* and Carol Rollyson, *A Higher Form of Cannibalism?*

11. The phrase is Judith Butler's. She writes of confession: "To say 'Yes, I did it,' is to claim the act, but it is also to commit another deed in the very claiming, the act of publishing one's deed, a new criminal venture that redoubles and takes the place of the old" (*Antigone's* 8).

ments from multiple parties about the fiction in question, as in the dispute between Hanif Kureishi and Tracey Scoffield. These cases are sufficiently well-known that simply to draw attention to them once again seems minimally invasive, especially when the concern is not to link real people with characters but to examine arguments about literary ethics made in texts such as reviews, biographies, and legal decisions. Also open to scrutiny are interviews and essays in which authors identify the rationales underlying their decisions about what to write. But in deference to D. H. Lawrence's dictum, in some respects it seems better to trust the tale than the teller. Therefore, fiction itself is my principal object of attention—in particular, texts that explicitly raise the question of autobiographical fiction's ethics. Like Kureishi's "That Was Then," these are fictions featuring protagonists who are typically writers of autobiographical fiction themselves, ones who have offended their intimates by writing about them. This sort of metafiction has affinities with the philosophical dialogue, creating scenarios in which characters reflect on and debate the ethical dilemmas they confront; it finds a dramatic impetus in the interplay of accusation and self-defense between intimate and writer. In these texts one might hope to find real-life authors more honest and deliberative about fiction's autobiographical transgressions than they can be in the course of promotional performances.

Although my choice to approach autobiographical fiction's ethics by examining metafiction is itself ethically motivated, still it must be said that there is something risky in writing about ethics at all. One confronts the danger of slipping into stringent moralizations or an overly detached treatment of issues that are quite visceral for those dealing with them directly. One of the first volumes devoted entirely to the ethics of literary production, H. M. Paull's 1928 book *Literary Ethics,* furnished future critics with a less than salutary model by falling precisely into the trap of conservative prescription. Surveying practices such as plagiarism, libel, and invasion of privacy, Paull makes condemnations along the way that are often paternalistic, reductive, and skewed by idiosyncratic assumptions about literary ideals, not least when damning *roman à clef* outright on the grounds that it is a novelist's business "to create a character, and a copy cannot claim to be a creation" (251). In a more recent account of literary ethics, *The Company We Keep,* Wayne Booth is wisely more interested in reflecting on the impulse to judge fiction than in actually judging it. However, he sets aside the question of autobiographical fiction's ethics, writing: "Biting as it may be for a given author, it does not arise for readers except when they have more or less accidental knowledge about the author's life" (130–31). In making this judgment, Booth fails to recognize that the desire to treat fiction as autobiographical often extends well beyond an author's intimates, especially in a confession-oriented, scandal-obsessed culture where authors can be as of much interest as their literary texts. In suggesting that a reader's knowledge of an author's life is "accidental," Booth ignores the fact that such knowledge is often sought out by audiences and easily found in a culture that in manifold ways generates information and innuendo about the people who write fiction.

Accordingly, with this book I seek to fill a significant gap in ethical criticism. Taking on board the meta-ethical approach developed by critics such as Booth, I avoid prosecuting or defending individual cases. Instead I examine the production, content, and reception of autobiographical fiction for their social and ideological underpinnings on the assumption that understanding these factors breeds the possibility for better encounters between readers, authors, and their intimates. My work is also informed by two further principles: first, that the consideration of an ethical poetics cannot proceed without regard to the ethics of hermeneutics; and second, that literary ethics requires attention to the social and historical contexts in which ethical issues become manifest.

With these principles in mind, the main concern of chapter 1, "A Short History of Transgression," is to establish how autobiographical fiction has evolved through a dialectical game that involves exploiting readers' expectations of literature's referentiality. Surveying instances of apparent authorial trespass from antiquity to the present, I argue that although the explicit opposition of "fiction" and "nonfiction" is a recent one, fiction has long playfully crisscrossed the border between fact and fabrication, while readers have developed complex strategies for discerning texts' truthfulness and inventions. More particularly, readers have been conditioned to read fiction with an eye to identifying traces of the author's private life. The consequence is that fiction constitutively involves multiple transgressions: not least on the part of authors, who are taken to embed details about real lives in ostensibly nonreferential narratives; and on the part of readers, who commit the "biographical heresy" by looking for such details despite authorial and critical insistences that fiction should not be treated as significantly referential. I argue that at least since the eighteenth century, readers have been taught to be skeptical about such insistences, and a key master plot of fiction has been one of biographical detection: that is, a crucial question propelling readers through a fictional narrative is not just "What happens next?" but "How autobiographical is this story?" The fact that a fictional text is itself unable to answer that question—any avowal or disavowal might be itself fictive and ironic—means there is something inherently scandalous about fiction. I argue further that fiction's scandalous quality has been a longstanding part of its appeal and that authors have exploited this quality, provoking or dramatizing attempts to pin down their work and take it to task for its referential slipperiness as well as its possible ethical failings. In this regard, important to fiction's development has been the evolution of various devices for catalyzing scandal, from magazine interviews to talk-show revelations. If fiction itself does not evoke outrage in intimates and reviewers, frequently its authors produce paratexts to do the same, or they write metafiction that dramatizes such outrage. As they do, they compel their readers to take an ethical and referential interest in their fiction.

Fiction's unclear relationship to reality has allowed it to court controversy in other ways as well: for instance, by venturing into the world of private life before other cultural forms dared to follow. As it has done so, authors have repeatedly situated their work at the borders of the permissible. They have also adapted to cultural developments affecting autobiographical fiction's reception, from Romantic poetry's self-expressive ethos to Hollywood's creation of a star system preoccupied with artists' private lives. In the present confessional age, when people are publicly disseminating personal narratives all the time, privacy is at once rampantly defended, relinquished, and invaded. In this context, autobiographical fiction's currency emerges less from the revelations it makes and more from its strategic ambivalence: the simultaneous disguises and confessions it offers reproduce a broader social ambivalence about public disclosure and private life.

This ambivalence manifests itself not least in the relations between authors of fiction and their audiences, relations that are both highly mediated and rendered apparently proximate through textual and paratextual confessions. Indeed, if this book documents a love story, it is one involving a fraught triangle between authors, their intimates, and their readers. Chapter 2, "Biographical Desire," focuses on the side of that triangle involving authors and readers, with each reaching out to the other through the phantasmatically interpersonal activities of writing and reading. From this perspective, it is not surprising that so much autobiographical fiction deals with love affairs, for it is modeling the kind of relationship into which readers and authors enter together: one involving intimacy, secrets, and desire. However, for readers this love affair is distinguished by the absence of authors from the very texts that evoke them. The poverty and promise of fiction in this regard send readers and authors alike into the realm of paratexts, where authors supplement their fictions with further confessional stories. I argue that while literary critics have largely neglected the role of paratexts in fiction's circulation and semantics, it is an estimable one, and it is crucial to apprehending the power of readers' biographical desire. In turn, that desire is an insufficiently recognized motor of contemporary literary culture. To make sense of it, I track the remarkable reception history of one book, Elizabeth Smart's "cult" novel, *By Grand Central Station I Sat Down and Wept*, through the second half of the twentieth century, investigating the processes whereby the author, narrator, and text came to be identified with and subjugated to one another. In this investigation, I pay particular attention to paratextual performances. Through such performances, authors maintain a flirtatious intimacy with readers, both satisfying and stimulating biographical desire. I argue that a striking transformation in the twentieth century lies in the proliferation of mass-media paratexts, such that present-day fiction cannot be considered an autonomous discourse so much as one node of a confessional matrix in which the authors circulate as texts alongside their literary work. Accordingly, paratexts are fundamental to the semantics of fiction, as well as to the marketing, ethics, and erotics of it. In particular, they are a key mediator of the author–reader relationship, fostering a sense of intimacy that both supplements and informs the intimacy of reading fiction.

Alongside the twentieth-century proliferation of paratexts was a growth in metafiction commenting on the ethical issues attending autobiographical fiction. Often this metafiction challenges readers' sense of intimacy with authors even as it nurtures it. I give special attention to the metafiction of Philip Roth, who presents readers with innumerable fictional versions of himself. As he does so, he suggests that such doppelgängers instantiate modes of self-invention in which everyone participates and that the self is always performative, fragmentary, closely bound to fantasy. I do not take up the task of taxonomizing the various self-representations and self-improvisations in Roth's work. Instead I argue that he tempts his readers into doing so precisely in order for them to fail in their attempts. He practices a poetics of exhaustion that underscores the ultimate indeterminacy of fiction's referentiality, as well as the endlessly proliferative character of self-fashioning. But although Roth's writing might seem to deconstruct the border between fiction and autobiography, I argue that this border remains a predicate of his work and of other border-blurring autobiographical fiction. For all the conflations of fact and fantasy enacted by such texts, the controversies they create inevitably produce reaffirmations of the boundary between fact and fabrication in the mass media, if not in courts of law. Consequently, I argue, autobiographical fiction operates not outside the conventional hermeneutic order but as part of it, serving as a foil against which verificationist discourse defines itself.

In a sense, the first two chapters of this book are instrumental to the latter two, providing the historical and cultural contexts necessary for an examination of conflicts between authors and their intimates. In another sense, though, the first chapters inaugurate an argument that chapters 3 and 4 take up: namely, that ostensibly dyadic conflicts between authors and intimates are imbricated with the biographical desire and paratextual production attending literature in a confessional culture. It is with these phenomena still in mind that chapter 3, "Fiction's Betrayals, Intimacy's Trials," turns to the matter of how intimates are offended by fiction and how authors justify giving such offense. For intimates, fiction can suggest a cruel detachment on the part of authors, and it can threaten a paralyzing loss of control over one's life story. Moreover, fiction's ambiguous referentiality and depictions of its characters' inner lives can make it even more mortifying than nonfiction. Through a reading of A. S. Byatt's novel *The Game*, I argue that fiction also wounds insofar as it rehearses and hyperbolizes preexisting struggles for intimacy and autonomy. In that respect, writing fiction based on intimate experience can involve a desire not only to engage with otherness but also to efface and diminish it. Similarly, although metafiction addressing such desires might seem ethical insofar as it presents multiple perspectives on the harms and benefits of autobiographical fiction, it can be a further appropriation of intimates' voices.

Against these charges of betrayed intimacy, authors such as Hanif Kureishi have argued for the need to challenge the privileging of intimacy itself, given its associations with censorship, repression, and possessiveness. From this perspective, fiction's infidelities are not ethical failures but remedial actions exposing problems with norms of intimacy. Autobiographical fiction so conceived stands as a repudiation of narrative monogamy and its demand that people owe to their intimates an exclusivity with regard to the stories they tell about themselves and each other. Kureishi, Roth, and other authors of autobiographical metafiction insist that this narrative monogamy traps people in single, static identities leading to deceptions and self-deceptions. In contrast, fictional self-representation embraces the multiplication of selves and the freedom to fantasize. However, I argue that authors who position themselves as social rebels are often reliant on the very norms they are protesting. Even while they identify their fiction as speaking out against a culture of reticence, they make use of reticence themselves to deny their texts' referentiality and court readers' biographical desire. What is more, if there is a tendency among authors to claim for themselves a special ethical license as dissenters, their privilege with regard to the public dissemination of their words means they have greater, not fewer, responsibilities to their intimate relations.

With an eye to those responsibilities, in chapter 4, "In Bed with an Author," I scrutinize various strategies that have been enacted or suggested to help authors and their loved ones get along. The chapter begins by examining the options available to intimates who wish to correct what they see as misrepresentations of them in fiction. A reading of Alice Munro's metafictional short story "Material" makes it clear that public responses risk further betraying the very intimate relationships the respondents wish to preserve. Moreover, when intimates attempt to write corrective narratives, they often reveal themselves as prone to the same sorts of misrepresentations, elisions, and caricatures that have upset them. Similarly, the controversy that arose from Claire Bloom's publication of *Leaving a Doll's House,* a memoir partly about her relationship with Philip Roth, speaks against retaliatory publication as a productive way of responding to injurious fiction. Although intimates might be attracted to gaining a voice through the same confessional field that authors have exploited, a lesson one might draw from Bloom's example is that this field has its own coercive narrative predilections. In particular, the public's biographical desire includes a taste for scandal and third-party judgments of all parties concerned, such that intimates who speak out subject themselves to more of the misunderstandings, condemnations, and invasions of privacy they felt the initial fiction inflicted on them.

At the same time, the confessional field offers possibilities for authors in terms of ethical action with regard to their intimates. Taking a cue from Munro's story, chapter 4 conceptualizes a collaborative, creative model of intimacy that exploits biographical desire and the erotics of fiction. This is an intimacy wherein authors and their intimates take pleasure from interrogating and embracing fiction's fantasies together in private discussion and public performances. Even if fiction's currency depends in part on its tantalizing ambiguity and the staging of conflict, I argue that authors need not fear this currency's debasement through private reckonings in which they and their loved ones jointly untangle lines of referentiality, making productive use of misunderstanding to augment rather than detract from intimacy. In imagining such relations, I posit a poetics of responsible indiscretion, one that does not see ethical intimacy as an impediment to the creation of socially transgressive literature. Indeed, I argue that for those authors who identify themselves as social rebels, their very stance against repression and silence demands such a poetics. While autobiographical fiction always risks being unfaithful, many of the conflicts arising between authors and their close relations might be minimized or avoided through greater self-consciousness on the part of both. I call for ethical engagement that is especially attentive to particularity, unpredictability, and contingency, not only due to the variety and mutability of intimate relations but also due to the nature of fiction itself, in which the unconscious colors the text's production and reception, the narrative's referentiality is indeterminate, and the text's effects in the world are unpredictable.

By considering historical, theoretical, and practical aspects of autobiographical fiction together, I hope to facilitate better dialogue about such fiction. In the most fundamental terms, this book represents an attempt to determine why fiction continues to matter: how it manifests compelling, ongoing social concerns about truth and reality, about intimacy and infidelity, and about the public and private realms. The pages that follow present a complex picture of the causes, functions, and effects of biographical desire. They have implications for how people read, write, and talk about literature, whether in scholarship or gossip. In attending to such matters, I also aim to shed light on how people conduct themselves in their most intimate relationships, with all the storytelling, silences, and desire those relationships involve.

1

A Short History of Transgression

> Bring down the fog of the imagination! What are novelists for? Go just so far as is necessary, set up camp inches beyond the reach, the fingertips of the law. But no one knows these precise distances until a judgment is handed down.
>
> —Ian McEwan, *Atonement* 370

> Fiction is like a spider's web, attached ever so lightly perhaps, but still attached to life at all four corners.
>
> —Virginia Woolf, *A Room of One's Own* 41

Since the introduction of the word "fiction" to the English language in the late fourteenth century, the term has been used to denote both pure invention and literature relating more ambiguously to reality. The word did not come to be associated with prose narratives in particular until the eighteenth century, but by that time prose fiction was already an established form, even if it went by other names. Likewise, although the term "autobiographical fiction" is an even more recent coinage, there has always been an interest among readers in connecting stories with the lives of their writers, and there has always been controversy attending those connections. Fiction has long involved a dialectical game of evasion and guesswork played out by authors and audiences, with the writers making oblique or contradictory claims about the referentiality of their texts, while their readers have treated those claims with suspicion. However, the ethical issues raised by autobiographical fiction were never quite so publicly considered or complex as they have been in the last fifty years. Not least, fiction's production and reception have been influenced greatly by the growth of mass media, which provide opportunities for people to offer intimate details about themselves in public and be criticized or praised for doing so. Even in classical Greece, people were upset by the thought of being represented in fictional narratives, but the significance and content of such representations have changed with shifting economic, legal, and social stakes. To examine the ethics of autobiographical fiction in the twenty-first century, one needs to appreciate how current understandings of authorship, creativity, and privacy have taken shape and how discourse about the autobiographical dimensions of fiction has developed. Philippe Lejeune's assertion about autobiography also obtains for autobiographical fiction: what we need is "a history of its mode of reading" (30). Because readers' expectations influence the ways in which authors write and discuss fiction, this chapter takes up the task of historicizing those expectations.

What emerges is that autobiographical fiction has made a name for itself through transgression. If Jago Morrison and Susan Watkins are right to observe the presence in the twentieth century of "an institutionalized demand for the literary novel to enact a kind of scandal, to articulate what is not banal, expected or conventional" (19), this demand was one that fiction helped create through a long history of bad behavior. In the case of autobiographical fiction, the most obvious transgressions have been referential ones, as texts have courted readers' credulity by blending fact and imagination. Fiction has a history of operating at the border of the permissible in terms of its correspondences with real life. As much as its claims to nonreferentiality have constituted a defense against prosecution, often those claims have also been disbelieved. Nevertheless, ethical and legal proscriptions against fiction have tended to galvanize authors more than discourage them. Authors have also broken ground in crossing from the public into the private sphere, and from the polite to the unseemly, breeding a taste for confession and glimpses of intimate life that nonfictional forms such as biography and autobiography have only more recently begun to satisfy. Meanwhile, authors have preserved a cultural niche for fiction by drawing out the social tensions of their times: for example, between personal advancement and intimate obligations, empiricism and fantasy, free speech and libel, as well as between the public performance of identity and the concealment of inner life.

EARLY LIBELS AND DENIALS

It is a truism that what the ancient Greeks took for fact, people in the contemporary West take to be fiction. More accurately, one might say that with regard to certain kinds of literary narratives—the epics of Homer, for example—the Greeks were concerned less with the verification of the story's basis in reality than with its other meanings. Still, they did distinguish between fact and imagination: they cared very much whether reports of imminent attack were true, and they condemned historians for inaccuracies or inventions.[1] Moreover, they were keenly aware that fictive stories were ethically charged in their ambiguous relationship to the real world. For example, Aelian tells the story of Socrates' reaction to Aristophanes' play *The Clouds,* in which a character called Socrates is represented as a comical mouthpiece of the Sophists. When the real Socrates attended the play and heard someone behind him ask about the model for the character onstage, he stood to identify himself and remained upright for the duration of the performance so that the audience could appreciate the differences between the invented character and his original.[2] The anecdote provides confirmation that Greek writers of the day were as wont to caricature real people as modern authors are and that consequently their art could become an object of dispute. However, Greek drama tended toward public and historical rather than clearly autobiographical subject matter, and literary criticism of the time followed suit by steering clear of biographical readings. M. H. Abrams points out that when Aristotle discusses literature, he does not bother accounting for an artist's "personal faculties, feelings, or desires,"—or, one might add, life history (11). No ancient Greek exegesis suggests that *Oedipus Rex* rehearses the oedipal drama of Sophocles' childhood.

In medieval Europe, poets such as Geoffrey Chaucer and Dante Alighieri intermingled fact and invention more personally by putting not just other people but also themselves into their tales. When Chaucer named himself as one of the pilgrims in *The Canterbury Tales,* and when Dante sent himself through hell in his *Commedia,* neither clearly intended to fool anyone into believing he actually made the journey he describes. Instead these acts of self-inclusion imbue the texts with a more abstract autobiographical quality. By depicting himself as interacting with his characters, Chaucer naturalizes himself as an observer of humankind in all its

---

1. See Walton 101.
2. See Aelian 85.

diversity, while Dante's self-representation as a literal voyager through the realms of the afterlife legitimized him as a poet of religious vision. At the same time, these authors' choice to represent themselves in their poetry signaled an expectation that their texts would not circulate anonymously. Rather, readers approached the poems with an awareness of their authors that the poems themselves fostered. But as the poems did so, their evident fabrications destabilized any notion of a straightforward authorial self-representation. There is an ironic distance between the writers as characters in their texts and as narrators of them. Indeed, such narrative personae were not uncommon in the later Middle Ages, and medieval scholarship attending to them shows considerable sophistication in apprehending their ambiguous referentiality.[3] To be sure, this scholarship did not extensively discuss how literature such as Chaucer's and Dante's might reflect those writers' life stories; rather, scholars' primary interest lay in assessing an author's rhetorical intentions and moral standing. Nevertheless, their attention to authorial distance in fictional narratives demonstrates how literature was already conditioning its readers to view autobiographical literature as at once a revelation and a masking of its author.

This concomitantly confessional and coy quality of self-dramatizing literature was later rehearsed by Elizabethan poets who wrote for an audience they knew would be familiar with them. Such was the case when Sir Philip Sidney gave the titular hero of his sonnet sequence *Astrophil and Stella* a name similar to his own. The gesture insisted at once on the sequence's connection to reality and its prerogative to depart from the real. For Sidney, linking himself to a fictional character was largely a playful gesture that he could expect to be embraced as such by his close-knit aristocratic audience, but in other cases, correlations were interpreted as dangerously transgressive. King James VI of Scotland, for one, was outraged when he took Edmund Spenser to have depicted his mother, Mary, Queen of Scots, as the evil Duessa in *The Faerie Queene*. Two decades later, having been crowned King of England, James became involved in another literary scandal with the publication of Lady Mary Wroth's romance *The Countess of Montgomery's Urania*, when he received a complaint from Edward, Lord Denny that the narrative contained an account of Denny's marital infidelities. Wroth defended herself in a letter to Denny, insisting: "I never thought on you in my writing, nor meant you or any nor did I never speak any such thing" (qtd. in Carrell 86–87). Eventually she withdrew the book, though, and it was not reprinted in her lifetime. Even so,

---

3. See Gust 20.

in 1641 she received a blithe request from George Manners, Earl of Rutland, that she supply him with the "key" to her text so he could read it with an eye to the real people on whom its characters were based.

Such a request was not unusual, insofar as by that time the *roman à clef* was an established genre. For example, in John Barclay's early seventeenth-century satire *Euphormionis Lusinini Satyricon*, the author admits that his story depicts "a few known and living men," and by 1608 a key was circulating that listed the real-life models for the text's characters (qtd. in Fleming 96). The introduction of such keys signals an important shift in literary culture: the readership for fiction was expanding beyond courtly circles to include people who were not personally acquainted with the texts' authors or the putative models for characters. As a result, authors who wished to flirt controversially with referentiality in their fiction required their audiences to gain familiarity with the texts' models not just through informal, oral modes of communication such as gossip but also through published paratexts. Given paratextual accompaniment, *romans à clef* could maintain a posture of nonreferentiality, even warning their audience against biographical interpretation, while they went about depicting lives that nonfiction would have had to represent more cautiously. Indeed, denials of referentiality were liable only to increase readers' biographical curiosity.

The proliferation of *romans à clef* affected audiences' expectations such that by the time the novel began to appear in English, reading between the lines already often meant reading biographically. One of fiction's crucial plots became one of biographical detection: that is, a significant force compelling readers through a text was their desire to discern connections between the narrative and the lives of real people. Whether accompanied by keys or only implicitly inviting readers to engage in biographical detective work, fiction presented riddles to be solved. What is more, honing one's skills in solving them was especially appealing given the context of an increasingly capitalist, urban culture. In a society requiring citizens to engage daily in a variety of exchanges with friends and strangers, colleagues and competitors, things such as commercial achievement and personal reputation depended on successfully sharing and guarding secrets. Fiction resonated in this regard because it both kept its secrets and promised to reveal them.

At the same time, the growth of print culture meant that people represented in literature could be exposed to ignominy in more widely disseminated ways than before, a change that led to broader applications of libel statutes. While medieval defamation law in Britain had been predominantly concerned with seditious offenses against the state, by 1600 it had begun to resemble its current shape, with courts also censuring false and derogatory statements about private citizens.[4] How, then, to discuss individuals in print without ending up in court? Fiction, with its claims to nonreferentiality, was one solution. Because libel laws of the era generally required people's actual names to be printed in order for defamation charges to be brought against an author, even the use of initials could serve as the sufficient foundation for a defense.[5] Consequently, libel laws were seldom brought to bear on texts that today would be called works of literature.[6] Still, as Catherine Gallagher points out, early eighteenth-century fiction was sometimes written not to escape libel charges but to attract them, with the understanding that the controversy would help the author's reputation, even as writers were careful to disguise their targets to a degree that would provide them with a viable legal defense (103). This was the case with Delarivier Manley's *The New Atalantis*, published in 1709, which deployed what Manley would later describe as "Romantick Names, and a feign'd Scene of Action" as it went about defaming various public figures (*Adventures* 114). Manley's fictional veil was sufficiently thin as to prompt a libel case. According to one report of her examination by prosecutors, Manley resolutely maintained her innocence:

> Her Defence was with much Humility and Sorrow, for having offended, at the same Time denying that any Persons were concern'd with her, or that she had a farther Design than writing for her own Amusement and Diversion in the Country; without intending particular Reflections or Characters: When this was not believ'd, and the contrary urg'd very home to her by several Circumstances and Likenesses; she said then it must be *Inspiration*, because knowing her own Innocence she could account for it no other Way. (113)

This report was offered by Manley herself in *The Adventures of Rivella*, a *roman à clef* published five years later. It is striking that in the wake of a prosecution for one referential fiction, Manley defended herself by writing yet another. It is even more striking that Rivella's self-justifications in the latter text are less than ingenuous, something made clear when Rivella privately admits that *The New Atalantis* includes stories about real people (110). Accordingly, *The Adventures of Rivella* offers a deeply ironic

---

4. See Helmholz 103.
5. See Kropf 159.
6. See Franta 151.

defense of Manley. At the same time, its account of Rivella's self-exculpating words during her prosecution suggests that juridical testimony, too, can be ironic, an imposture, no more trustworthy than fiction. The text implies that the only solution for readers bent on hearing the true story is simply to keep reading Manley's textual supplements, not with the expectation of straightforward revelation but to enjoy the twists and turns of scandal, with its sequence of offense, accusation, denial, and yet more flirtatiously referential narratives.

THE PRIVATE LIFE OF NOVELS

The drive to tell possibly biographical, potentially libelous stories in fiction is not surprising in the context of social changes that occurred during the early modern period. For one thing, various factors strengthened the impetus to distinguish between fact and falsity. William Nelson asserts that in the Middle Ages, a common attitude toward apocryphal tales was that they "could not be warranted as true, but they might be true, and in any case could be read without danger to the soul, perhaps with profit" (111–12). By the seventeenth century, this was no longer clearly the case. The scientific revolution was generating a new empiricist methodology for knowledge acquisition, and historians became more stringently focused on facts, too, affecting an ethos of transparent reportage while abandoning traditional devices such as imagined speeches and ornamental details. Many literary writers followed suit, giving up the use of fantastical literary elements, so that fiction moved toward realism, at least in the sense that Samuel Johnson described when he observed in *The Rambler*, No. 4, that fictional works of his day "exhibit life in its true state, diversified only by accidents that daily happen in the world, and influenced by passions and qualities which are really to be found in conversing with mankind" (*Yale* 19). But fiction and history parted ways insofar as historians seeking authenticity could no longer plausibly narrate life's unobserved, unverifiable moments. Their principal object of study was largely limited to the public sphere. Biographers were similarly constrained, if for reasons of decorum as much as methodological ones.[7] In contrast, fiction explored private life so often that by the end of the eighteenth century, Madame de

---

7. Debora Shuger observes that early biographers "characteristically maintain an obdurate silence on matters of absorbing interest to modern biographers and autobiographers, several thousand pages yielding barely a handful of phobias, fantasies, perversions, or traumas" (64).

Staël could define the novel precisely in terms of its focus on the private, distinguishing it from history by observing that the latter "does not reach down into the life of ordinary people and to feelings and personalities that have no effect upon public affairs" (280). Although it would still be some time before social mores evolved sufficiently for novelists to be censured publicly for writing about their intimates, fiction was already opening the door to look in upon domestic life.

The novel's trade in the lives of "ordinary people" was not merely a consequence of history defaulting on the private realm. Rather, as the European bourgeoisie enjoyed new opportunities to change their station in life and, along with it, their self-definition, narratives of individual difference and transformation gained currency. What is more, such narratives gave public accounts of lives that were otherwise increasingly hidden, as the private sphere was becoming more distinctive, prestigious, and susceptible to curiosity. Earlier, the private had been demeaned: the English word shares its root with "privation." Through the early modern period, though, the private sphere became privileged, its transformation emblematized by the advent of the courtly park, which, according to Jürgen Habermas, permitted a "life sealed off from the outside world" (10). In the seventeenth and eighteenth centuries there was a further trend toward one-story residences housing nuclear families, and Habermas argues that these buildings facilitated a new kind of intimacy between family members, with rooms devoted to individuals instead of maintaining the communality of the extended family (44). As for the character of relations within those families, historians have rejected the claim that companionate marriage based on love was something new in the eighteenth century, but it remains clear that spousal intimacy was strengthened by the seclusion afforded by single-family homes.[8] These new living arrangements brought expectations of privacy, loyalty, and confidentiality—precisely the expectations that autobiographical fiction would come to be seen as betraying.

From the novel's beginning, it lifted the veil on privacy ostentatiously. For instance, the subtitle of Samuel Richardson's *Clarissa* declares the text's subject to be "the most Important Concerns of Private Life," and

---

8. In *Romantic Love and Society*, Jacqueline Sarsby sets out to refute Edward Shorter's *The Making of the Modern Family*, which depicts free choice in marriage and affective intimacy as arising from capitalism and individualism. She also takes issue with Lawrence Stone's *The Family, Sex and Marriage in England 1500–1800*, which claims that the sixteenth century witnessed the beginning of a movement from arranged to companionate marriage.

Carolyn Steedman observes that early novels such as Richardson's angled for readers' interest by pretending to present letters and other documents not intended for strangers' eyes (75). The fact that the novelists were nevertheless publishing them created a moral complication that trailed the epistolary novel as a genre; such fictions drew attention to the unstable relationship between private and public life in a print culture where intimate correspondence was alarmingly susceptible to mass dissemination. In fact, eighteenth-century authors' willingness to trade in scandal could even involve turning invasions of their own privacy to their advantage. Such was the case with Alexander Pope. Spurred on by the significant sales greeting Edmund Curll's publication in 1726 of various letters by Pope—a publication that Pope himself had privately encouraged, even though publicly he feigned outrage at the act—Pope went on to publish other letters himself. Ian Hamilton argues that doing so offered Pope "a means of showing to the world a humbler, kinder, much more human Pope than it may have grown used to from a reading of his verses and his controversial pamphlets" (51). Pope's staging of his own outrage echoes Manley's self-presentation as wrongly aggrieved by her accusers; in both cases, the authors sought to associate literature with conflict and betrayal. Moreover, Pope's epistolary publications constitute an early example of a phenomenon that is now common: namely, writers offering autobiographical material to the public for the sake of promoting interest in them as well as their work.

The publication of Pope's letters signaled a shift toward the installation of authors at the center of literary discourse. In the age of the commercial press, with the diminishing likelihood of face-to-face encounters between authors and most of their readers, writers became known predominantly through the texts that circulated by and about them. As they gained reputations in this way, commentators began to treat their fiction as one more source of information about them. For instance, Charles Gildon criticized Daniel Defoe's *Robinson Crusoe* by claiming that Defoe had created a protagonist who shared the author's own "Rambling, Inconsistent" personality (72). Such a condemnation, with its recognition that a narrative could be psychologically revealing of its author, pointed the way to the kind of biographical interpretation that would gradually gain a foothold in discourse about fiction. At the same time, the fact that Gildon viewed the novel's putative autobiographical quality as a failing was consistent with an increased valuing of literary "originality" in the eighteenth century, the corollary of which was a denigration of "mere" self-representation. Richardson expressed this set of literary values in a 1752 letter in which he castigates Henry Fielding's fiction for borrowing too much from Fielding's personal experiences and those of his acquaintances. Richardson complains that Fielding's "brawls, his jarrs, his gaols, his spunging-houses, are all drawn from what he has seen and known" and that he "has little or no invention" ("To Anne" 197). However, even as novelists such as Richardson condemned autobiographical fiction per se, others exploited the biographical curiosity of their audiences by blurring the line between fiction and autobiography. For instance, after Laurence Sterne found success with the initial volumes of his novel *Tristram Shandy,* the former pastor published his sermons under the name of Mr. Yorick, the parson from his novel, thus playfully encouraging readers to wonder what else in *Tristram Shandy* might be taken from its author's life. As Sterne embraced the notoriety his fiction brought him, he made it evident that for novelists, fame could be had not just by publishing fiction but also by becoming distinctive characters themselves and performing identities with a conspicuous relationship to their literary work. Such authors became a manner of paratext, further fictions to be "read" by the public, supplements to their writing, while fiction grew conversely to resemble a biographical extension of its author.

Later in the eighteenth century, an association between authors and their fiction that had been established by literary practice was corroborated by literary commentary, as the Romantic movement foregrounded literature's autobiographical aspects. Previously, critics had been explicitly dismissive of biographical interpretation. For example, in his "Life of Thomson," Johnson provides an anecdote to refute the notion "that an author's life is best read in his works":

> Savage, who lived much with Thomson, once told me, how he heard a lady remarking that she could gather from his works three parts of his character, that he was a "great lover, a great swimmer, and rigorously abstinent"; but, said Savage, he knows not any love but that of the sex; he was perhaps never in cold water in his life; and he indulges himself in all luxury that comes within his reach. (*Lives* 297–98)

Still, the reported reading habits of the woman in question show that Johnson's distaste for biographical readings was not uniformly shared. And in Germany, Johann Gottfried Herder was among the Romantics formulating a view of art virtually antithetical to Johnson's, one in which great literature testifies intrinsically to the life of its creator. Herder declared:

> Each poem, especially a great and complete poem, a work of the soul and of life, is a dangerous betrayer of its author, and often when he believes that he is betraying himself least. Not only do you discern, as the populace will have it, the poetic talents of the man; you also discern which of his faculties and propensities were the ruling ones; the manner in which he got his images; how he regulated and disposed these and the chaos of his impressions; the most intimate places of his heart and often the fated course of his life as well. (qtd. in Abrams 236)

Herder's evocation of poetry's betrayals is notable not merely for its attention to the possibility that a work of literature reveals its author's psychology, but also for its implication that literature should be read precisely to unravel the secrets of the author's mind. This view quickly gained widespread support, and it bred a broader interest in authors' lives, such that in 1816, William Wordsworth could refer to third-party publications about the private life of Robert Burns as examples of "the coarse intrusions into the recesses, the gross breaches upon the sanctities, of domestic life, to which we have lately been more and more accustomed" (122). If there was an unwitting irony attached to Wordsworth's comment, it was that he was himself one of the English Romantics whose introspective poetry cultivated a desire for intimate authorial confessions.

Meanwhile, as Herder was redirecting lines of inquiry into poetry, Jean-Jacques Rousseau's *Confessions* remade standards of self-revelation in prose. Rousseau had already courted biographical curiosity with his fiction; for instance, in the prefatory note to his 1761 novel *Julie, or The New Héloïse,* he writes: "Although I bear only the title of Editor here, I have myself had a hand in this book, and I do not disguise this. Have I done the whole thing, and is the entire correspondence a fiction? Worldly people, what matters it to you? It is surely a fiction for you" (*Collected* 3). By emphasizing his own involvement in the text, Rousseau encourages his audience to relate their readings of the narrative back to him. Moreover, in accusing readers of being unable or unwilling to treat the text definitively as "true," he entices them precisely to view it as referential and, by extension, possibly self-referential in some manner. Later, the publication of *Confessions* revolutionized the degree of intimacy readers would come to expect of authors. While the text's frank descriptions of Rousseau's past transgressions violated the age's norms of decorum, the book also participated in shifting those norms, such that the next century would be marked by a dynamic tension between the valorization of reticence and a drive toward exposure. What is more, Rousseau became a precursor of the *poète maudit* whose transgressive, iconoclastic lifestyle is of no less interest than her or his writing and whose life is often taken to be inextricably connected to that oeuvre.

NINETEENTH-CENTURY PUBLICITY

After Rousseau, the *poète maudit* found an English incarnation in Lord Byron, whose reputation depended on his licentiousness as much as his poetry. Byron's notoriety heralded the beginning of a nineteenth-century transformation that made living authors famous through an expanding print culture preoccupied by transgression. For example, when Lady Caroline Lamb published her novel *Glenarvon* in 1816, it was perceived to depict her affair with Byron, and word of the controversy traveled as far as continental Europe, where it was reported in *Galignani's Messenger*, a periodical of English news for tourists in France. Through the development of such widely disseminated journalism, the modern *succès de scandale* became possible. Joe Moran attributes the rise of the "star system" of authorship in the nineteenth century predominantly to innovations in media technology, from the telegraph to the rotary press (16); one might also note the growth of library networks and the introduction of universal elementary education, which raised literacy rates substantially. With these expansions came a change in literary discourse: for instance, the century saw the advent of the New Journalism, with its exposés, gossip columns, and human-interest stories. In this manner, the way for more intensively biographical readings of fiction was paved by the increased production of paratexts and the nurturing of public interest in authors. Acceding to interviews in their homes, they became celebrities who provided readers with access to their intimate lives. In Richard Salmon's words, "rather than offering a refuge from the public domain, the 'private life' of the author became the very sign of celebrity" (110). And where journalists went, audiences followed: in the late nineteenth century, the new industry of literary tourism took visitors to the locales of Scott and Burns, not to mention the homes of living authors such as Alfred, Lord Tennyson. Meanwhile, photography, mass-produced portraiture, and illustrated newspapers allowed for the dissemination of authors' faces, as well as for the arrival of the first paparazzi, who sought to capture "candid" photographs of writers engaged in private pastimes.

The media made figures such as Charles Dickens famous on both sides of the Atlantic and facilitated public discussion about biographical aspects of their fiction. This was the case with *Bleak House*, in which Dickens modeled the character Harold Skimpole on his friend Leigh Hunt. After an American newspaper remarked on the resemblance, word of the portrait spread quickly. The incident evinces an early public recognition that fiction was a threat to personal relations and that for individuals seeking privacy, authors of novels might not make such fine bedfellows. Indeed, Karen Chase and Michael Levenson view the tension between intimate life and scandal as endemic to the Victorian period, which they characterize as "the great domestic epoch" but also "the first great age of information" (7). Family life was celebrated as the foundation of community, but the prioritization of familial virtue required a foil: namely, public stories of domestic failure against which people could define themselves as socially upright and successful. With the advent of realism and naturalism, fiction satisfied this interest in the more sordid aspects of human existence. William A. Cohen asserts that by the nineteenth century, the novel had come to be installed as a strictly fictive entity, so that "the danger of novels being taken for stories about real people had virtually evaporated" (18). However, even if novels in the Victorian era seldom tried to convince anyone they were true, the referential skepticism and curiosity that the form had created in readers was still prone to be channeled into questions about how much a novel's characters were based on actual people.

Such speculation was abetted by a growing amount of biographical material in the mass media. In fact, the media's intrusions into authors' lives catalyzed a backlash from those who—like Wordsworth before them—worried that standards of decorum were being eroded by a new culture of exposure. Appearances in American newspapers of "idle gossip" and "details of sexual relations" with regard to the country's social elite were one motivation for Samuel D. Warren and Louis D. Brandeis's watershed *Harvard Law Review* article of 1890, "The Right to Privacy," the first published attempt in America to establish a legal basis for privacy rights (77). In the essay, Warren and Brandeis defend what they take to be traditional standards of public reticence, but their acknowledgment of the transformations effected by new technologies verges on an admission that society has been altered irrevocably. They complain: "Instantaneous photographs and newspaper enterprise have invaded the sacred precincts of private and domestic life; and numerous mechanical devices threaten to make good the prediction that 'what is whispered in the closet shall be proclaimed from the housetops'" (76). Imagining a legal bulwark against such exposure, Warren and Brandeis argue for defending what they called a person's "inviolate personality" (82). By grounding their conception of privacy in this notion, Warren and Brandeis privilege privacy's psychological dimensions, insisting that feelings such as embarrassment and shame are a legitimate injury against which people should have protection. However, Warren and Brandeis fail to interrogate the social norms that made people in the nineteenth-century so susceptible to such feelings. Instead they focus on protecting what they famously refer to as the "right of the individual to be let alone" (82).

In fictional narratives and the practices of certain writers, late nineteenth-century literature reflected this anxiety about privacy. Henry James, for one, was exquisitely attentive to the growing public curiosity about authors, and he cast a critical light upon its ethics in stories such as "The Aspern Papers," "The Death of the Lion," and "The Real Right Thing."[9] These texts can be read as morality tales that deem a preoccupation with authors' lives to be misguided. However, insofar as the stories themselves focus on authors in the private sphere, they also cater to and implicitly legitimize the very biographical curiosity they castigate. Indeed, these stories are joined in James's corpus by several others in which authors are either the protagonists or the objects of a protagonist's interest, making James one of English literature's most rigorous investigators of authorial psychology.[10] Even while his fiction endorses the sanctity of the private, it offers a way of intimately exploring—without necessarily violating—authors' personalities. In doing so, it anticipates the self-reflexive attention to authorial psychology in various confessional fictions of the modernist era. At the same time, James was careful to guard his own life from public view. He burned his letters, banned posthumous publication of his remaining papers, and insisted that no biography of him be authorized after his death. If James's efforts were inversely paralleled by other authors' industry with regard to self-promotion, it is because the respective endeavors were two sides of the same coin. Both stand as attempts to control the circulation of the authorial image in an era of unprecedented publicity.

At the end of the nineteenth century, most of the mechanisms were in place for a confessional society resembling today's, in which fiction is often read as autobiographical and sometimes as transgressively so. Not least, a mass readership participated in a print culture that produced celebrities and featured competition to tell interesting stories about them. In 1901,

---

9. Elsa Nettels notes that James's early fiction is preoccupied by "the rights of the subject, the responsibilities of the biographer, and the effects of biographical revelation upon the judgments of the reader" (120).

10. See, for instance, "The Figure in the Carpet," "The Lesson of the Master," "The Private Life," "Sir Dominick Ferrand," and "The Middle Years" in *The Collected Stories*.

Augustine Birrell remarked: "In these noisy days of literary newspapers and literary interviewers, publishers' puffing catalogues, illustrated with portraits, and communicated paragraphs, it is difficult to avoid knowing perhaps too much about authors" (qtd. in Waller 327). Moreover, the literary marketplace promised people that they could grow wealthy and change their social position through the stories they told. The reading public's desire for true or verisimilar accounts encouraged would-be authors to mine their own lives to produce these narratives. Long before the proliferation of creative writing programs, people were encouraged to "write what you know." In the 1903 book *How to Become an Author,* Arnold Bennett suggests tongue-in-cheek that people treat even family misfortune as material for published stories. Of the aspiring journalist he says: "When his uncle is killed in a great railway accident, he should be moved to write an illustrated article on the differences between ancient and modern railway accidents for the *Strand Magazine*" (78).

The moral ramifications of such advice were not lost on some observers. In fact, questions about the ethics of autobiographical fiction were beginning to be tabled by authors themselves. In O. Henry's turn-of-the-century story, "Confessions of a Humorist," the titular narrator calls himself a literary vampire and says his home became a "hunting ground" when he began to seek out *bons mots* from his wife for the sake of his literary career:

> I began to market those pearls of unwisdom and humor that should have enriched only the sacred precincts of home. With devilish cunning I encouraged her to talk. Unsuspecting, she laid her heart bare. Upon the cold, conspicuous, common, printed page I offered it to the public gaze.
> A literary Judas, I kissed her and betrayed her. (55–56)

The narrator confesses only to stealing the products of his family members' wit, not to exposing their personal lives, but his recognition that he has been treacherously detached while listening to private conversations anticipates the growing public discourse around autobiographical fiction's ethics later in the twentieth century. The irony here is that the same democratization of literature which allowed an unprecedented number of people to provide for their loved ones by writing also brought with it a democratized interest in ordinary lives that made intimates more susceptible to betrayals in print.

Literary culture at the turn of the century was already expressing an anxiety about authorial rebellion, free speech, and privacy rights. As a result, recent cases in which authors have been accused of unethically writing about themselves and their intimates in fiction might be seen as reiterations of the controversies involving earlier authors like Dickens, Wroth, or even Aristophanes. Indeed, given the explicit biographical curiosity surrounding authors in the Victorian period, it may be surprising that scandals dealing with fiction's autobiographical aspects did not surface more often. However, social injunctions against self-exposure and invasions of others' privacy were still largely operative. Personal reputation had a different valence, family life had a greater sanctity, and although the press was quick to pounce when an individual's wrongdoing seemed to legitimize public inquiry, most people would have considered it unthinkable to invite such scrutiny of their intimate relations. With the advent of modernism, though, fiction would challenge this state of affairs by setting new standards for candor and self-revelation.

MODERNISM AND THE CONFESSIONAL AGE

The proliferation of public confessions, both true and invented, voluntary and involuntary, across a range of media in the last one hundred years suggests that the twentieth century witnessed the inauguration of a confessional era. As Virginia Woolf declared: "We live in an age when a thousand cameras are pointed, by newspapers, letters, and diaries, at every character from every angle" (*Death* 195). With the Hollywood star system already nascent before World War I, the celebrity of literary authors was on the brink of being eclipsed by that of artists in other forms, but writers were still sufficiently prominent that during the twenties, British *Vogue* featured portraits and cameos of T. S. Eliot, Gertrude Stein, and others.[11] Meanwhile, many authors courted further attention through their literary self-revelations. Michel Foucault claims that in modern society "one confesses one's crimes, one's sins, one's thoughts and desires, one's illnesses and troubles; one goes about telling, with the greatest precision, whatever is most difficult to tell" (*History* 59). This statement might be taken as an after-the-fact manifesto for modernist fiction, which in many cases set about erasing the boundary between authors' art and their lives while daring to disclose private details that courted not just readers' biographical curiosity but also their indignation and disgust. At the same time, the early decades of the twentieth century featured the birth of the New Criti-

---

11. See Jaffe 199.

cism, which seemed to create a countervailing force by moving the author outside the boundaries of literary criticism. Through the introduction of concepts such as "biographical heresy" and "intentional fallacy," the New Critics dismissed authors' aims and backgrounds as irrelevant to literary study, thereby arrogating hermeneutic authority to a growing number of professional scholars, even while many of these academics took an unprecedented interest in the writing of living authors.

Certain ironies in this dismissal of authors from critical discourse were evident not least in the "poetics of impersonality" advocated by T. S. Eliot, whose essays on literature were foundational documents for the New Criticism. To be sure, Eliot's insistence in 1928 that "poetry is something over and above, and something quite different from, a collection of psychological data about the minds of poets" seems to sideline biographical considerations (ix). However, Eliot and the New Critics were preoccupied with the author in ways they did not articulate, and they owed a greater debt than they were usually willing to admit to the Romantic ethos they derided. For example, in "Tradition and the Individual Talent," Eliot's picture of the author is of a "man who suffers," one whose mind must "digest and transmute the passions which are its material," in order to write poetry (54). Eliot follows the Romantics in presenting poets as quasiprophetic figures who stand apart from contemporary society, high priests of Art with a special relationship to literary canons that may seem dazzling, if not mystical, to the uninitiated. Because this depiction makes authors into objects of interest, Eliot's seemingly arbitrary insistence that they are out of bounds for criticism sets the stage for an even more intensively biographical hermeneutics. In the same vein, Eliot's New Critical legatees W. K. Wimsatt and Monroe C. Beardsley do not dispute the Romantics' characterization of literary composition as involving an imperative to "surrender yourself to yourself, search for the truth in your own soul, listen to the sound of your own inside voice"; they only reject the notion that poems should be read as though they are inscriptions of this process (8). If one accepts the validity of a Romantic poetics, though, one might think it artificially and unnecessarily restrictive to treat that poetics as inconsequential to readings of the literature it produces. Indeed, Eliot's privileging of "impersonality" can be taken as a literary reformulation of Warren and Brandeis's emphasis on the "inviolate personality" three decades earlier. Each formulation serves prescriptive purposes better than descriptive ones, and each seeks to remediate the behavior of the biographically curious. Accordingly, Eliot's poetics of impersonality is less a poetics than a hermeneutics, a way not of proscribing confession but of facilitating and protecting it by imposing on readers a tacit obligation not to take a poem's admissions as referential. This imposition helped writers such as Eliot to explore intimate material while keeping their sometimes tumultuous private lives more or less secret. At the same time, Eliot's injunction against biographical reading made a biographical hermeneutics more attractive by opening the door for readers to betray the author's wishes and enjoy the thrill of transgression. What is more, given the long history of ironic authorial disavowals with regard to the referentiality of their work, it is not surprising if certain readers took Eliot's emphasis on impersonality to be a veiled admission that his poetry contained confessional material.

Even while Eliot was making impersonality a hallmark of modernist poetic discourse, fiction writers such as James Joyce were writing novels that provocatively drew on their acquaintances' lives along with their own.[12] The transgressive use of personal material became as much a modernist tenet as impersonality, although it was less often explicitly formulated as one. Earlier, proponents of aestheticism had declared literature to be immune from ethics—as Oscar Wilde put it, "There is no such thing as a moral or an immoral book" (3)—but modernists often appeared eager to align fiction with intentional impropriety, not least through bald depictions of private citizens. Joyce, for one, gave the names of real people to characters in *Ulysses,* and he was sufficiently unkind in certain representations that one of the models sued successfully for defamation. Meanwhile, as Sean Latham has noted, *romans à clef* proliferated in the modernist era, with prominent examples including Aldous Huxley's *Those Barren Leaves,* Somerset Maugham's *Cakes and Ale,* Wyndham Lewis's *The Apes of God,* and Jean Rhys's *After Leaving Mr. Mackenzie.*[13] In certain ways, this brand of *roman à clef* was not so different from earlier ones: for instance, it often traded in satirical portraits of well-known figures. However, modernists' targets were not just the aristocracy but also the artistic coteries of Bloomsbury and the Left Bank. Such targeting served at once to consolidate those circles' cultural cachet, confirm that the authors of the *romans à clef* were members of the avant-garde, and assert the authors' critical distance from those cliques. Given that these circles served in the popular imagination as what Latham calls "icons of imagined bohemian

---

12. Max Saunders situates such autobiographical novels in the context of a broader modernist trend toward the writing of "autobiografiction": that is, narratives that complicate the line between fiction and life writing while construing the self as "something that needs to be constructed" (502).

13. See Latham 11.

autonomy and sexual liberation," the authors of novels skewering them managed to appear doubly transgressive, both depicting taboo-breaking lifestyles and betraying those who cultivated them (127).

The mass media did not hesitate to accompany novelists down the paths they were opening into their own and each other's private lives. For example, in 1922 the *New York Tribune* commissioned a review of F. Scott Fitzgerald's novel *The Beautiful and Damned* from his wife Zelda, as if hoping for a glimpse into the couple's relationship and for public confirmation that his writing was autobiographical. Such hopes were not without foundation, given that the previous year in a magazine interview, F. Scott himself had aligned Zelda with his fiction, avowing: "I married the heroine of my stories" (qtd. in Bruccoli, Smith, and Kerr 79). In her review for the *Tribune,* Zelda corroborated this association of her husband's art with their lives, mentioning the novel's "uncanny fascination" for her and then revealing: "On one page I recognized a portion of an old diary of mine which mysteriously disappeared shortly after my marriage, and also scraps of letters which, though considerably edited, sound to me vaguely familiar" (*Collected* 387–88). Here was something new: the popular press putting an author's loved one in the public eye and encouraging conflict by facilitating an indirect public dialogue between the two. It was not simply that fiction was making a public spectacle of private life, as it long had. Rather, now fiction was attended by a media-disseminated spectacle of betrayal and grievance. With the couple in the spotlight like this, and with literary fame dependent partly on the satisfaction of the public's biographical curiosity, there were ramifications in terms of authorial intimacy. For instance, considerable discord arose when F. Scott sought to stop Zelda from publishing her 1932 autobiographical novel, *Save Me the Waltz*. He did so claiming sole prerogative to use their common history as material, on the grounds that he was the more established author.[14] The situation made it clear that intimate experience had public currency, that it was an asset to be exploited, and that ownership of it was something to be contested.

The fact that Zelda wrote *Save Me the Waltz* as a part of her treatment for mental illness is also significant. If fiction was now expected to plumb an author's interiority and intimate relationships, that expectation was nurtured by the new field of psychoanalysis. In foregrounding the role of the unconscious and insisting that human beings did not know their own minds as well as they thought they did, Sigmund Freud made

---

14. For an account of the conflict, see chapter 3 of Felber.

people—and especially authors—newly estranged, curious interpreters of themselves. The protagonist of Marcel Proust's *In Search of Lost Time* goes so far as to claim that the entire project of writers is to examine their "inner book of unknown signs" (6: 187). And as authors took on this project, they often embraced psychoanalytic tenets and techniques. It was not uncommon for novelists to undergo psychoanalysis and even, as with Zelda Fitzgerald, to write fiction at the behest of their physicians. Rebecca West drafted her autobiographical novel *Sunflower* while under analysis, and H.D. wrote a *roman à clef, Bid Me to Live,* at the suggestion of Freud himself. His reliance on talk therapy emphasized the efficacy of words as a vehicle for greater self-knowledge and mental health, so it was no surprise that the confessions of psychoanalysis came to overlap with those made in fiction.

Another consequence was that fiction gained a new impetus to address sex. "The accent on sex has changed within living memory," wrote Woolf, and the change could be attributed in part to Freud (*Death* 194). By naming sexual desire and early family life as linchpins of psychology, Freud made both interesting in unprecedented ways. He triggered a greater frankness in discussions of sexuality, and he created new possibilities in terms of treating fiction as a vehicle for learning about its authors. Psychoanalysis connected sexuality to autobiographical writing inextricably, yet because the persistence of taboos around sex made it an unlikely topic for nonfiction, the novel stood as an especially viable form in which to represent it. At the same time, because Freud saw fictional writing as a sublimation of its authors' unconscious desires, he offered a new hermeneutics of suspicion to readers. Fiction was apt to be "truer" than autobiography insofar as psychoanalytic theory viewed nonfictional narratives as rife with distortions and denials, while in fiction, as in dreams, the unconscious mind was more liberated to express itself, if indirectly. As a result, although audiences had long taken fiction to be intentionally disguised confession, now readers of a psychoanalytic bent could also treat fiction as betraying its authors' psyches unintentionally.

It was with a psychoanalytically informed notion of the connections between art and life that certain writers in the mid-twentieth century went a step further than their early modernist forbears and identified themselves explicitly with their protagonists, as Henry Miller did in his 1934 sexually explicit novel *Tropic of Cancer*. The book's fallout was protracted. *Tropic of Cancer* was not a bestseller when it was originally published in Paris, but it did make it into the hands of Lawrence Durrell, whose first novel, *The Black Book*—also published in Paris and also subsequently banned on both sides of the Atlantic—bore the mark of Miller's confessional style.¹⁵ *Tropic of Cancer* was smuggled across the ocean in sufficient numbers to influence the Beat poets too, and later it enjoyed commercial success in the wake of a 1961 obscenity trial sparked by its first American publication. Media coverage of the case helped to sell 100,000 copies of *Tropic of Cancer* in hardcover and a million in paperback. Erica Jong, whose novel *Fear of Flying* was strongly influenced by Miller, argues that writers of her generation such as John Updike and Philip Roth owed to Miller's efforts their own relative freedom to write graphically and autobiographically (*Devil* 15). These later authors cemented the association of the transgressively confessional with the transgressively sexual. Meanwhile, Miller's influence might also be seen in his indefatigable promotion and explication of his work. Not least, he created endless textual supplements to his literary corpus, including essays in which he encouraged biographical interpretations of his fiction.

Miller was not alone in his determination to direct people's attention toward his novels and himself concomitantly. His enterprise was paralleled by other self-interpreting, self-celebrating writers, including Norman Mailer. As the title of Mailer's 1959 collection *Advertisements for Myself* indicates, there was a growing emphasis in literary culture on the promotion of authors along with their texts, and Mailer, for one, participated with unapologetic energy, admitting in print to being among "that overcrowded mob of unconscionable egotists who are all determined to become the next great American writer" (18). Such ambition was hardly new; the novelty lay in Mailer's sense of freedom to confess his ambition publicly and in his audience's apparent willingness to accept this rhetoric. Both phenomena suggest a culture in which authors were being not only identified as rebels but also celebrated as such, and in which authors' performances of a particular personality were no less texts to be consumed than their fiction was. Indeed, the mass media allowed for unprecedented conflations of the two. Crime novelist Mickey Spillane went so far as to play his hardboiled detective Mike Hammer in an audio drama, a motion picture, and Miller Lite beer commercials, while posing as Hammer for the covers of his books. Spillane's self-promotion fit a stereotype of U.S.

---

15. Durrell had introduced himself to Miller in 1935 with an adulatory letter that commended Miller's novel as one of the few books "which men have built out of their own guts" ("To Henry" 3). In an interview years later, Durrell claimed: "Henry Miller and T. S. Eliot gave me myself" (qtd. in Jong, *Devil* 34). Durrell was speaking about literary influence, but Miller had also provided concrete assistance by helping him secure a publisher for *The Black Book*.

commercialism, and indeed it seems more than coincidental that Miller, Mailer, and Spillane were all American. To be sure, their shared nationality bespeaks a longstanding American embrace of unapologetic self-advancement. It may also suggest that, as Loren Glass argues, America differed from Europe in its "much-less-established tradition of high culture and a far-more-developed mass cultural public sphere." Consequently, American authors were more attuned to "the marketing strategies and audience sensibilities of large-scale production" (6).[16] They evinced a recognition that the mass media had created a confessional industry which needed to be fed and that journalists were eager to promote certain authors in part simply because of the need for personalities to discuss. The Hollywood star system had played no small role in creating a mode of journalism dedicated to investigating the private lives of famous people, and this demand spilled over from film into the other arts.[17] Biographical curiosity about authors was arguably even more intense—if less prevalent—than curiosity about actors, given that increasingly in the twentieth century, the literary texts that brought writers into the public eye were construed as intimate confessions.

THE SCANDAL OF CONFESSIONAL POETRY

Readers' biographical curiosity became particularly evident in the 1960s when a wave of autobiographical literature led by American confessional poetry responded to and reshaped public discourse about privacy, referentiality, and ethics. It did so in part through a network of media that was structured around the facilitation and dissemination of confession. The previous decade had prepared the ground for these changes: not least, as Diane Wood Middlebrook argues, Cold War anxieties about the "enemy within" had shifted boundaries around privacy, so that "ordinary citizens were encouraged to keep an eye on their neighbors and report deviant behavior or suspicious activity to the FBI" (647). Meanwhile, even as new technologies such as eavesdropping devices and telephoto lenses offered

---

16. One might also consider Mark McGurl's hypothesis that the imperative in American creative writing classes to "write what you know"—not to mention America's leadership in establishing creative writing programs in the first place—is partly a product of 1920s educational reforms that sought to "re-gear U.S. schools for the systematic production of original persons," such that "the practice of self-expression became paramount" (83, 85).

17. Daniel Boorstin comments about such a system: "In the creation of a celebrity somebody always has an interest—newsmen needing stories, press agents paid to make celebrities, and the celebrity himself" (74).

unprecedented means to violate privacy, other technologies fostered greater privacy than before. Among them was television, which allowed people to be entertained by confessions on talk shows, game shows, and the like without having to leave their living rooms. As a result, although confessional poetry was innovative in changing expectations of literature, it was meeting an already existent demand for confession.

Robert Lowell's controversial and influential 1959 poetry collection, *Life Studies,* met that demand by presenting a speaker who was taken for the poet himself and who flouted decorum by testifying to his family history in ways that were not always flattering. The book produced an outcry among critics: for example, M. L. Rosenthal characterized *Life Studies* as "a series of personal confidences, rather shameful, that one is honor-bound not to reveal" ("Poetry" 64). Rosenthal's use of the word "personal" is not innocent here, given that in style and subject matter, *Life Studies* broke decisively with the "impersonal" modernist style of which Lowell himself had been the decade's foremost American practitioner. *Life Studies* set the tone for the work of many authors in the next decade, perhaps most famously Lowell's students Anne Sexton and Sylvia Plath. Literary critics have differed as to what exactly constitutes a "confessional" poem, but nearly all would agree that it features a first-person speaker identified with the poet who testifies to her or his own intimate, usually painful experiences, and that these confessions have been taken by some to be transgressively self-revelatory.[18] For example, mental illness, alcoholism, and divorce were previously more or less taboo topics in public conversation, but they were among the issues that confessional poetry of the 1960s addressed.

The willingness to treat these subjects in literature was partly due to Freud's continuing currency. Lowell and Sexton were both introduced to psychoanalysis in the fifties when suffering from depression, both were encouraged by doctors to write for the sake of their mental health, and both went on to read much of Freud's work. The influence of psychoanalysis on Lowell's writing is observed by Alan Williamson, who comments that the poet's "principal techniques—the resurrection of early memories, the unsparing objectivity about present behavior, and the increased conscious awareness of interpersonal dynamics—are all common features

---

18. Rosenthal describes a confessional poem as one in which "the private life of the poet himself, especially under stress of psychological crisis, [is] a major theme" (*New* 15), and Alan Williamson observes "a thematic concern with disclosure or shock" (*Introspection* 7). Middlebrook characterizes the genre more contextually as "middle-class postwar art—produced by WASP writers—that violated the norms of decorum for subject matter prevailing in serious literature" (632–33).

of the analytic experience" (*Pity* 68). One might add that such poetry also rehearses the analytic experience by positioning readers as akin to therapists, offering them an unusually powerful sense of intimacy with the author by making them privy to apparently uncensored confessions. However, the psychoanalytic influence on confessional poetry did little to simplify its ethics. For one thing, the Freudian narrative of identity emphasized early relations and encouraged patients to examine them, so that autobiographical exploration gained an impetus to have an interpersonal scope. What is more, psychoanalytic theory construes family relations— and, through transference, subsequent intimate relationships—as riven by ambivalence, so that bonds of love are inextricable from rivalries and resentments. If a foundational early stage of a child's development involves its desire to sleep with one parent and kill the other, the pattern of intimacy being established is not an entirely tidy one. The therapeutic setting offered a relatively safe environment in which patients could explore such patterns, but it was quite another thing for poets to publish psychoanalytically inflected narratives that explicitly discussed their friends, family, and lovers. Indeed, the ethical complications of doing so were not lost on the public.

Such was the case with Lowell's 1973 sonnet sequence, *The Dolphin*, which incorporated excerpts of letters from his ex-wife, Elizabeth Hardwick, prompting complaints by reviewers that he had betrayed her by appropriating her voice. Donald Hall, for one, characterized Lowell as a "cannibal-poet" who dined "off portions of his own body, and the bodies of his family" (44), while Adrienne Rich called the appropriation of Hardwick's words "one of the most vindictive and mean-spirited acts in the history of poetry" (186). Apologists for *The Dolphin* countered by foregrounding what they saw as its salutary public effects; for instance, Diane Wakoski argued that questions of personal betrayal were subordinate to the matter of Lowell's moral contributions to society as a whole. Emphasizing the latter, she claimed that Lowell had published "a document in which we, the readers, can derive a morality, understand some lives, give credence to our humanity" (188). With regard to the history of literary ethics, these arguments for and against Lowell's book are notable not for the novelty of their reasoning but for the fact that they were occurring in print. The license that critics felt in addressing the matter was abetted not least by the changing sexual politics of the time, as the women's movement slogan "The personal is political" had taken hold, and not only poets were treating private issues in public. At the same time, changes in the divorce rate and in the terms of marriage during the sexual revolution had created a period of social turmoil in which there was an audience hungry for stories to help make sense of the zeitgeist.

It was in this period that the confessional age reached maturity. As never before, connections between intimate literary details and real people's lives were being identified by third-party commentators in an array of media, and these commentators were willing to castigate the authors in question for their putative transgressions. This phenomenon of third-party commentary was not incidental to the creation and character of confessional poetry in the first place either. Authors in the sixties and seventies could predict with some assurance that although most of their audience would not be familiar with their life stories at the outset, the reception of their writing would be supplemented by readings, interviews, reviews, and articles. For that reason, poetry and fiction could afford to be both more self-revelatory and coyer than before. If literature seemed to be confessional, there would be more interest in it, but because authors could expect to be called upon to explicate their writing, they did not need to make its autobiographical basis fully clear in the text itself. Rather, a certain amount of flirtatious confessional obliquity might well be more successful in drawing the media's gaze. Accordingly, confessional poems often took the shape of autobiographical puzzles that required a paratextual key to solve them, and poets became inextricably enmeshed in a field of confessional commentary.

Public discussions about the ethics of autobiographical writing were not long confined to the scandals of confessional poetry. Novelists and story writers, too, were increasingly accused of having written treacherous autobiographical narratives, as in the cases of Philip Roth's *Portnoy's Complaint* and Erica Jong's *Fear of Flying*. The debts of these novels to confessional poetry and psychoanalysis were clear enough: for instance, Roth's novel takes the form of an extended monologue by a patient to his analyst, while Jong's novel includes sections of Plath-like confessional poetry written by its narrator. What is more, each novel teasingly invites biographical readings: *Portnoy's Complaint* by giving its Jewish male protagonist a New Jersey childhood not entirely dissimilar to Roth's, and *Fear of Flying* by making its female narrator a writer named Isadora Wing. Both novels became bestsellers and generated significant commentary about their putative autobiographical qualities as well as their sexual explicitness. To be sure, the controversy of these novels and confessional poetry was a relatively minor cultural phenomenon compared to the kinds of scandals that were the bread and butter of Hollywood reporting and that would become increasingly common in American politics after the

Watergate affair. Nevertheless, they set the tone for the literary scandals that have since reached the mainstream press with regard to autobiographical fiction. Clearly it was no new thing for literature to be controversial; the relatively unprecedented aspects in the case of confessional poetry and subsequent fiction were the exposures of authors' loved ones and the degree to which both authors and commentators were willing to discuss publicly the writers' intimate relations.

Since *Portnoy's Complaint* and *Fear of Flying,* the public appetite for details of people's private lives has only grown, and with the advent of phenomena such as Facebook, cell-phone cameras, Internet hacking, and CCTV, it is harder than ever for people to maintain control over those details. At the same time, the financial and cultural rewards of confession have created a marketplace for genres such as the "tell-all" autobiography. Western culture has embraced confessional poetry's ethos of self-exposure and has dismantled barriers with regard to what can be said in public about previously taboo subjects, so that fiction's traditional cachet in terms of frankness has evaporated. The daily nonfictional confessions on reality TV shows, YouTube, and blogs are no less shocking than what fiction used to offer as transgressive. The extent to which fiction remains scandalous has come to depend less on its candor than on its referential ambiguity. As William A. Cohen observes, the perpetuation of scandal requires a continued inconclusiveness about what actually happened; scandal "captures public attention only to the extent that such a determination is deferred" (9). Given this quality of scandal, autobiographical fiction is inherently scandalous in its refusal to confirm the extent to which it is true. Instead, it appears to present only hints and clues as to its basis in reality. With regard to Catherine Millet's 2001 autofiction, *The Sexual Life of Catherine M.,* for example, the ostensible controversy of its sexually graphic passages was shaded, if not eclipsed, by readers' fascination with the text's simultaneous referentiality and coyness.

The term "autofiction" was first used by the novelist Serge Doubrovsky to describe his 1977 book *Fils.* Since that time, autofiction has become a much-discussed genre, in particular with regard to French writers. For Doubrovsky, the term both foregrounds and complicates the relationship between autobiography and invention. I take autofiction to be interesting less for its formal characteristics—which hardly seem innovative if one considers writers such as Proust and Miller—than for the public use of the term by authors to classify their work. The production of autofiction as such is a paratextual phenomenon: it involves not simply writing fictively about oneself in a literary text but extending the autobiographical act into paratextual commentary and establishing a public self that provides a foil for the self depicted in the autofiction. As this chapter has shown, authors of fiction have long involved themselves in such paratextual industry, from the creation of prefaces to courtroom disavowals, and they have done so not least to publicize their work by fomenting scandals. But there have been important changes in terms of the cultural norms and discourses that have shaped paratextual confessions, as well as in the media through which paratexts have been disseminated. As the next chapter argues, one consequence of these shifts is that it is difficult to read contemporary fiction independently of authors' paratextual confessions and self-inventions. For many readers, a literary text in itself is impoverished without paratextual framing that somehow connects the author to the work.

As becomes clear in chapters 3 and 4, this shift in literary culture also has ramifications for authors' intimates, who sometimes find themselves named if not shamed as the originals of literary characters, and who—in the manner of Zelda Fitzgerald—may be tempted to enter the paratextual fray. When they do so, though, they perpetuate a cultural preoccupation with scandal; indeed, they facilitate a new kind of scandal in which the scandalous material is not simply a work of literature but the subsequent public war of words between authors and their intimates. If authors such as Lady Mary Wroth and Charles Dickens largely remained in the private sphere as they allayed their putative victims' feelings, defended themselves against accusations of libel, and made their own identifications of characters with originals, contemporary writers are apt to go about such business in public, and not only in the wake of causing offense but also anticipatorily, as if to court controversy by intentionally wounding their loved ones. Such paratextual performances draw attention to the imbrication of fiction's semantics, ethics, and erotics. To understand this imbrication better, and to provide greater context for the dilemmas that authors and their intimates face as they negotiate the ethics of fiction, the next chapter examines literary culture in the present day more closely, attending in particular to the relationships that authors and readers develop with each other through the mediations of fiction and paratexts.

2

Biographical Desire

> I myself cannot (as an enamored subject) construct my love story to the end: I am its poet (its bard) only for the beginning; the end, like my own death, belongs to others; it is up to them to write the fiction, the external, mythic narrative.
>
> —Roland Barthes, *A Lover's Discourse* 101

> Of course, by projecting essentially fictional characters with manic personae out into the world, you openly invited misunderstanding about yourself. But because some people get it wrong and don't have any idea of who or what you really are doesn't suggest to me that you have to straighten them out. Just the opposite—consider having tricked them into those beliefs a *success*; that's what fiction's *supposed* to do.
>
> —Philip Roth, *The Facts* 167

Searching fiction for references to its author's life is not an innocent mode of reading, nor are writers without motive when they use personal material in their stories, discuss their work in relation to themselves, and otherwise facilitate or advocate biographical readings of literature. Readers and writers alike are susceptible to the pull of biographical desire. For readers of fiction, this is a desire to know authors through their texts; for authors, it is a desire to be sought out in that fashion. Biographical desire is stimulated when fiction presents protagonists who resemble their authors in physical appearance and background, or when it otherwise gestures back to the people who produced it, suggesting authors' wishes to be recognized not merely for but in their texts. Tobias Wolff's novel *Old School* offers an astute description of this desire with regard to the later fiction of Ernest Hemingway: a character asserts that every year, Hemingway became "harder to separate from the work. He loomed over it . . . drawing up into himself the love and honor he demanded for his characters. . . . This deliberate blurring had always been in play, but now it seemed anxious, greedy" (184–85). The love described here need not be merely platonic, either. Wayne Booth describes books as readers' friends (*Company* 169)—a description that, in Lawrence Buell's words, aims "to restore plenitude to the reading relationship and offset the one-sidedness of a hermeneutics of suspicion" ("What" 12). But this rather cozily asexual description of the reader–author relationship elides the presence of other kinds of desire while ignoring the referential hide-and-seek games that go on in and around fiction. Rather than thinking about fictional texts as the reader's friend, it may be more apt to consider them as a kind of Pandarus who mediates between separated lovers. That possibility informs this chapter's exploration of biographical desire in literary culture. In particular, I focus on the importance of paratexts, arguing that they have not been sufficiently recognized in accounts of contemporary fiction. This is surprising, given their ubiquity and manifold influence on fiction's aesthetics, erotics, and marketing. Paratexts are sites of phantasmatic interpersonal relations between authors and readers, a form of mediated intimacy involving flirtation, betrayal, and a sense of loss. As such, they are crucial to the creation, expression, frustration, and satisfaction of biographical desire.

An emblematic case demonstrating the evolution of paratextual production and biographical desire through the latter twentieth century is that of the Canadian-born author Elizabeth Smart and her 1945 "cult" novel *By Grand Central Station I Sat Down and Wept*. While the author's and book's places in literary canons are marginal, the story of the novel's changing fortunes makes for a fascinating study, not least because those fortunes have been so closely aligned with Smart's own as an author, while the renown of both the writer and her work has been tied closely to the public circulation of stories about Smart's romantic experiences. *By Grand Central Station* enjoyed successive rounds of republication and publicity during the later decades of Smart's life, and it attracted significant attention because of its autobiographical content. Smart's appearances in the mass media show her to be addressing a complicated set of desires on the part of her audience, as the public's wish for the book to be confessional runs alongside a shared ambivalence about the propriety and literary merit of including personal history in fiction. The impulse to identify Smart with her novel's protagonist can also be read as expressing an anxiety that fictional texts are in fact radically independent of their authors, reminders of authors' absence as much as evocations of them. In this regard, the narrative of *By Grand Central Station* prefigures the novel's public life by focusing on the same kinds of desire that would come to frame the book's reception. Smart's narrator, abandoned at the end of the novel by her poet lover, stands in a place that also comes to be occupied by her readers as they, in their relationship to Smart, enter their own intimate and estranged affair with an author. Accordingly, the love story the novel describes is mirrored by the love story between Smart and her readers. This mirroring is not merely coincidental, either. Rather, in multiple ways the novel's account of the narrator's affair has shaped the attraction readers feel to Smart.

Because it is nearly impossible to encounter *By Grand Central Station* without also encountering paratexts that facilitate or even demand biographical readings of the book, a strictly formalist approach to it would fail to recognize how readers actually engage with the text. Indeed, the novel raises questions about its own referentiality that cannot be solved without resort to paratexts. As a result, the book's narrative serves as a catalyst for interactions between reader and author in paratexts and media commentary, where curiosity about the novel's autobiographical character makes the author as much an object of attention as the text she produced. It would be one thing if this were true only of *By Grand Central Station*, but I take the dynamics of the novel's reception to exemplify the workings of biographical desire in the confessional age. As I argued in the previous chapter, a key transformation in literary culture since the 1960s has been in terms of paratextual production and the public discourse about fiction. Novelists earlier in the twentieth century were not shy about writing with sexual candor and drawing on their loved ones' intimate experience; the change has been that third-party commentators are now more willing to make public identifications between fictional characters and real people, as well as to excoriate authors publicly for creating these correspondences. What is more, authors use paratexts more pervasively, in particular to avow and disavow their fiction's referential content, and more generally to cultivate and respond to biographical desire.

If the nature of this desire is mapped implicitly by Smart in *By Grand Central Station,* other authors have explored it more explicitly and at greater length. In this chapter I also focus on the work of Philip Roth, which, rather than suggesting there is a "real" Roth to be uncovered behind his fiction, encourages readers to think of personal identity in terms of the fantastic, plural, protean, performative, and hypothetical. Within this framework, biographical desire can appear to be merely a reductive and misguided hermeneutic phase that leads to more sophisticated kinds of reading. Indeed, some readers might consider biographical desire to be beneath them, a form of middlebrow taste for titillation, gossip, and scandal that fails to recognize the imaginative, depersonalized nature of fiction. However, it would be difficult *not* to be biographically desirous given that, as the previous chapter makes clear, frequently even the most "highbrow" literature breeds such desire and, in fact, cannot help breeding it, given the confessional culture in which contemporary literature is situated. Accordingly, I suggest we might understand biographical readings of fiction as a form of play, with readers oscillating between referential curiosity and the suspension of it, and with each approach conferring various benefits. Meanwhile, I consider arguments that the entire confessional culture in which biographical reading takes place is morally suspect, devoted to scandal and narcissistic narratives. I argue that we need to recognize the advantages as well as the drawbacks of such a culture, but that we should also notice how authors of fiction are frequently made into social scapegoats, castigated for their indecorous revelations and defamations by commentators who are themselves often invested in scandal. Rather than simply condemning autobiographical fiction for its treacheries, I suggest it occupies a social space which, to use Michel Foucault's term, might be considered heterotopic: that is, it both stands apart from and confirms the predominant social order. As such, it expresses not the intrinsic decline of culture but the tensions inherent in a culture's functioning.

ELIZABETH SMART AND CONFESSIONAL CULTURE

In the field of paratexts, commentary, and promotion, authors are both creators of and servants to readers' biographical desire. The coercive force of this desire is perhaps baldest in moments when authors speak publicly about the extent to which their fiction is based on their lives. The cultural yearning for such discussion may discomfit writers, not least because an attraction of writing autobiographically in fiction rather than nonfiction is that the former promises them greater control over public adjudications of their texts' referentiality. With fiction there is less risk than with autobiography that someone else will emerge to say of the narrative, "It didn't happen that way." However, readers' biographical desire means that more often than autobiographers, authors of fiction are asked a version of the question: "How much of the story is true?" At such moments they confront a demand that they do for their fiction what it cannot do for itself: that is, testify reliably to its referential character. Authors are also facing a demand that they tell a story about themselves and reveal personal details, if not about their intimate relations, then at least about their relationship to their writing—a relationship that, of course, might be one of the most private and personal they have. To be sure, readers do not all equally approach fiction biographically, but in the confessional age, one seldom encounters fiction without also encountering paratexts that encourage biographical curiosity. If Gérard Genette is right that "a text without a paratext does not exist and never has existed," this is especially true in the age of television, radio, and the Internet (3). Although Carla Benedetti has called paratextual commentary by authors "secondary labor," in practice it has come to be a sufficiently consuming task that in many cases, literature can seem to be primarily the catalyst for the production of commentary (27). Consequently, paratexts are not external to a literary text in terms of its semantics; rather, they are part of the apparatus that shapes its meaning. Moreover, paratexts participate in a field of discourse that at one level supplements literary texts and, at another level, exists for its own sake, both economically and culturally. From this perspective, the literary text can be an instrument of paratexts, enabling an industry that produces interviews, profiles, reviews, and other materials as commodities in themselves.

In this industry, the impetus to focus on authors is both hermeneutic and commercial. As Michel Foucault argues, to speak of the "author" is to reify a subject who can claim proprietary rights to a piece of writing and provide an organizing principle by which to associate a group of otherwise diverse texts (*Foucault* 107). Literary culture enacts this process by systematically yoking individual authors to texts—on covers and title pages, in biographical blurbs, in interviews and scholarship, and so forth—while generally ignoring or diminishing the role of editors and other collaborators in those texts' production. The author function also cedes to the principal writers of texts a certain authority in interpreting those writings. But at the same time that authors are interpellated as the sole creators of literature, they are, as Joe Moran points out, "themselves (whether they like it or not) the intertextual creations of promotion and publicity" (66–67). In the process of being so constituted, authors are made into subjects appropriate for study in biographies and criticism, performers to be heard discussing their work, and personalities to be discovered through their fiction. Frequently reviewers discuss the authors as well as the books they are considering, speculating about their lives or intentions, while the New Critics' "biographical heresy" is committed rampantly in interviews when journalists ask authors to explain the personal background of their stories. The writer A. L. Kennedy has described literary culture as one preoccupied by "de-fictionalization" and has said she wants to scream when asked for the "eight hundredth time what real people something I've written is based on" (qtd. in Gibbons). Authors are also required to craft public personae for themselves that are associated with their literary texts. The authorial persona is hardly new, but the variety of forums in which authors are called upon to speak about themselves in these personae, along with the expected degree of self-revelation, is without precedent.

Few can follow Shakespeare who, in Henry James's phrase, "slunk past in life," stealing away from posterity with his life story more or less unknown (*Literary* 1219). And should authors protest against imputations that their fiction is autobiographical, they still become complicit in confessional culture, given that their protests provide grist to readers whose understanding of the fiction comes through weighing its seeming confessions against authorial commentary. Indeed, even readers who take authorial denials of autobiographical content at face value only confirm the centrality of the authors to their fiction, insofar as those readers are implicitly accepting that writers' views of their work are authoritative. In a similar paradox, those contemporary writers who, like the famously reclusive American novelists Thomas Pynchon and J. D. Salinger, seek to extricate themselves from confessional culture end up drawing attention to themselves precisely through their efforts to avoid the spotlight. Likewise, anonymously published texts tend to beget rampant speculation about their authorship. Because the choice for authors seems to be either to cede framings of their texts and their lives to journalists and publicists or to produce confessional paratexts themselves, it is not surprising if many exhibit what Genette calls a "great conscientiousness" in performing "their paratextual duty" (409). By doing so, they are able at least to participate in, if not control, decisions about what aspects of their lives will be explored and exposed. After all, as Moran argues, a paradoxical effect of the media's author-centered textual supplements is the removal of agency from authors: "The author becomes gradually less in control not only of her work but also of her image and how it circulates" (61). Commentary is a way for authors to continue "producing" a text even after its publication, foregrounding their own interpretations of it and implicitly asserting the authority of those interpretations. Still, a confessional culture requiring authors either to endure biographical speculation silently or to provide preemptive confessions presents them with a significant dilemma.

This dilemma faced Elizabeth Smart as she responded to media curiosity about the autobiographical qualities of her first novel, *By Grand Central Station I Sat Down and Wept*. The book documents how its unnamed narrator, a young Canadian woman, falls in love with a married man while living with him and his wife in California during World War II. Guiltily but ardently she enters into an affair with him, eventually ending up pregnant and abandoned, first living solitarily in British Columbia, then traveling to the titular station in New York and lamenting her situation. A short, lyrical narrative, spare in plot and details about its characters, the novel is a *cri de cœur* focusing on the narrator's desire for her lover and her agony in his absence. The book is now recognized as a "cult" classic for its poetic prose and charged, candid expression of female desire, which feminists of the 1960s embraced as ahead of its time. *By Grand Central Station* is also inevitably understood to fictionalize the beginnings of Smart's decades-long romantic relationship with the English poet George Barker. To be sure, there are more than incidental parallels between the book's narrator and her author: Smart, too, was a young woman during World War II, and she began an affair with Barker while living with him and his wife at a writers' colony in Big Sur. Moreover, Smart relocated to British Columbia while pregnant with Barker's child. What is interesting about the book, however, is not these points of identification so much as the ways in which they were made explicit with increasing candor and frequency by media commentators as well as by Smart herself in the later years of her life.

This commentary was catalyzed partly by changes in the preoccupations of the mass media and partly by the self-revelatory semblance of Smart's novel. In that regard, Smart was participating in a newly confessional form of fiction that had already emerged in Europe. By attending to her narrator's erotic life and making a novel out of her own private history, Smart was influenced by the work of self-fictionalizing authors such as Lawrence Durrell, Henry Miller, and Anaïs Nin. In the early forties a direct connection developed between Smart and these writers when Durrell accepted some of her poems for his magazine *Booster* and then wrote to Miller about her while also arranging an initial correspondence between her and Barker. But just as Smart first came to know Barker through his poetry, she also knew and admired these other writers' work before contacting them. In 1939 Smart wrote in her journal: "I do not want, I am irritated with the devious method and hidden indirectness of the novel, for instance, or even the short story, or a play. Poems, notes, diaries, letters, or prose such as 'The House of Incest,' in The Black Book, only meet my need" (*Necessary* 201–2). And indeed, the writing of Durrell, Miller, and Nin, which blurred the line between them and their fictional protagonists, would come to inform *By Grand Central Station,* as Smart chose to leave her narrator unnamed. This decision implicitly created what Philippe Lejeune has called a "phantasmatic pact" with readers, who are left to decide for themselves whether to view Smart's narrator as an incarnation of her author (27). Readers who feel uncomfortable with such ambiguity have the option of adjudicating the narrative's referentiality by drawing on the paratexts and commentary that have proliferated since the 1970s and 1980s, when reviewers and journalists repeatedly enlisted Smart in their attempts to conjure the young woman who had fallen in love and written a book about it.

Upon the initial publication of *By Grand Central Station* in 1945, its few reviewers exhibited no interest in or awareness of the book's autobiographical aspects. Indeed, the book caused very little splash of any kind. Released by a small London publisher during wartime, it disappeared quickly from the public eye. It was not until 1966 that a second edition was published in Britain, where Smart was still living, and then it was Smart herself—now the mother of four children by Barker, although the two of them never married or lived together—who made the first public suggestions that the book was based on her own experience. A review in the *Evening Standard* quotes her as saying: "It's not just a play title. I sat down by Grand Central Station for a whole day crying and writing the novel." This comment marked the beginning of a series of flirtations with the press in which Smart alternately embraced and challenged biographical readings of her book. Such readings came to the fore in 1977 when the novel was republished again alongside Smart's first poetry collection, *A Bonus.* Notably, the praise from reviewers that greeted *By Grand Central Station* at this time was concomitant with the first widespread discussions in print of the novel's autobiographical aspects. These discussions sometimes offered interpretations of the book that were self-contradictory, in one sentence speaking of it as fiction and in the next as straightforward autobiography. For instance, Leland Bardwell's review in *Hibernia* describes the plot as a love affair between an anonymous woman and an anonymous poet during World War II and then notes of the decades since: "Ms. Smart has spent that time rearing the poet's children" (20). Catherine Stott's article in *Cosmopolitan* presents an equally seamless shift from discussing Barker and Smart to declaring that the novel "chronicles one of the strangest love stories of our time," eliding any sense that the narrative might be at least partly nonreferential (6).

This sudden attention to the book's autobiographical background is hardly surprising, given that it occurred in the wake of confessional poetry's advent, not to mention the controversy of such novels as Philip Roth's *Portnoy's Complaint* and Erica Jong's *Fear of Flying*. It is even less surprising if one considers that the cover of the 1977 edition of *By Grand Central Station* features a photograph of Smart and Barker. The cover served as an equivalent of the keys that had long circulated to supplement *romans à clef* and reveal the real-world originals of fictional characters. Of course, the cover was hardly a surprising promotional choice in terms of seeking to pique readers' biographical curiosity. Other paratexts, including prefatory disclaimers that claim "Any resemblances to people living or dead are purely coincidental," often serve to stimulate rather than stifle biographical desire. Given the long history of authorial irony with regard to such statements, readers can hardly be blamed for viewing their invocation as a sign there is a crime to be denied. The pseudo-legalistic phrasing of the standard disclaimer provides further reason for suspicion. As Thomas Jones points out, such disclaimers paranoiacally overstate their case because the law does not prohibit defamation of the dead and because it is not intrinsically libelous to base characters on real people (18). Such overstatement conspicuously undermines the disclaimer's authority, thus activating the hermeneutics of suspicion it ostensibly seeks to disarm. Accordingly, although a disclaimer is legally useless, it can be effective as a literary device. Before the narrative has even commenced, the disclaimer sets in motion a plot of biographical detection. The very language that would indemnify the fiction against legal action instead positions readers as quasi-juridical investigators and frames a reading of the text as a manner of court case wherein from the beginning the text pleads innocent even while unilaterally—and thus suspiciously—raising the specter of its guilt. In that regard, it is notable that if the disclaimer evokes the text's potential referentiality, it does so in a way that also suggests the text's potential ethical transgressions. By seeming to anticipate legal action, the disclaimer serves as a sensationalizing device that reminds readers of fiction's relationship to scandal. Meanwhile, the disclaimer's hollow legality and potential disingenuousness are reminders that paratexts, too, can be a sort of fiction, performances that are not strictly to be believed and that are thus also susceptible to ethical scrutiny.

In Smart's case, commentators did not condemn the photograph on the cover of the 1977 edition of *By Grand Central Station* for its biographical flirtatiousness. Rather, they took it as a cue to treat the book as autobiography and, when interviewing Smart, to seek clear delineations of the novel's real-life background. Only a few journalists showed much self-consciousness about the novel's referential ambiguity. One, Eleanor Wachtel, expressed such self-consciousness in a 1979 letter to Smart. Enclosing an article about Smart that she had published, she wrote: "I fear you will not approve. I too have some misgivings which I tried to assuage by quoting from your own articulation of disdain for 'mere gossip' and personality. Compromise is seldom admirable but I wished you to reach a wider audience than the academic journals have so far provided." Implied here is a divide between a mainstream readership interested in authorial confessions and a more refined, if limited, audience attentive to aesthetic matters such as form and style. Such a hierarchy presents a challenge to writers seeking both commercial and critical success: they are compelled to satisfy biographical desire, even while critical acclaim seems to depend upon embracing a commitment to impersonal craft. In this regard, it is notable that Wachtel refers to finding an audience for Smart, not for her fiction. Despite Wachtel's skepticism about a popular interest in personality, she does not pretend that the author is anything but central to literary promotion. At the same time, due deference to New Critical values means that the author being promoted must be publicly self-effacing. As Wachtel's letter hints, in such cases it is left to journalists to perform the role of eliciting and disseminating the authors' nonfictional confessions.

The letter underscores the importance of paying attention to the novelist–journalist relationship if one wishes to take stock of how autobiographical fiction functions in contemporary culture. Whatever real or apparent antagonisms that relationship involves, it can be a highly symbiotic one. Indeed, a certain public antagonism between a journalist and a literary author can be mutually beneficial insofar as the author can be seen to confess only reluctantly, at the behest if not the coercion of her interrogator, while the journalist's probing questions and unabashed unveilings give the appearance of objectivity and investigative acumen. Wachtel's letter seems meant to reassure Smart that despite the appearance of a zero-sum game between the two parties, the interests of both can be served. It is telling that Wachtel should have sent Smart a letter at all, confirming the bond between her and her subject. Wachtel justifies her public exposure of Smart by emphasizing their shared "misgivings" and interest in gaining the novelist a "wider audience." As Wachtel identifies these affinities, her medium reinforces her message, the personal letter affirming the intimacy she shares with Smart while opposing that intimacy to an externalized, faceless demand for salacious confession. Even while Wachtel's publicly disseminated article risks destabilizing the journalist–novelist relationship, her letter creates a separate, private space for her and Smart to occupy together—a space paralleled by what Wachtel implicitly identifies as their shared moral and aesthetic concerns. And as Wachtel asserts a critical distance from her article, her use of a letter to explain herself is not so different from Smart's use of paratexts in the same period to insist that she was not identical with her novel's protagonist.

Such nonidentification was difficult for Smart to establish in the later 1970s and early 1980s. Repeatedly in interviews she sought to answer personal questions without reducing *By Grand Central Station* to autobiography. Some degree of complicity in critics' conflations of her life and fiction was inevitable, and she did not usually shy from discussing her affair with Barker. She even fueled biographical speculation by giving readings with him, including an appearance together at the 1980 Edinburgh Festival, where she read from *By Grand Central Station* and Barker read from his book *The Dead Seagull*, also viewed as a fictional treatment of their affair. An article in an advance publicity bulletin for the Edinburgh reading claimed Smart was "afraid that she and George might argue for the whole time" (Brown 2). However, in a review of the event for the *Scotsman*, Allan Massie observed that the two writers "refused to play the game" expected of them by organizers, and he wondered what kind of conflict or confession had been anticipated. At the same time, Smart and Barker's coyness might be seen as part of the "game" itself, since uncertainty about the exact autobiographical nature of their books was no doubt part of the stories' appeal.

If authors of fiction are often inconsistent or disingenuous when accepting or repudiating identifications with their characters, sometimes the reason is that the exact relations are unclear to the authors themselves. For example, in the final years of Smart's life she confessed that she could not remember which parts of *By Grand Central Station* were true and which were made up. But such relations might be murky even sooner after the fiction's composition if the text is sufficiently personal and involving to influence the author's self-conception. Philip Roth makes this point in his border-blurring autobiography *The Facts* when he has his alter ego, Zuckerman, address him in a letter, saying: "My guess is that you've written metamorphoses of yourself so many times, you no longer have any idea what *you* are or ever were. By now what you are is a walking text" (162). Such authorial uncertainty about the distinction between fact and fantasy is likely to grow, not diminish, in the course of paratextual performance. Even as interrogators demand clarification of a fiction's referentiality, authors are required above all to tell interesting stories and present compelling versions of themselves. Consequently, it would be wrong to look to paratexts as a site for the authorial reclaiming of an authentic identity after the self-inventions of fiction. Rather, paratexts encourage further fictive improvisations in a discourse that, while holding authors to higher verificationist standards of truth-telling than fiction does, seldom approaches the juridical. In fact, often the most theatrical and hyperbolic personae thrive best in a mass media environment: consider the dandyism of Tom Wolfe. With regard to such authors, more important than their performances' authenticity is the maintenance of a distinctive identity that can be easily recognized, commented upon, even parodied. In this environment, it is not surprising that an author such as Roth should feel his factual and invented selves melding. Rejecting the model of single-direction causality, Roth reminds readers that characters can remake the authors who create them—a process that, as we shall see in the next chapter, can be especially disorienting and injurious when an author's intimates find themselves caught up in it as well. In the meantime, it is unsurprising that Smart should have claimed to be unsure about her novel's relation to her life. Her assertion was at once an evasion of her audience's biographical desire and a move to ally herself with them as just one more bewildered reader of her fiction and her life.

As might be inferred from Wachtel's letter, Smart's uncertainty also refracted a longstanding cultural unease about the aesthetic implications of writing autobiographical fiction. Although there is an expectation that novelists often draw their plots and characters from their own lives, there is a common denigration of those who do so transparently. For instance, Leo Gurko observes the critical consensus that developed by 1940 around Thomas Wolfe: namely, that "his novels are autobiographical, and he could not handle experiences that were not directly his own" (1). Because of such diminutions, some writers have feared writing autobiographically, or at least admitting to doing so. Women in particular, who historically have faced aspersions when writing about female experiences at all, have had to combat the further prejudice that women's fiction is "merely" autobiographical—what Mary Jacobus calls "the autobiographical 'phallacy'" (520). Smart herself grew increasingly wary of discussing the autobiographical aspects of her work even while she continued to evoke them. As early as 1977, she claimed in an interview: "They've made far too much of the autobiography. Naturally, you have to use your own life—even Mary Shelley used parts of her own life when she was writing about Frankenstein. But I only took things out of my own life which I felt were relevant" (qtd. in A. Jones 5). On other occasions, she struggled to assert the imaginative qualities of her novel. For instance, a 1979 stage adaptation in St. Louis consternated her by naming its characters Elizabeth Smart and George Barker. Similarly, after Metropolis Pictures bought the film rights to the novel in 1980 and Smart was shown the screenplay, she was horrified by its biographical emphasis, declaring: "I sold the rights to my book. Not to my life" (qtd. in Sullivan 340). Still, it might seem difficult to sympathize with Smart's complaint that she was "sick of those who assume that the woman is me and the man is George" when in her own script for a film version of *By Grand Central Station* she named her protagonists Elizabeth and George (qtd. in Layton 2). Perhaps the gesture was a subversive complication, not a simplification, of the novel's relationship to reality, but it seems Smart was less prone to see such gestures in so charitable a light when they were made by others. In that respect, her participation in confessional culture can be understood as a desire for control over her text's reception, even if exerting that control meant occasionally contradicting herself in the course of negotiating her audience's various desires.

One desire in readers that Smart could not satisfy, however, was for her to remain the young woman of the early 1940s who had written *By Grand Central Station* and was identified with the book's protagonist. When Smart returned to her native Canada in 1982 to become writer-in-residence at the University of Alberta, having been an expatriate most of her adult life, Canadian media commentators continued to discuss her first novel while rehearsing the history of her affair with Barker. Through such discussion, the book became a metonym for Smart's vanished youth and its attendant passions. Meanwhile, the sixty-nine-year-old Smart became a figure confirming the loss that the metonym evoked, a launch point from which commentators could commemorate that absence. Repeatedly, interviewers and reviewers attended to the discrepancies between the present-day Smart who was available for interviews and the young woman whom critics saw preserved in the text but otherwise lost to history; for example, Ken Adachi observed in the *Toronto Star* that Smart's face carried a reminder of its "youthful beauty" (17). One could say that Smart was construed as a modern-day Tithonus, granted eternal life through her novel but tragically having continued to age before she could be properly appreciated. Implicitly, journalists saw in the reception history of *By Grand Central Station* an allegory of its author: just as the novel's narrator is abandoned by her lover, the young Elizabeth Smart had been abandoned and ignored for decades by literary culture on both sides of the Atlantic. The reemergence and repatriation of the living Smart were taken to betoken a past to lament rather than a present to celebrate, as though her growing older were the fault of an ignorant, indifferent audience. The tendency of readers to identify Smart's life story with her novel's narrative threatened to relegate her to the past along with her protagonist and, in effect, bury the present-day Smart alive. The title of Adachi's article, "'Conformist' Was Years Ahead of Her Time," might as well have headed an obituary. Although Smart in her youth may have wished to gain immortality through the publishing of a novel, in her later life she could have been forgiven for feeling as if *By Grand Central Station* had effected a kind of early death for her through her effacement by her fictional alter ego. To resist this annihilation, she was compelled to testify repeatedly in paratexts that she was alive, after all, and she could prove it precisely by identifying with her novel's protagonist, insisting that the two of them were one and the same.

Referring to paratextual performance as a struggle to stave off annihilation might seem hyperbolic, but it is not implausible given how often contemporary authors of fiction find their life stories becoming bound up with their fiction's reception. The public fortunes of those fictional texts affect the writers' prospects for fame, wealth, and a literary afterlife. Accordingly, authors seek through paratexts to control not just interpretation of their texts but also narratives about themselves; they struggle to have an influence on who, if anyone, will remember them, and what forms remembrance will take. With those stakes in mind, it is not much of an overstatement to suggest that paratextual performance can feel like a matter of life or death. An irony of authors' performances in this regard, then, is that even as they seek to secure for themselves a particular literary stature—an authoritative public voice, a connection to their texts, literary immortality—they create for themselves public personae that not only vivify them in their readers' minds but also threaten to supersede them, circulating beyond their control while being subject to reworking and reconstitution by others.

INTIMACY WITH THE ABSENT AUTHOR

Some authors are bound to feel misidentified by readers who have come to "know" them predominantly through fiction and paratexts. Because of such mediations, readers' desire is less often for the embodied author than for an author figure whom they have mentally constructed. In Michel Foucault's terms, this figure is not a human being but "a projection, in more or less psychologizing terms, of the operations that we force texts to undergo" (*Foucault* 110). An author's name gains a certain independence from the person it identifies, standing in not just for her or him but also for a textual corpus, as when one refers to reading "all of Shakespeare." Wayne Booth observes that the authorial name can further come to identify a "public myth, a kind of super-author," a figure who might have a certain reputation and cultural valence even for those unfamiliar with her or his body of work (*Rhetoric* 431). Many readers install this figure at the center of their hermeneutics, even though the figure may bear little resemblance to the living person sharing the authorial name.

The point is made dramatically in Henry James's short story "The Private Life" when it is discovered that Clare Vawdrey, an author rather unremarkable in person despite the genius suggested by his literary output, has a doppelgänger who works alone in a dark room writing wonderful prose that is published under Vawdrey's name. The day after a public reading of that prose by Vawdrey, one of his audience members says to another: "Do you know what was in my mind last night, all the while Mr Vawdrey was reading me those beautiful speeches? An insane desire to see the author" (*Collected* 2: 27). That is to say, the audience member wants to encounter the ideal author whom the words evoke but whom Vawdrey in the flesh does not personify. As it turns out, the existence of Vawdrey's embodied doppelgänger makes the audience member's wish less than crazy. However, the phrase "insane desire" also implicitly applies to the desire of readers in the real world, where author figures do not find such corporeal instantiation except in the bodies of the people who actually write the texts, and who—however charming, insightful, and articulate they may be—inevitably do not quite match the expectations audiences have developed through reading.

Because of the disparities between the embodied author and the author figure, it might seem that the former could be omitted easily from the reading process. Such an excision has been imagined by the New Critics and more recently by Roland Barthes. In declaring the death of the author, Barthes asks readers to think of even an autobiographical text as offering not a representation of its author but a "figuration" (*Pleasure* 56). This is an implicit rejection of Lejeune's "autobiographical pact": Barthes argues that when a protagonist's name is also the author's, one should still not be tempted to view the protagonist as referring to an embodied human being.

But if ignoring such a temptation may be semiologically valid, pragmatically it seems like wishful thinking. The reception history of *By Grand Central Station*, which reveals readers' recurring preoccupation with the young Elizabeth Smart, demonstrates that many readers will not so easily abandon an interest in the living person whom they understand to have produced the text and of whom they take the text to be an autobiographical trace. Instead, embodied authors lurk as lost love objects. They are imagined to be the creators rather than the spectral effects of the texts that conjure them, while their texts are embraced as conduits back to them. Even Barthes admits of his own reading practices, "[I]n a way, *I desire the author*," although he insists that this desire is merely for the author figure, not for an embodied author (37). For other readers, the embodied author is indeed the object of desire, even though for most of them, she or he is primarily a back-formation, created imaginatively in the course of reading.

Although such readers may have approached *By Grand Central Station* with hopes of finding Smart at the heart of her novel, they may have been better off searching for themselves. The book's narrator has been seen as a version of her author, but it is just as fruitful to consider her as a figure of the novel's audience. When one approaches the novel with this possibility in mind, *By Grand Central Station* stands as an anticipatory allegory of its own reception. The narrator's adulterous relationship with her lover, their transgressive border-crossing travels together, and his eventual abandonment of her all serve as tropes for the experience of the book's readers, who similarly desire Smart and are abandoned by her, not only because of her aging and death but also because of the necessary distance between any text and its author. In this way, the narrator's yearning for her absent lover echoes the reader's quest to find Smart in the language of her book. An identification of Smart with the absent lover in *By Grand Central Station* is corroborated by the lover's status as a writer; his exact vocation is unclear, but the "literary letters" he exchanges with the narrator, along with the book he is typing, support the biographical assumption that like George Barker—and like Smart—he is a poet (50, 25). The lover's penchant for storytelling is also on display when the narrator first meets him: he speaks for himself and his wife as he "recounts their adventures," and later, alone with the narrator, he regales her with a narrative of a past love affair (17, 20). By dramatizing the narrator's infatuation with him, *By Grand Central Station* demonstrates the validity of René Girard's observation that a text can mediate the desire of readers by providing models whose desires the audience may emulate (5). Smart's depiction of the narrator's unsatisfied yearning anticipates readers' reactions to Smart's own absence from her text.[1]

The first and last words of the novel's opening sentence, "I . . . desire," also frame *By Grand Central Station* as a whole. In the first scene, as the narrator waits for a bus that is carrying her future lover and his wife, her state of mind is the same as at the end of the novel: she is expectant and desirous. Meanwhile, from the opening sentence, readers are also expectant; indeed, Smart creates this expectancy by withholding details of character and situation. Who is this narrator? For whom is she waiting, and why? Because the narrator does not provide answers right away, readers are immediately allied with her in a state of anticipation, their curiosity piqued less by narrative events than by a plot of biographical detection. In some ways this desire is fulfilled, as details accrete into a portrait of a young woman who has parents in Canada. But in other ways the reader is left unsatisfied, not least with regard to the narrator's name. Lejeune's formulation of the autobiographical pact suggests that readers decide whether a text is autobiography or fiction based on the correlation or noncorrelation of the author's name on a text's title page with the name of the text's narrator. But until the final sentence of *By Grand Central Station* passes without the divulgence of the narrator's name and it becomes certain that the text proposes a "phantasmatic pact" instead, readers cannot even be certain about what attitude toward the text they are being asked to adopt. Accordingly, their movement through Smart's text is in part an investigation of the author's intentions and, by extension, a pursuit of the author herself. If *By Grand Central Station* frustrates the desire of readers who would prefer to have a stable sense of the book's referentiality, they can at least take pleasure from speculation about Smart's relationship to her novel, as well as from the anticipation of autobiographical disclosure. Autobiographical fiction's ability to sustain its readers' biographical desire through the building of such anticipation has an analogue in the way a

---

1. This anticipation need not have been intentional. Just as all fiction can possibly be read as autobiographical, one might also say that all fiction is potentially metafictional. If metafiction is defined with an attention to explicit formal conventions, it denotes texts that mediate in some way on the writing, reading, or function of fiction. For instance, Patricia Waugh defines metafiction as "fictional writing which self-consciously and systematically draws attention to its status as an artefact in order to pose questions about the relationship between fiction and reality" (2). However, given Linda Hutcheon's observation that metafiction can occur covertly (*Narcissistic* 7), one might identify a continuum of progressively more oblique, thematic, allegorical, or implied self-consciousness in texts, such that metafiction can be considered not a set of formal qualities but a way of reading. One reads through a metafictional lens when one wants to consider what a fiction might have to say self-reflexively about fiction.

scandal's currency in the popular imagination depends on the possibility of further revelations. Indeed, so crucial is the anticipation of revelation to scandal that often the failure or refusal of a party to reveal all becomes a key component of the scandal. Fiction is intrinsically scandalous insofar as it never fully confesses its precise relationship to reality or to its author but instead leads the reader to seek out paratextual revelations in that regard. However frustrating the failure of fiction to provide referential certainty can be for readers, that failure often successfully develops, sustains, and channels their biographical desire.

If readers want to understand the relationship between Smart and her narrator, they also desire a sense of intimacy with the author through the words she has left behind. In the same manner, the relationship between the narrator of *By Grand Central Station* and her poet lover is thoroughly linguistic in nature. Aside from the letters they write each other, their first intimacies are textual ones: to be together, they "sit at the typewriter, pretending a necessary collaboration" (25). The narrator's symbol-laden, allusive prose style in recounting the subsequent affair further underscores the fact that the relationship is conducted at the level of language even in its most carnal moments, as when she describes a sexual encounter by saying, "[W]e wrote our ciphers with anatomy" (34). In fact, the poet's appeal for the narrator lies partly in his relationship to language: she first desired him "when he was only a word" and produced in her "shivers of intimation" (20). Her initial infatuation with him lies specifically in the referential promise of language, which suggests a chain of signification that will lead from words to a living body. Before he first meets her at the bus stop, the poet exists in the narrator's mind only as a signifier; when he arrives in person, he becomes whole, both word and referent. Consequently their affair permits her a fantasy of empowerment in which she confers upon herself the ability to unite signifier and signified, claiming, "I can compress the whole Mojave Desert into one word of inspiration" (43). Readers of *By Grand Central Station* may find themselves similarly infatuated with Smart through the sense of intimacy her narrator's language engenders. However, the difficulties they encounter when attempting to locate Smart precisely in her text are also anticipated by the portrait of the poet lover, who is represented as elusive and protean, geographically peripatetic and sexually promiscuous, virtually defined by his mobility and transformative capacity, a "hermaphrodite whose love looks up through the appletree with a golden indeterminate face" (20). Taken as a figure for authors more generally, and for Smart in particular, the lover's ambiguous, metamorphic character speaks to the complications of treating fiction—or, indeed, any writing—as a biographical conduit to its author, when textual signification refuses to sit still, when interpretations differ, and when the author behind the text is also a construction of it, at once absent and proximate.

Meanwhile, given readers' wish to locate authors in their texts, the audience gains not only an object of desire but also a rival: namely, the unnarrated and unsignified, those private aspects of authors' lives that are not written and that accordingly withhold from readers a more complete sense of intimacy with the author. In *By Grand Central Station*, the narrator's equivalent rival is her lover's wife. From the beginning, the woman is associated with the unspoken—"her silence is propaganda for sainthood," the narrator says—and in this silence the wife, too, becomes an object of desire (18). Just as readers might lust after knowledge of Smart's private, hidden life, so is the narrator of *By Grand Central Station* fascinated by the poet's wife from the moment she steps off the bus. As a figure for the unwritten, she is both a threat to intimacy and herself attractive, not least because she occupies a place the narrator wishes to inhabit. In the same way, Smart's reader might hope to enter the private space of the author's life. Moreover, if the narrator and the wife in *By Grand Central Station* seem destined to compete in a zero-sum game where intimacy with the poet comes at the other's expense, so too is there an ineluctable conflict between Smart's maintenance of a distance from her text and her satisfaction of readers' biographical desire. In that respect, it is notable that the poet in *By Grand Central Station* eventually flees back to his wife, abandoning the narrator and leaving her disoriented, "caught without a polestar" (84). The novel ends with the narrator alone at Grand Central Station, where she imagines the poet to be asking his wife for his notebook so he can write again. The narrator thinks: "Give it to him, O my gentle usurper, whom I also have usurped, my enemy whom I have both killed and been killed by. Let him write words that will acquit him of these murders" (111). At once she recognizes her rivalry with the unwritten along with the wife, her undoing by both, and her victory whenever the poet once more takes up a pen to transform his life into a text the narrator might possess. Likewise for biographically desirous readers of *By Grand Central Station*, Smart's every act of public commentary stands as a satisfaction and a reminder of defeat, another indication that the novel in itself cannot provide them with the complete intimacy they desire.

The only hope of Smart's narrator with regard to her abandonment is to embrace language itself and, in particular, its ability to provide substitutes. As Judith Butler points out, if desire comes from a retrospective postulation by the subject of an initial unity with a love object, then "[d]esire is thus defined as displacement, but also as an endless chain of substitutions" ("Desire" 380). The final full paragraph of *By Grand Central Station* articulates a provisional, if ironic, attempt to embrace this substitutive reality from the narrator's own displaced position in Grand Central Station. She thinks: "I myself prefer Boulder Dam to Chartres Cathedral. I prefer dogs to children. I prefer corncobs to the genitals of the male. Everything's hotsy-totsy, dandy, everything's OK. It's in the bag. It can't miss" (112). For her, everything has a counterpart; even her final affirmations stand in near-synonymous relation to one another. At the same time, there is an implied dissatisfaction with this game of switching. Everything is not okay, and language does "miss." Like desire, language comes to be associated with loss and lack; it can be found wanting. It is appropriate, then, that sometimes when Smart defended *By Grand Central Station* against reductively biographical readings, she claimed the novel was not about her affair with George Barker, but about her "love affair with the English language" ("Fact" 193). Whether or not this was true for her, it is certainly the case that for the narrator and readers of *By Grand Central Station* alike, their love affair is just such a romance with language, even if that language testifies to the absence of the author who produced it.

BIOGRAPHICAL READING AS PLAY

Because readers may take pleasure not only from the autobiographical aspects of fiction but also from the process of seeking them out, biographical reading might be considered a form of play. To be sure, some might view such reading as a rather tedious game, too bent on reducing fiction to its factual content, and enjoyed only by those with rather unsophisticated notions of fiction's relationship to reality. Yet biographical desire thrives not least among the *literati,* who may define themselves as elite readers in part because they believe themselves better able to distinguish the referential elements of fiction from the nonreferential ones. If biographical reading can be a game, then, it is one readers might play with greater or lesser facility. Indeed, there is a case to be made that biographical reading is socially useful play insofar as it develops the ability to discern between fact and fabrication. The psychologists John Tooby and Leda Cosmides argue along these lines, claiming that the disposition to read fiction is a human adaptation which has helped to "develop, calibrate, or tune" neurocognitive systems faced with the task of processing large varieties of narratives (15). They observe:

> Humans live with and within large new libraries of representations that are not simply stored as true information. These are the new worlds of the might-be-true, the true-over-there, the once-was-true, the what-others-believe-is-true, the true-only-if-I-did-that, the not-true-here, the what-they-want-me-to-believe-is-true, the will-someday-be-true, the certainly-is-not-true, the what-he-told-me, the seems-true-on-the-basis-of-these claims, and on and on. (20)

Given this flood of disparate everyday truth-claims, reading fiction biographically affords people valuable practice in evaluating material with regard to its referentiality. As Sissela Bok recognizes, for people only to accept others at their word would leave them open to exploitation, so they have a vested interest in knowing more about others than others choose to reveal. People hope to "go beneath the surface of what is said and shown, and try to unravel conflicting clues and seemingly false leads" (90). Biographical readers aim to reach a privileged epistemological position in which they know more about a fiction and its author than naïve readers do, and often more than the author meant for them to apprehend. Accordingly, biographical reading is not only educative but also transgressive, as readers learn to distrust authorial commentary. The figure of the author fundamentally shapes biographical readers' orientation toward fiction, but they refuse to be faithful to the author's apparent desires with regard to how the fiction should be read.

As a game, biographical approaches to fiction can also have a soothing effect, reducing any anxiety that arises from material that is referentially ambiguous. The writer Javier Marías observes in certain readers a "distrust of the imagination and the inventive faculties," as if those readers "needed something to hang onto" to avoid "the strange vertigo of that which is absolutely invented and without experience or basis" (*Dark* 12–13). For such readers, a "decoding" of fiction into biographical fact is a necessary demystification of creativity, reassuring them that authors do not have occult powers to conjure stories from nothing, that narratives have a distinct, discrete source, and that for all fiction's vertiginous disorientations, it can ultimately be mapped and mastered. Moreover it can be mapped in relation to another person. In this sense, biographical desire is not merely a desire for truth; rather, it seeks a connection with another human being, even if that connection is phantasmatic. Autobiographical fiction further promises access to truths that non-fiction cannot or will not disclose, truths intimately confessed by people with interesting stories to tell. At the same time, the ambiguous referentiality of autobiographical fiction presents a challenge to readers in terms of getting to know those people. Confronting this challenge offers the opportunity to become more skilled with regard to social epistemology, which involves not only becoming acquainted with people but also reading between the lines of their narratives to figure who they really are.

Given the interpersonal character of biographical reading, it is not coincidental that such an approach to fiction should have a sexual component. As readers seek to identify sources for fictional narratives, the authorial body can seem a plausible germinal site. Peter Brooks identifies in human beings a general "'epistemophilic' project" manifesting a "desire to know," one that is linked to sexuality and the child's question "Where do babies come from?" (*Body* 5, 9). In the case of autobiographical fiction, the equivalent question is "Where do characters come from?" This equivalence is underscored in Thomas Wolfe's novel *You Can't Go Home Again* when the protagonist is castigated by his community for having written a novel depicting it. A friend consoles him by saying that the offended people are like "children who had not yet been told the facts of life. They still believed, apparently, in the stork. Only people who knew nothing about the world's literature could be surprised or shocked to learn where every good book came from" (277). The friend's statement begs the question of fiction's relationship to reality, reaffirming the reductive tendencies of biographical desire, but in comparing fiction to reproduction the character recognizes a certain sexualization in the act of biographical reading. The authorial body is a site of desire both as an absent love object and as the apparent procreative source of fiction.

The idea that the authorial body is the originary site of fiction is also attractive insofar as it suggests readers might extend the pleasures of engaging with a work of fiction beyond readings of the narrative. A desire to prolong such pleasures is understandable given fiction's concomitant verisimilitude and incompleteness. Fiction offers worlds that can seem comprehensive and believable, but they are confined to words on a page, and there is always the ending to remind readers that the fictional world is radically incomplete. As Catherine Belsey writes:

> The last page of a book which has been a really good read can break hearts, because it compels us to recognize what, of course, we have really

known all along . . . , that it wasn't *true*, that the whole experience was a textually induced illusion. The end of the story is desolate, with or without a happy ending, because it reaffirms the textuality of the text. The world we have inhabited *was not real*. Some of the intensity of reading is the longing to make it real. (37)

Given such limitations, a biographical approach to fiction promises an appealing expansion of the reading experience. Biographical reading denies the finality of the text's ending by reaching toward intimacy with the author through other means on the assumption that the fictional world has an analogue in the author's life. The life becomes another narrative to pursue, an extension of the game, leading from fiction's hints and intimations to paratexts and commentary, which serve as prequels and sequels to the fiction.

But even as biographically desirous readers seek to connect fiction to real lives and confirm its referentiality, they can also take a pleasure in uncertainty, enjoying the frisson that comes with recognizing fiction's referential indeterminacy. Such a conception of reading has affinities with that of Roland Barthes, who defines the reader "at the moment he takes his pleasure" as someone "who abolishes within himself all barriers, all classes, all exclusions" (*Pleasure* 3). Among the possible abolished barriers is the one between fact and invention, such that readers may abandon their usual verificationist practices in favor of reading through an ironic double lens, flirting with biographical interpretation but not committing to it. Notably, readers of *By Grand Central Station* who remain uncommitted in this way have affinities with the novel's narrator, who often conflates her concrete reality with a figurative, even mythological one. The irreverence with which she treats the boundary between realities imperils her when she and her lover find themselves stopped by the Arizona border police while traveling across America. The police appear as representatives of a culture that demands strictly referential confession: in true constabulary form, the officers who interrogate her want "[t]he truth, the whole truth, and nothing but the truth" (49). Unsurprisingly, they are dissatisfied by the metaphoric tendencies of the narrator, whose response is to challenge "the nature of Truth" itself, and whose replies during their interrogation take the form of quotations from the Song of Solomon (52, 49). In this way, Smart offers readers an alternative to a verificationist hermeneutics.

Smart's insistence on the irreducibility of metaphorical reality also challenges readers to reconsider the extent to which fiction provides the kind of quasi-juridical training in the assessment of truth-claims that Tooby and Cosmides suggest. It might be observed that fiction equally provides an education in accepting uncertainty, and that as it does so, it plays a rather unique social role. In an empiricist culture that often appears to insist on everything being known, fiction's indeterminate referentiality affirms the power and intractability of secrets. Even biographically desirous readers who discover significant, compelling links between a fiction and its author's life will find that their work is not finished. Instead they create for themselves an endless hermeneutic project. To achieve a totalizing biographical reading of a text they would need to know not merely all the details of the author's life but also his or her intentions, both conscious and unconscious, at the time of composition. Because such a reading remains an impossible but imaginable ideal, fiction is a fitting vehicle for desire, always gesturing toward something it never quite reaches, and a compelling example of play in which the game may never end.

PHILIP ROTH'S FICTIONAL SELVES

The notion of fiction as an endless, exhausting game is explored to a decidedly exhaustive degree in the work of Philip Roth. With its playful autobiographical intimations, Roth's fiction both inflames and forestalls readers' desire. Moreover, because the writer-protagonists of his novels often create confessional fiction themselves, Roth's books offer a study of authors' own biographical desire. The commonplace injunction in creative writing classes to "write what you know" no doubt does its share to nurture such desire in writers, implying a belief that fiction is more distinctive, more authentic, and easier to write if it emerges from personal history. The dictum also expresses a market imperative for authors to present themselves and their fiction as a package that can be promoted together. However, autobiographical fiction can function in other ways for authors too. Not least, writing it can be therapeutic, helping them to achieve psychic order by coming to terms with their past and their identities. In Roth's *My Life as a Man*, for instance, the protagonist Peter Tarnopol calls the novel he attempts to write during a disastrous marriage "the major part of the daily effort to understand how I had fallen into this trap and why I couldn't get out of it" (104). Insofar as such self-understanding becomes possible through fiction, it is in no small part due to the objectivity about the self that it affords, one not equally available through nonfiction. Emmanuel Levinas argues for "the radical impossibility of seeing oneself from the outside and of speaking in the same sense of oneself and of the others," but fiction allows writers to imagine versions of themselves precisely in this way (*Totality* 53). Tarnopol, for one, counters the charge that his autobiographical fiction is a product of narcissistic navel-gazing by insisting that "the artist's success depends as much as anything on his powers of detachment, on *de*-narcissizing himself" (242). Moreover, authors can feel equipped to describe their own psychic states more candidly if they do not consider themselves to be speaking *in propria persona*. Autobiographers are expected to take responsibility for the confessions and selves they present to the world, and the drive toward representing certain truths about those selves may be at odds with the need to appear socially acceptable. Novelists solve this problem by projecting uncomfortable truths onto characters from whom they are able to claim some distance. In Roth's *The Counterlife,* Zuckerman admits as much, saying: "I can only exhibit myself in disguise. All my audacity derives from masks" (275).

Because fiction allows authors to represent experience from the outside or through disguises, it can also be a mode of exploring the provisional, fragmented, theatrical, and protean aspects of identity. In that regard it promotes a view of selfhood espoused by theorists such as Erving Goffman, who argues that the self is not a coherent entity prior to social experience. Rather, the self is preeminently a character, "a dramatic effect arising diffusely from a scene that is presented" (252–53). If there is no essential self, no ultimate face behind the masks people use to perform identities, then fiction, with its fabricated characters and uncertain referentiality, speaks to this fact foundationally. On this point fiction can be further contrasted with autobiography, which conventionally requires that its authors restrict themselves to the presentation of a single subjectivity.[2] Authors of fiction are under no such obligation; they can create innumerable versions of themselves, either in successive narratives or in a single story. This capability to proliferate selves moves fiction closer than autobiography to everyday life, given that people inevitably fashion for themselves various roles to suit changing contexts, and they often tell different stories about themselves—in bars, diaries, therapy, the workplace, or at family dinners—that are often significantly disparate, even contradictory. What is more, the counterfactual license of fiction allows its authors to shift beyond representations of the selves they have been into depictions of the people they might have been or could become. Commenting on this

---

2. J.-B. Pontalis has argued against adherence to this convention, asserting: "One shouldn't write one autobiography, but ten of them, or a hundred because, while we have only one life we have innumerable ways of recounting that life to ourselves" (qtd. in Phillips, *Flirtation* 73).

hypothetical quality of fiction, Lee T. Lemon writes that often the novel "presents the shadow, the other, the lesser self that one has just barely escaped falling into or, alternately, the better self that one cannot hope to rise to" (67).[3] Fiction featuring such suppositional figures complicates biographical desire by replacing its ostensible love object—the embodied author—with a more ontologically ambiguous one. Instead of being encouraged to chase after the author directly, audiences are invited to occupy the same estranged, exploratory perspective on the fiction's characters that the author has assumed in creating them.

Perhaps no author has explored fiction's autobiographically suppositional quality more rigorously, or presented readers with a greater number of alternative selves, than Roth, whose ruminations on the process of writing versions of oneself in fiction began to take public form in the wake of the *succès de scandale* and sudden fame brought to him by his 1969 novel *Portnoy's Complaint*.[4] A sexually frank and exuberant confession on the part of its titular protagonist, a Jewish American man, the novel was taken by many to be autobiographical. Roth responded to such assumptions by producing the 1974 novel *My Life as a Man*, in which Peter Tarnopol writes various fictional versions of his life using an alter ego, Nathan Zuckerman. Subsequently Roth continued to use the Zuckerman persona, and in the novels *Zuckerman Unbound* and *The Anatomy Lesson* he gave his protagonist problems that resembled ones Roth seems to have encountered himself. Not least, Zuckerman's novel *Carnovsky* is a *succès de scandale* that is taken to be autobiographical, bringing both the author and his family a troubling public notoriety. Roth's 1986 novel *The Counterlife* explores the literary transformation of identity further by creating a complicated *mise en abyme* of Zuckerman's life and fictions. For instance, one chapter has Nathan mourning his brother's death, but then in another it is the brother mourning Nathan. Readers confronted with such conflicting narratives might attempt to rank them hierarchi-

---

3. Similarly, Jerome Bruner argues that fiction functions by "subjunctivizing reality" and "trafficking in human possibilities rather than in settled certainties" (26). Both Lemon's and Bruner's conceptions of fiction owe a debt to Aristotle, who claims in his *Poetics* that "the function of the poet is not to say what *has* happened, but to say the kind of thing that *would* happen, i.e. what is possible in accordance with probability or necessity" (16).

4. It should be noted that Roth is hardly the first novelist to explore the multiplicity of selfhood. As Lynette Felber observes, modernist writers such as Anaïs Nin, Rebecca West, and Radclyffe Hall "sometimes move away from a unified, singular identity to explore a kind of destabilized, multiple, various subject" (5). A more recent landmark is Doris Lessing's 1962 novel *The Golden Notebook,* in which Anna Wulf uses separate notebooks to explore various facets of herself while also writing autobiographical fiction.

cally, identifying one as the cause of or frame for another, but Roth's novel offers few signposts by which to do so. Instead it seems intent on confounding and even exhausting biographical readers, outwitting them with innumerable leads, contradictions, and dead-ends. Near the end of *The Counterlife*, a narrative voice declares: "I am a theater and nothing more than a theater" (321). Mark Shechner argues that the voice here is Roth "speaking in propria persona," but by this point in *The Counterlife* it is no longer clear exactly what it would mean for Roth to write in his own voice ("Zuckerman's" 226). Instead the self appears as a layering of playful performances, whether on the page or in person, none more authentic than the others.

Roth's *The Facts*, subtitled *A Novelist's Autobiography*, is similarly playful, concluding with a letter allegedly written by Zuckerman to Roth in which Zuckerman advises against publishing the autobiographical text Roth has just produced because it lacks the energy and honesty of Roth's fiction. Moreover, in an attack on audiences' preoccupation with the factual basis of fiction, Zuckerman complains that facts do not provide the solid hermeneutic foundation a biographically desirous reader would prefer. Instead they are "refractory and unmanageable and inconclusive, and can actually kill the very sort of inquiry that imagination opens up" (166). Of course, the fact that Zuckerman is a fictional character addressing his author cautions readers against a too-easy identification of Zuckerman's opinions with Roth's. Instead, one is encouraged to view Zuckerman as at once wholly Roth—in the sense that the former is a product of the latter's imagination—and as a refraction of Roth, a vehicle for the sort of imaginative inquiry Zuckerman identifies, one through which an author can voice ideas without any obligation to defend them. This poetics is likewise evident in Roth's next novel, *Deception*, which takes up the game of ambiguous referentiality more directly by depicting a writer named Philip whose wife and lover are angry with him for his conflations of life and invention, especially in a previous novel that sounds much like *The Counterlife*. And if *Deception* defies its readers to accept it as nonreferential despite the fact that its protagonist shares the name of its author, Roth's 1993 book *Operation Shylock* dares readers to accept its story as autobiography, with Roth claiming in a preface that his narrative of becoming a Mossad spy is true, even while a "Note to the Reader" at the end insists otherwise. Given such a range of self-referentiality, it is not surprising that in *Deception*, Philip's imagined biography of his character Zuckerman is called "*Improvisations on a Self*," for Roth has been occupying himself and his readers repeatedly with just such improvisations (93).

Roth's performances have been no less complicated in paratextual commentary. For example, during interviews about *Operation Shylock,* Roth rather improbably insisted on the narrative's veracity, further undermining the border between his fictional and embodied selves. He has also flummoxed and exasperated various readers by declaring that he is uninterested by questions about the relationship between his life and writing—a declaration that would seem to be patently refuted by the pervasive meta-autobiographical preoccupations of his fiction. The critic Leland de la Durantaye sees in Roth's disavowals an "apparent bad faith" (320). However, it would be a mistake to expect a greater degree of sincere referentiality from Roth's paratextual performances than from his fiction. It makes more sense to treat these performances as co-extensive with his fiction, the same sort of referential play he exhibits in his novels. In this regard, Roth distinguishes himself from modernist writers such as Marcel Proust and Henry Miller. While they also wrote fiction that blurred into autobiography, they were not writing with the expectation that a significant amount of third-party biographical material about them would circulate publicly. In contrast, Roth's fiction and paratextual commentary after *Portnoy's Complaint* are strikingly contemporary in responding to, analyzing, and exploiting a culture in which such material proliferates and inevitably informs readings of fiction. Roth recognizes how the mass media at once stimulate biographical desire and provide an arena in which authors might manipulate that desire.

Accordingly, in interviews as in his novels, Roth evinces a poetics of confusion and exhaustion, presenting his audience with contradictions and inconsistencies that tease but do not satisfy, creating the appearance of referentiality and then pulling the rug from beneath readers' feet, reminding them that fiction retains the right to deviate from factual reality at any moment, and that precisely when a narrative seems most real it might be completely invented. While Roth does not hesitate to stimulate biographical desire by creating similarities between him and his protagonists, he often does so to derogate, complicate, and ultimately transform that desire. This is the case in the Zuckerman novels, where the protagonist repeatedly encounters people who take his fiction to be autobiographical and turn out to be wrong in some way. Through such dramatizations, Roth's metafiction models but also outmaneuvers biographical desire, showing it to itself over and over as if to force its collapse under the burden of its own reflection. Roth's novels suggest that only when readers have given up hope of sorting out fact from invention can they properly join him in his games of improvisation. With regard to the various stories of *The Counterlife*, for instance, readers are encouraged to embrace the idea that there will be no simple resolution of the novel into a concrete sequence of events, and that, as Marie A. Danziger puts it, "this blurry uncertainty is our only reality" (16). There may still be a desire in readers for a biographer to delineate the factual basis for Roth's fiction. However, Roth insists that the desire to reduce fiction solely to this level of signification is to ignore the persistence of what *The Counterlife* identifies as "the accidental and the immutable, the elusive and the graspable, the bizarre and the predictable, the actual and the potential, all the multiplying realities, entangled, overlapping, colliding, conjoined—plus the multiplying illusions!" (306). Like Elizabeth Smart's narrator in *By Grand Central Station,* Roth's fictional alter egos model an ethos in which desire and expectation with regard to referentiality are set aside in favor of the pleasures of negative capability.

If everyday life often requires a subordination of fantasy in order to privilege certain facts that fix the self in place, Roth's fiction presents itself as a reprieve from such exigencies. In a manner that might be called paradigmatically postmodern, it celebrates the fragmentation of identity over its unity, performance over authenticity, and a desire to cross borders over the desire to patrol them.[5] In *The Counterlife,* Zuckerman lauds "the performing selves that the author indulges, the slipping irresponsibly in and out of his skin, the reveling not in 'I' but in escaping 'I'" (210). Reading such fiction opens a space in which one can explore these performances with regard to other people's stories, embracing noncommitment as authors do. It also encourages readers to rethink the constitution of their own multiple, fragmented selves as they shift between the here and now and the world of "what if?" in telling their own stories. Such fiction invites them, as Judith Butler does in her nonfictional writing, "to question the line according to which the distinction between the real and the unreal is drawn; to ask: what is it that passes as the real, that qualifies the extent or domain of 'reality'? are the parameters of the real acceptable, contestable?" (*Judith* 185).

As Roth's fiction puts this challenge to readers, it takes on the attributes of a heterotopia, Michel Foucault's term for a site that operates ostensibly outside the logic of systematized space but is also an intrinsic part of that system ("Other" 24). In a society where people want a secure

---

5. Linda Hutcheon identifies crossing boundaries as a primary characteristic of the postmodern impulse, observing a "move to rethink margins and borders" (*Poetics* 58). Likewise, Danziger sees the "refusal to choose between conflicting narratives" as "the essence of the postmodern" (104).

sense of the "real," autobiographical fiction is both an intervention and a symptom. A play-space of indeterminate referentiality that foregrounds the importance of the hypothetical and phantasmatic, it thwarts the verificationist drive of biographical desire, but simultaneously its referential flirtations provoke that desire, thereby touching off an ever more intensive hermeneutics of suspicion. Brian Sutton-Smith observes that play in general has both practical and autotelic functions (197). Biographical readings of fiction in particular can involve both an epistemological game of detection and a more flirtatious game that emphasizes fiction's fantastic, hypothetical aspects. Thus, the relationship between autobiographical fiction and its readers is characterized by a dynamic tension between instrumental knowledge-acquisition and autotelic play. Readers can take on a flirtatiously noncommittal hermeneutics that alternates between the two approaches in the course of reading a single text.

MORALIZING CONFESSIONAL CULTURE

In addition to promoting a ludic attitude toward autobiographical fiction, Philip Roth's writing puts on trial the culture that creates biographical desire in the first place. For instance, his self-professedly final Zuckerman novel, *Exit Ghost,* includes an author's letter to the editors of *The New York Times* lamenting the "biographical reductivism" of cultural journalism and labeling it "tabloid gossip disguised as an interest in 'the arts'" (182). The letter further bemoans this journalism's hypocrisy, calling it "hypersensitive to the invasion of privacy perpetrated by literature over the millennia, while maniacally dedicated to exposing in print, unfictionalized, whose privacy has been invaded and how" (182). It is true that in cases where the media have criticized authors for writing about their intimates in fiction, journalists have often become complicit in the supposed crime by publicly identifying the ostensible victims with fictional characters. Similarly, biography and biographical criticism are complicated ethically when they treat fiction as veiled autobiography that can be decoded to reveal its factual basis. Even if the presumption of autobiographical content is correct, such decoding may involve invasions of private lives that authors have tried to protect precisely by writing fiction instead of nonfiction. Conversely, biographical readings may abet the malign intentions of authors who have presented shoddy fictional veils with the expectation that third-party identifications will expose the originals of certain characters to scorn or ridicule.

As though to meet such expectations, there is a cottage industry of volumes presuming to offer comprehensive biographical keys to fiction: examples are William Amos's *The Originals: An A–Z of Fiction's Real-Life Characters,* Brian Busby's *Character Parts: Who's Really Who in CanLit,* and André Bernard's *Madame Bovary, C'est Moi! The Great Characters of Literature and Where They Came From.* Busby, for one, is careful to assert that "the real people found between these covers are character *parts,* and may have lent nothing more than a name or physical appearance" to the character in question (5). However, despite this prefatory caveat, Busby's book is more or less a catalogue of one-to-one identifications. Such volumes corroborate a common perception that, as Nadine Gordimer phrases it, literature is "a tatty guise to be gleefully unmasked" (*Writing* 1). By documenting cases in which literature has been accused of being improperly autobiographical, these books also allow their readers to reaffirm their own sense of propriety even while participating in invasions of privacy. For that reason, when an author's intimates find themselves exposed publicly as the models for fictional characters, responsibility lies not just with the author but also with a readership hungry for authorial revelation, as well as with the voices in the mass media that hypocritically both feed and condemn biographical appetites.

Then again, authors such as Roth who seem to criticize literary culture for its biographical desire can appear equally hypocritical. Loren Glass asks with regard to Ernest Hemingway's resistance to biographical criticism: "How can an author forbid a critic from analyzing a life that the author himself has so carefully fashioned in the public sphere?" (166). Those who embrace public platforms for speaking should expect to be asked questions or otherwise scrutinized while there. Authors are on particularly unstable ground when they make autobiographical insinuations about their fiction and then complain about others reading their publications biographically. As Joseph Epstein has said of Roth's resistance to "voyeuristic" readings of his work: "if a writer doesn't wish to supply such kicks, perhaps he would do better not to undress before windows opening onto thoroughfares" (64). Likewise, Christopher Lasch, identifying in 1976 what he called a "culture of narcissism," offered mordant words about authors of autobiographical texts:

> Instead of working through their memories, many writers now rely on mere self-disclosure to keep the reader interested, appealing not to his understanding but to his salacious curiosity about the private lives of famous people. In Mailer's works and those of his many imitators,

> what begins as a critical reflection on the writer's own ambition, frankly acknowledged as a bid for literary immortality, often ends in a garrulous monologue, with the writer trading on his own celebrity and filling page after page with material having no other claim to attention than its association with a famous name. Once having brought himself to public attention, the writer enjoys a ready-made market for true confessions. Thus Erica Jong, after winning an audience by writing about sex with as little feeling as a man, immediately produced another novel about a young woman who becomes a literary celebrity. (17)

Lasch's account of the reasons for Jong's success is hardly satisfactory, and the brush with which he paints confessional narratives is breathtakingly broad. He seems right, though, to suggest that there is a dialectical relationship between confession and celebrity whereby one produces the other through the mass media. Having said that, if his suggestion is correct, then authors cannot be held solely accountable for their texts' autobiographical emphasis, given that they are meeting a preexistent demand for self-revelatory prose. Although critical movements from the New Criticism to deconstruction have attempted to draw readers away from biographical desire, this desire is intransigent, its roots sufficiently deep and complex, its catalysts and fertilizers so pervasive, that one cannot expect individual authors, readers, and critics simply to suppress it. It is also doubtful that the invasions of privacy and libels attending a confessional culture can ever be entirely eliminated—or, for that matter, that they should be, given the difficulty of doing so without having a chilling effect on free speech.

The scandals that arise from transgressive fiction also serve a cultural function in addressing unclear norms around intimacy, privacy, and narratives of the self. James Hull and Stephen Linerman argue that scandal can be "a popular forum for public awareness and debate of moral questions" (28). In the case of autobiographical fiction, when conflicts between authors and their intimates play out in public, those who consume such scandals confront issues that affect them personally even as they participate vicariously in debate and judgments regarding the figures and issues involved. Scandal happens when someone seems to be caught doing something we do ourselves, want to do, or suspect everyone else is doing. In that regard, authors of fiction are not alone in struggling to balance the needs of intimacy with those of confessional culture. Contemporary intimacy makes distinctive demands of everyone with its psychology-inflected vocabulary, its proliferation of socially viable romantic and familial configurations, and its technological possibilities for communication. Such intimacy brings with it unprecedented demands for exclusivity, loyalty, and confessional candor, even as people are increasingly able and even compelled to confess widely and intimately to non-intimates, as well. Accordingly, the scandals in which authors of autobiographical fiction become involved tend to touch on important broader social questions. For example, how much should we believe other people's confessions? How should we manage the need to play different roles in different situations? How much information about ourselves should we reveal to others, and how should we divulge it? How can we best protect ourselves and others as we do so? How much control do we really have over the material of our lives? Because autobiographical fiction is both revelatory and coy, a single person's story yet often contested by others, it is a resonant form in the present day.

This is not to suggest that the scandals autobiographical fiction creates are intrinsically salutary for those who participate in them vicariously. Such participants can become mired in the particularities of a case without seriously considering the underlying issues. They might also find themselves scapegoating authors for the sins of the many with regard to betrayals of intimacy and decorum. But by expressing what a culture defines as transgressive, scandal serves usefully to identify not only which norms the culture holds but also which ones it is unable to maintain. As a result, scandal has the potential to challenge and even change the norms being violated. For example, as was seen in the previous chapter, contemporary authors such as Erica Jong have credited their predecessors' scandalous fictions with granting them the license to write about controversial subject matter, thus suggesting that autobiographical fiction's transgressions have had an effect in producing a more candid, tolerant society. What was scandalously confessional in the 1960s is now conventional.

Whether or not autobiographical fiction effects such change, its association with controversy has meant that it continues to have social currency. Not least, it captures attention because it draws out certain contradictions of the confessional age. It is an age that

- offers new possibilities for privacy but also violates privacy in unprecedented ways;
- privileges the intimacy and confidentiality of friendships, family life, and erotic relationships but also rewards people for public confessions about those relationships;
- prioritizes free speech but protects personal reputation through defamation laws;

- has available to it a psychoanalytic vocabulary recognizing the constitutive role of fantasy in everyday psychic life, even while the boundary between fabrication and fact is policed in manifold ways;
- privileges creativity but has a particular penchant for "real-life" stories;
- celebrates authors as dissenters and taboo-breakers but also censures them for taking up those roles;
- creates celebrities and renders their personal lives accessible to an audience that is increasingly globalized and distant from those lives.

As we shall see in the next chapter with regard to philosophical debates about privacy and intimacy, there have been arguments over how this culture might be altered for the better, but these are arguments in which utopian ideals are offered more easily than practical solutions. With regard to biographical approaches to fiction in particular, some will always push for an emphasis on formalist and poststructuralist readings in which authors are de-centered. However, in a confessional culture, hermeneutic habits cannot so easily be divorced from biographical desire. After all, a culture has its unconscious too, one that does not obey rational prescription but instead persistently informs what we find intriguing. This is not to deny the possibility of changing cultures but to describe its challenges.

Lest one be tempted to join Christopher Lasch in condemning confessional culture as a whole, it might be said that biographical desire is hardly without its merits. For instance, as well as abetting the admission of previously taboo subject matter into public life, biographical desire has often been evident in the expansion of literary canons to include previously marginalized voices, not least those of women: Molly Hite observes that "much American feminist criticism has concentrated on the woman who writes and the female experience represented" (16). However, a biographical approach to literature can also limit the appreciation of fiction by attending only to those aspects of it that seem confessional. Moreover, publishers and booksellers may exploit readers' curiosity about authors for crass commercial purposes. As Carla Benedetti notes: "peculiarities about the writer, real or fictitious . . . are the most commonly used ingredients in sales strategies" (4). Especially in the case of authors who are identified as "other" in some way, promotional material often implies that their fiction is autobiographical and will provide readers with educational benefits by offering them an authentic glimpse into the lives of people with nationalities, ethnicities, religions, sexualities, etc. different from their own. Although this might sometimes be true and praiseworthy, such a literary culture risks producing fiction that panders to demands for simplistic notions of otherness, providing a sort of cheap literary tourism.

Moreover, in a culture where people treat fiction as founded on the authenticity of its author's unique experience, there is an inevitable backlash when it turns out that a story was invented after all. An example is offered by the case of J. T. LeRoy, who was introduced to the world in 2001 as an American teenage, transgendered, HIV-positive sex worker turned author. Quickly he became something of a celebrity among celebrities, gaining Hollywood admirers after the publication of the novels *Sarah* and *Harold's End* as well as the story collection *The Heart Is Deceitful Above All Things*. These books' success lay in part due to a fascination with their "autobiographical" content, but in 2005 LeRoy himself was revealed to be fictive, the invention of a writer named Laura Albert, who was sued for fraud by a production company that had bought the film rights for *Sarah*. At one level, the fabrication merely hyperbolizes authors' frequent adoption of public personae. Indeed, during Albert's trial she insisted that she had taken on LeRoy's voice as a way to be able to speak with suicide hotline operators and, later, as a way to write, saying: "He was my respirator. . . . He was my channel for air. To me, if you take my JT, my Jeremy, my other, I die" (qtd. in Feuer). That persona was considered fraudulent insofar as Albert's self-invention crossed the line from performance into outright lies: for instance, unlike LeRoy, Albert was not HIV-positive. However, any outrage over this deception might be read as carrying an unconscious undercurrent of self-blame on the part of people who had been taken in by LeRoy, building a picture of him through his novels and stories despite the fact that these were always labeled fiction. In my previous chapter, I presented a picture of fiction as gaining cultural capital through transgression. Occurrences such as the LeRoy scandal reveal readers' biographical desire as transgressive too, unfaithful to authors in its violation of the pact those authors have offered by calling their work fiction. In this light, biographical desire emerges through a flirtatious game in which both readers and authors are active participants, sometimes collaboratively, sometimes oppositionally.

As this game is played out, autobiographical fiction often seems to traduce authors' intimates, not least when such flirtatiousness between authors and their readers appears to usurp the intimacy of authors' personal relations. A disjunction between authors' playful performances of identity in public and their private identities can suggest to intimates that they know the authors less well than they thought. At the same time, often they fear that they themselves will be represented in fiction and exposed publicly. In *Deception,* Philip defends the use of his and his wife's names in his fiction by declaring with regard to his fictional alter ego: "It is *not* myself. It is *far* from myself—it's play, it's a game, it is an *impersonation* of myself. Me *ventriloquizing* myself. Or maybe it's more easily grasped the other way around—everything here is falsified *except* me. Maybe it's *both.*" His wife's response is to ask him: "*But who would know that, aside from us?*" (184). She fears that readers, recognizing the use of real names, will take Philip's book to be referential; she fears embarrassment and misunderstanding. My account of biographical desire and paratextual production in the preceding pages suggests that she is right to be worried, but also that one needs to remember structural contexts when considering how such fiction might offend. In paratexts, for instance, authors might draw attention to or away from their use of loved ones' lives; they might speak truthfully or engage in fabrication; they might even pull their intimates into public with them. As we will see, the paratextual field is especially fraught for such intimates, who may be tempted to respond to offensive fiction publicly but who, once in public, are liable to face further exposure as well as third-party attacks, and whose relationship to the author is apt to become only more estranged, reduced to a zero-sum conflict in a scandal that, maddeningly, helps to sell more copies of the offensive text.

3

Fiction's Betrayals, Intimacy's Trials

> We might envy museum pieces
> that can be pasted together or disfigured
> and feel no panic of indignity.
>
> —Robert Lowell, "Home" 824–25

> A book is a great cemetery where the names have been
> effaced from most of the tombs and are no longer legible.
>
> —Marcel Proust, *In Search of Lost Time* 6: 212

When authors' intimates identify themselves with characters in fiction, some may be expressing their own form of biographical desire: a wish to be the object of an artist's attention, to serve as a muse, to be immortalized, to be given a flattering portrait. For instance, when Bharati Mukherjee's father encountered his fictional double in her novel *The Tiger's Daughter*, he is said to have told her: "Oh, I like what you've done with me" (qtd. in Busby 21). After all, for intimates to find themselves in fiction proves that the author has at least considered them interesting enough to represent. As a character in Philip Roth's novel *The Counterlife* observes: "If you're written about, if you're turned into a character in a book, unless it is really crushingly derogatory, the very fact of being focused on like that is somehow curiously romanticizing" (249). For some intimates, autobiographical fiction can even have the ludic function it often has for authors and its wider readership. They can indulge in guessing which of the author's acquaintances are the models for characters, while taking pleasure in resemblances as well as transformations; they can playfully speculate about the author's intentions and psychology. They can also enjoy their own privileged hermeneutic position, given that unlike most readers, they may possess inside information about the author's relationships, experiences, motives, and so on. For many intimates, though, the same referential indeterminacy that allows a fiction's other readers to engage in hermeneutic play is a source of anxiety, anger, and humiliation.

Tellingly, a favorite trope of writers to describe autobiographical fiction's offensiveness is adultery. Like "That Was Then," the short story by Hanif Kureishi discussed in the introduction, metafictions that dramatize the writing of transgressively personal fiction also often depict sexual infidelities, as though to draw attention to the fact that the two activities share the same triangular structure, as well as similar impetuses, rewards, and risks. To be sure, family members can feel betrayed by autobiographical fiction as much as authors' lovers do, but if adultery in particular has been a popular metaphor for such fiction's crimes, it is not least because monogamous sexual relations are seen as paradigmatic of intimacy. Lovers and life partners choose each other as family members do not, and often they agree to choose each other exclusively. As a result there is all the greater potential for betrayal when one's significant other goes on to choose intimacy with someone else, as authors do when they make their confessions to readers. Even worse for authors' loved ones, it can seem that they are being dragged into the public spotlight, too. Autobiographical fiction feels like something done apart from them and, at the same time, something done *to* them without their consent. For that reason, it is not surprising that autobiographical fiction has also been compared to rape. For example, in Kureishi's novel *The Buddha of Suburbia*, one character asks his friend, an actor, not to base a character on him, saying: "Now promise you won't enter me by the back door and portray me in your play" (185). Although the metaphor seems overblown, it draws attention to the fact that autobiographical fiction has an erotic aspect in its relation to intimacy, desire, and control over personal boundaries.

The importance of such boundaries is especially evident in A. S. Byatt's 1967 novel *The Game*. The story of two sisters, Cassandra and Julia Corbett, who in childhood create stories together about a magical land of their invention, *The Game* would have readers believe that when the adult Julia writes a novel about a character based on Cassandra, her sister's instinctive reaction is to commit suicide.[1] Through this scenario, *The*

---

1. The reaction may seem implausible, but Byatt has claimed that she refuses to base

Game presents a metafictional case study offering insights not only about how intimate relationships are affected by fiction but also about how they catalyze its writing in the first place. The novel suggests that to understand people's feelings of injury, one must appreciate how autobiographical fiction challenges assumptions and expectations bound up with intimacy. In the face of these expectations, authors can seem like detached observers of intimate relations rather than merely participants in them, people who privilege autonomy above all. But while Byatt's novel pays attention to the kind of betrayal that fiction represents for family members, it also depicts the varieties of betrayal that family loyalty can require. The central conflict between Cassandra and Julia in *The Game* emerges from their attempts to accept the social constitution of the self even while establishing sovereignty over their lives. If in previous chapters I have argued that authors' desire to write autobiographical fiction has been informed by changes in literary culture, Byatt's novel suggests that such desire also emerges as a psychical response to intimate relationships and that to understand why people find such fiction injurious, one must look to the family as well as the desires and frustrations found in childhood. *The Game* makes the case that fantasy's impositions are inevitable with regard to intimate relationships and that fiction may serve as an attempt to bridge a preexisting interpersonal chasm between authors and their loved ones.

While the example of Julia's fatal novel implies that such attempts can be as problematic as the situations they seek to remediate, the self-reflexivity about fiction and intimacy found in *The Game* itself raises another possibility for the ethics of fiction: namely, that metafiction is a mode of writing ethically, one that diagnoses the problems of literature rather than perpetuating them. However, in this chapter I argue that there is nothing intrinsically ethical about metafiction and that, like autobiographical fiction, it is a symptom of confessional culture, not merely an intervention in it. As such, it is no less liable than other fiction to be biased in its creation of the world and to court biographical readings or give offense. Metafictions are wont to be self-scrutinizing, it is true, and some admit to their own potential ethical culpability, but such admissions risk standing as further acts of appropriation, stealing intimates' very possibility of protest out from under them.

---

characters on living people because she knows of "at least one suicide and one attempted suicide caused by people having been put into novels" (qtd. in Shriver). Moreover, the French novelist Serge Doubrovsky was accused of bearing responsibility for his wife's death after what one critic has called his "brutal" revelations about her in his autofiction *Le Livre brisé* (E. Jones 4).

This chapter also considers the arguments of writers who assert that the intimacy some people seek to protect is not something valuable in the first place. What is at first glance a debate about the ethics of fiction is also a debate about the ethics of privacy, intimacy, and decorum. Authors such as Kureishi have claimed for their fiction the role of challenging these values, which are criticized for suppressing fantasy life, trapping people in static identities, and insisting on silence. However, authors profit from the very culture of reticence they sometimes vociferously reject, and their framing of interpersonal infidelities as acts of social protest could be considered equivalent to adulterers calling their affairs ethical acts of rebellion against the oppressiveness of marriage. Accordingly, the pleasures as well as the politics of betrayal must be kept in mind when considering authors' claims to rebel status.

MORTIFICATION AND UNCANNY DOUBLES

To describe the kind of offense that autobiographical fiction gives, those whose imaginations do not run toward metaphors of adultery often turn to deathliness, even homicide. The ability of a visual representation to effect the figurative death of its object has been observed frequently, from Oscar Wilde's remark that there is "something fatal about a portrait" (112) to Roland Barthes's discussion in *Camera Lucida* of photography's sepulchral character. As we saw in the previous chapter with regard to Elizabeth Smart and her novel *By Grand Central Station I Sat Down and Wept*, narrative representations of people can likewise freeze them in place, reducing them to a particular self recorded at a particular moment and from a particular vantage point. Indeed, A. S. Byatt has observed that people who are fictionalized may be "haunted thereafter by an almost certainly unwanted doppelganger, a public image or simulacrum whose sayings, feelings, and even life history, will be confounded with their own" (*Portraits* 40–41). As these representations circulate, they can shape opinions about their subject and threaten to overwhelm or efface that person.

Portraits in fiction might seem innocuous enough, given that they are not necessarily true. However, fiction's lack of commitment to referentiality can be especially injurious, not only because people may feel inaccurately represented but also because the fictional portrait circulates with a greater degree of semantic autonomy. One cannot simply point to it and say "That is not me," because a representation in fiction almost never strictly claims to depict a real person accurately in the first place. Even when fictional characters have the names, traits, and life stories of real people, fiction retains a dramatic license. Accordingly, a fictional alter ego is not so much a copy of life but its own independent creature, akin to those uncanny doubles of oneself encountered in dreams, whom Sigmund Freud views as at once symbols of the self's immortality and usurpers of the self, harbingers of death (*Art* 211). By itself, the trope of homicide inadequately conveys the sense of intimate violation that can attend these doubles, and it is common to find autobiographical fiction described using metaphors of vampirism and cannibalism as well. These metaphors suggest that if authors steal people's stories, in some sense they steal the people themselves too, consuming them, so that what has been taken is digested and cannot be given back. What is more, tropes of vampirism and cannibalism touch on the uncanny transformation that authors of offensive autobiographical fiction can seem to undergo in the eyes of their intimates, changing into someone malevolent, parasitic, even monstrous. The shock of autobiographical fiction's transformations is a twinned one for intimates, then: at their own doubling, and at the author's.

Fiction's unique power to mortify is further coextensive with its ambiguous referentiality in the sense that often people who take offense at it cannot be sure exactly to what degree they are an object of representation in the first place. Alter egos in fiction frequently have significant differences from their putative originals, and in cases where the differences are significant, those who think they are the models may be confused about whether the authors have attempted to be mimetic and failed, chosen to fabricate details, or perhaps revealed something about their models that previously the models had not seen in themselves. Authors' motives can also be unclear: have they set out to wound or merely been reckless? Either way, the fictional doppelgänger is threateningly alive not only on the page and in public discourse but also in the imaginative life of the author, who has had some kind of intense relationship with it that challenges the exclusivity of the author's real-life relations. Accordingly, the authors of autobiographical fiction also haunt their work, their elusive intentionality heightening the uncanny nature of intimates' encounters with their doubles. To read fiction and identify one's doppelgänger therein is like walking into somebody else's daydream and encountering a strange version of oneself. Indeed, fiction can be especially mortifying when it goes so far as to represent characters' thoughts.[2] If, when intimates encounter such

---

2. Dorrit Cohn points out that "narrative fiction is the only literary genre, as well as the only kind of narrative, in which the unspoken thoughts, feelings, perception of a person other than the speaker can be portrayed" (7).

representations of their mental lives, they find that the authors have somehow managed to depict them with some accuracy, such an unexpected public rendering can leave them feeling exposed if not paralyzed by the invasion of their most private life.

Fiction can also mortify intimates by unilaterally divesting them of control over narratives of themselves. People inevitably understand themselves through stories—whether written, told orally, or only mentally scripted—and most want a say in which parts of these stories are narrated, disguised, glossed over, or omitted. However, we are not the sole manufacturers of our own narratives. Other people necessarily have a role in our self-definition, whether they are telling stories to us or others. As Nathan Zuckerman asserts in Philip Roth's *The Counterlife:* "The treacherous imagination is everybody's maker—we are all the invention of each other, everybody a conjuration conjuring up everyone else. We are all each other's authors" (145). It is not surprising, then, when intimates complain both that fiction takes too many liberties with the truth of their lives and that it takes too few, that it is libelous in its fabrications and an invasion of privacy in its facts, simultaneously a caricaturing mask and a revealing exposé. Underlying both these affronts is an appropriation of narrative control. People do not want certain narratives told by others, and with regard to those stories that do circulate, people often work hard to make sure those narratives are understood in a particular way. For example, in Raymond Carver's story "Intimacy," an author's ex-wife who is upset by his writing about their relationship explains that she is hurt less by any factual mistruths on his part than by his selection of events on which to focus. She implores him to write more about the good times in their relationship, telling him: "In my opinion you remember the wrong things. You remember the low, shameful things" (366). What upsets her is not just his attitude toward their shared past but, implicitly, his seizing of the prerogative to shape the public narrative of that past.

Intimates can also feel paralyzed in terms of the responses to fiction that are available to them. Protesting in public is a perilous option when most readers may not even be aware of the fiction's referentiality in the first place and when they may admire it for other qualities, making them the author's allies from the outset. Moreover, fiction's license to be nonreferential means that authors need not admit to its biographical qualities. For instance, the writer Javier Marías reports that one person's anger with him about his novel *All Souls* arose not just because she thought he had created a cruel caricature of her, but also because he denied that the character was based on her in the first place. She rebuked him by saying:

"You're not going to deny that the story is out to get me, are you? You're not denying that to me, Javier Marías" (*Dark* 83). Beyond the perceived libel is the offensive implication in Marías's denial that the woman cannot even recognize herself correctly. It is one thing for the book to cast her as a bad person; now she hears Marías implying that she is also a bad reader. The sense of lost agency attending her mortification by fiction only increases by her being told that her grievance is not legitimate. Such people feel doubly coopted, made involuntary objects of representation and then denied a right to judge those depictions. Their concomitant effacement and loss of agency explain why the language of death attends the discourse of autobiographical fiction's effects.

Fiction can be equally mortifying in the way it threatens to circumscribe intimates' sense of their future. As fictional characters circulate in public, they can lead readers to treat the characters' putative originals as though they are more or less identifiable with their fictional doubles. Linda Grant observes:

> It must be strange and infuriating to go through life having people think that because they have read your relation's books, they know who you are and what you came from. To be told, in effect, that strangers know you better than you know yourself, especially if you don't even agree that the "truth" of those fictions is true. (3)

Fictional representations can be especially imprisoning for intimates due to the static nature of representation. A person ineluctably changes over time, but such change may be frustrated if people continue to view the original of a fictional character through the prism of the fiction. Even if the character is an accurate, comprehensive representation, at best it depicts the original's past self, not necessarily that person in the present day, yet the character persists as a foil against which one must struggle to distinguish oneself. As people react to their fictional doubles and try to untangle themselves from them, it becomes clear that fiction does not only reflect, reveal, or distort the world but also has a hand in shaping it.

FAMILY AND FANTASY IN A. S. BYATT'S *THE GAME*

Concerns about fiction's impingements on the future are forefront in A. S. Byatt's novel *The Game,* and they are bound up closely with the nature of familial relations. *The Game* insists that the writing of autobiographical fiction gains an impetus as well as ethical complications from challenges of intersubjectivity that begin in early family life. However, the novel does not merely substantiate the psychoanalytic tenet that childhood family relations are crucial determinants of one's adult self. It also dramatizes how family relations in adulthood can continue to affect one's identity. The novel's protagonists, Cassandra and Julia Corbett, are sisters who since their early youth have told stories together. When they were children, their collaborations included a sustained imaginative exercise they called "the Game," which involved the creation of an elaborate fantasy world like the Brontës' Zamorna. As the sisters invented their fantasy world together, Cassandra thought of herself and Julia as "not quite separate" (230). Their eventual shift into adulthood is distinguished by the loss of this dyad and the taking up of individual creative work: Cassandra paints and keeps a journal, while Julia becomes a novelist. These activities partly symptomatize the siblings' shared desire to gain autonomy and shake loose the other, but each sister is painfully aware that much of what she possesses in terms of autobiographical material is possessed by the other too, such that completely sole ownership of experiences seems impossible.

This awareness become crushing for Cassandra when Julia makes her the main character in a novel. Even before the book's publication, Cassandra has been discomfited by Julia's narratives about her in their quotidian interactions. Not least, Cassandra feels that Julia still thinks of her as she once was rather than as the person she has become. Cassandra has attempted to cope with her sister's misprisions of her by letting her "store and catalogue the limp relicts of what had been Cassandra" (222–23). In other words, Cassandra has tried to slip free of her sister's misrepresentations by focusing on their dated quality and refusing to identify them with her present self. However, Julia's novel not only fictionalizes Cassandra but also imagines a future for her alter ego. In doing so, the narrative seems to anticipate the self that Cassandra will become, and she worries she will be unable to escape the future scripted for her. In this regard, the novel's offense does not lie simply in the possibility that others will take its version of Cassandra to be true. Rather, the novel seems to have foreclosed a certain range of possibilities for her, preventing her from viewing the years ahead as a narrative she might script for herself. Now that Julia has publicly envisioned her future, Cassandra feels destined either to fulfill that vision or to struggle against fulfilling it. Either way, the mortification of Julia's fiction lies in the sense of fatalism it produces. In that light, Cassandra's eventual suicide can be read as an attempt to reclaim her life: she is rejecting a future in which she would feel herself always in a dialectical relation to the narrative prophesied for her.

Cassandra's suicide also underscores a sense of fatalism attending family relations in general, especially when one's family includes a novelist. In the family, not only is one subject to others' narratives about oneself, but often one also has little or no choice with regard to clan membership. This fact distinguishes the family from other kinds of intimate relations. For instance, adults who become the friends or lovers of established authors would be foolish not to recognize the possibility that versions of them might turn up in those authors' fiction. *The Game* suggests as much when Julia's paramour Ivan says to her: "I'm laying myself open to appearing as the selfish lover in one of your books" (133–34). As a result, an option for those uncomfortable with the possibility of being fictionalized is not to pursue such a relationship in the first place. In contrast, parents and siblings can hardly be expected to recognize a future novelist in the child among them. Even if they did, it is not clear what they could do about it. Given the intransigent intimacies of conventional family life—with its shared living spaces, mutual care, and affective bonds—there may be little chance for members to protect themselves from the developing author's gaze. At the same time, the fact that so many experiences are shared by family members means that if a particular member goes public with stories of familial life, that person's right to do so unilaterally may be disputed, as it is in *The Game* when Julia publishes her novel. Because the experiences have been shared ones, others in the family are liable to view them as joint property and want a say in decisions about how those experiences are publicly narrated.

Such a situation reveals a broad tension in family life between intimacy and autonomy, as well as more a particular one between the predominantly individual work of autobiographical writing and the social constitution of identity. It is difficult for authors to avoid introducing representations of other people into autobiographical narratives, because any one life inevitably involves the lives of others in fundamental ways.[3] This is true with regard to life out in the world but also with regard to one's psyche, as Doris Lessing observes when she comments: "Writing about oneself, one is writing about others, since your problems, pains, pleasures, emotions—and your extraordinary and remarkable ideas—can't be yours alone" (13). Even one's language and worldview are informed by others'

---

3. Lynette Felber acknowledges this fact by referring to fiction that draws on personal experiences as "auto/biographical" (28). I take the slash to be implicit in my use of the same term.

perspectives. In *The Game,* after expressing strong opinions about her family's Quaker faith, Julia realizes: "Much of this speech was something Cassandra had once said to her in anger. It was also her own considered opinion" (85). Given such intricate connections with others in the very formation of one's attitudes and ideas, it is impossible to tell one's own story without telling others' in some way too. A corollary is that authors' depictions of their characters involve a certain amount of self-portraiture. In *The Game,* Julia insists that the protagonist of her novel is a "composite creature" partly modeled on herself (14); similarly, although critics of *The Game* have been tempted to see in the Corbetts certain echoes of the relationship between Byatt and her sister, the writer Margaret Drabble, others have claimed that Julia and Cassandra represent two aspects of Byatt herself.[4] But because an author's identity is relationally constituted, such a self-imposition still installs others in fiction, however indirectly. In *The Game,* Julia's novel is intensely autobiographical not despite but because of the degree to which the protagonist is based on Cassandra. The more thoroughly Julia represents her sister, the more she testifies to her own longstanding preoccupation with her.

One reading of *The Game* would see it as contrasting the idyllic imaginative play of childhood with the betrayals of adult individuation. However, the novel is at pains to demonstrate that even while playing the Game as girls, Julia and Cassandra are already suffering from a fundamental sense of lack, the kind which Jacques Lacan associates with an infant's lost sense of oneness with its mother.[5] From a Lacanian viewpoint, the Game represents the sisters' attempt to recapture that lost unity by bonding with one another. However, as a substitute for the maternal dyad of infanthood, the Game is destined to fail. Instead, the girls' joint imaginings create conflicts between them: for example, it is revealed that the young Cassandra repeatedly "twisted Julia's stories towards her own grim conclusions" and that the sisters privately wrote down individual versions of their collaborative narratives (47). The girls' supplements to the Game suggest that playing it is pleasurable but frustrating. Julia and Cassandra

---

4. For instance, Richard Todd sees the Corbetts as "representing two split facets of the creative writer's imagination" (10), and Drabble herself has remarked: "I thought that [Byatt] had made both characters herself in some strange way . . . which I think writers always do; they split their characteristics up and give little portions to their characters" (qtd. in Creighton, "Interview" 24).

5. Addressing sexuality in particular, Lacan writes that it is "established in the field of the subject by a way that is that of lack" (204).

are caught between two impossible poles; namely, complete unity with one another and complete independence. Growing older, each character becomes eager to distinguish her imaginative productions from the other's, but each is also unable to accept the other's assertions of individuality without feeling betrayed, as when Julia discovers that Cassandra has been writing private narratives derived from the Game. The ostensible dyad is further fractured when, at the age of sixteen, Julia wins a short-fiction competition with a story she has written based on a jointly conceived episode of the Game, one that Cassandra herself has tried privately to write down. Each sister appropriates shared narratives as a way to assert her identity, and each does so without consulting the other, as though to speak with her sister about the betrayal would be to betray the betrayal and to fall back into the very intimacy from which she is ambivalently trying to escape.

For Cassandra, an escape feels especially necessary to safeguard her personal boundaries against invasions by Julia. Because of the sisters' strongly interrelational identities, Cassandra cannot help assimilating Julia's view of her—with all its attendant fantasies and misrecognitions—into her own self-conception. Even before her sister's novel is published, she feels surveilled, studied, and narrated by Julia. Consequently, she believes her survival depends on creating a secret self that Julia and others cannot perceive. To that end, Cassandra lives a solitary life and remains a virgin, the latter choice literally and metaphorically suggesting her desire not to be known. She retreats to a world of private fantasy where she can feel hidden and maintain the illusion of complete autonomy. In this regard, the avoidance of surveillance is crucial. She writes in her journal: "We could not live if we were made to see ourselves more than conjecturally as others see us" (230). In making this claim, she speaks more to her particular anxieties than to a universal human condition, but she is right to the extent that individual flourishing sometimes requires a certain degree of unselfconsciousness. In contrast, when she confronts her alter ego in Julia's novel, she is doubly alienated from herself, left to ponder both the character's relation to her and the degree to which the character reflects Julia's perception of her.

However, *The Game* suggests that Cassandra has been complicit in her own wounding by Julia's novel insofar as her pursuit of separateness has paradoxically made her more, not less, vulnerable to others. While interrelationality is something she treats primarily as dangerous, it is also necessary to the formation and maintenance of healthy ego boundaries;

indeed, Ferdinand David Schoeman points out that "autonomy uncompromised is sociopathic" (*Privacy* 66). One learns one's contours, powers, and limitations through social interactions, and one's fantasies are usefully checked by external counterpoints. Cassandra's avoidance of interactions leaves her perilously in her own head, so that her sense of self becomes attenuated and flimsy. She has little idea of where her identity ends and the imagination—either her own or others'—begins, so she is ill-equipped to see Julia's novel as anything but an imposition on her. At the same time, Cassandra's self-isolation only fuels her sister's interest in her. As Julia says after her sister commits suicide: "She locked me out until I was crazy to get in" (233). What is more, Cassandra's self-protective withdrawal forces Julia to rely on her own imagination to engage with her sister. Accordingly, Cassandra's insistence on complete privacy makes her an ironic, unwitting coauthor of Julia's novel about her. *The Game* suggests that if writers recreate their intimates, intimates are all the time shaping the authors among them too, not least by positioning them as writers and telling stories in such a way as to catch their attention or evade it. The narrative insists that the kind of author one becomes is determined in part by the kind of author others direct one into being.

In this way, while *The Game* does not laud Julia for her use of fiction to engage with her sister, it also does not simplistically condemn her for the theft of Cassandra's life story, for the invasion of her privacy, or for misrepresenting her. Rather, it characterizes injurious autobiographical fiction as the result of a family dynamic that has failed to produce for both sisters a balance of intimacy and individuation, a sense of personal freedom that also allows for the accommodation of the other's needs and desires. For the Corbett sisters, the desire for autonomy is predicated upon a feeling of being too well-known by and too vulnerable to the other, but the gap that opens between the two characters as a consequence means that what one "knows" of the other comes to be constituted by fantasy rather than interaction. A paradox of Julia's fiction, then, is that it seeks to recover a past sense of unity with Cassandra but ends up effecting an even greater mutual alienation. In that regard, *The Game* suggests that both the desperate writing and the wounded interpretation of autobiographical fiction can hyperbolize everyday anxieties about intimate relationships: for instance, that the other's surveillance and narratives of us will not allow for independent self-discovery; that the other's love is not exactly for us, but for some illusion of us; that the other's interests are not ours, and that eventually when those interests come into conflict, our intimates are going to sell us out.

AUTHORIAL DETACHMENT AND IMPOSITIONS

In the previous chapter's discussion of Philip Roth, I identified various reasons for writing autobiographical fiction, not least the opportunities it provides for gaining distance from oneself and exploring hypothetical situations. The case of Julia and Cassandra in *The Game* adds a number of interpersonal motivations to the list. For one, fiction can be a means of engaging with intimates in the way that Julia's novel is an attempt—however misguided—to come to terms with her sister. Writing it helps her address the question that plagues her: "What was it like to be Cassandra?" (112). Because fiction allows authors to explore a character's internal life, it can be a particularly powerful way of entering another's shoes, facilitating a sympathetic apprehension of a close relation. For example, after the writer Margaret Laurence fictionalized her grandfather in her story collection *A Bird in the House,* she claimed: "I think I honestly kept on disliking him until I'd got all the way through these stories . . . and when I finished the last story I realized that I didn't dislike him anymore, but that there were things about him I greatly admired" (qtd. in Busby 58). However, *The Game* depicts the writing of fiction as a hazardous way of engaging with otherness. Because its authors are freed from nonfictional standards of referentiality, they might begin to merge representations of others with self-portraits, outrageous fantasy with facts, leading to exercises in domination. Julia hopes to know her sister better by writing about her, telling herself, "Knowledge, after all, was love," but the desire for knowledge of Cassandra might also be a desire to possess her (122). Indeed, Jean-Paul Sartre explicitly equates such a possessiveness with the creation of art, asserting:

> If I create a picture, a drama, a melody, it is in order that I may be at the origin of a concrete existence. This existence interests me only to the degree that the bond of creation which I establish between it and me gives to me a particular right of ownership of it. It is not enough that a certain picture which I have in mind should exist; it is necessary as well that it exist *through me*. (*Being* 736)

Julia's novel threatens to be an appropriation of her sister precisely in this way: its possession of Cassandra is even more complete because it is fiction and need not admit to presenting a partial, subjective view of her.

Fiction can also manifest a detachment in authors that is at odds with expectations of intimacy. By using fiction to gain a more distanced perspective on her sister, Julia is not unusual: Nadine Gordimer argues that being a writer involves an "excessive preoccupation and identification with the lives of others, and at the same time a monstrous detachment," so that there is a "tension between standing apart and being fully involved" (*Selected* 4). For Julia, the intimacy of writing about Cassandra is revelatory, and the detachment is a relief in the face of the sisters' otherwise suffocating interrelationality. For Cassandra, however, the intimacy of the fiction is stifling, and she takes the detachment it evinces to signal Julia's lack of care for her. In Erica Jong's novel *Fear of Flying,* the writer Isadora Wing's lover Adrian charges her with a similar crime, telling her: "You sit there the whole time keeping tabs, making mental notes, imagining people as books or case histories—I know that game. You tell yourself you're collecting material. You tell yourself you're studying human nature. Art above life at all times" (120). If such an activity really is a game as Adrian claims, then to intimates it seems to be a zero-sum one in which authors gain at their closest relations' expense. When autobiographical fiction is published, intimates are both implicated in the fictional text and alienated from it, readers like any others, forced to witness only retrospectively the author's imaginative treatment of them and subsequently estranged from the relationship themselves.

Meanwhile, authors' focus on engaging with others by writing fiction can hinder them from dealing with their intimates directly in all their uniqueness. In *The Game,* Julia finds herself viewing her life as a future fiction and "constructing a chain of near-sentimental thoughts about her father as though he was a character in a novel" (43). It might be said that Julia is simply performing a version of the everyday narrativization of experience in which all human beings engage. However, by bringing generic conventions of fiction to bear on her father, she risks failing to recognize his particularities. As she goes on to write her novel based on Cassandra's life, Julia's imagination similarly rules supreme; she does not have to collaborate or compromise with anyone. Effectively, she has become as closed off from social interaction as her sister, and thus she is equally subject to the pitfalls of scripting otherness rather than reckoning with it. Cassandra herself worries that imaginings in fiction "may be positively dangerous—not a lighting up of facts but a refusal to face facts" (68). To be sure, fiction may provide writers with a comfortingly mediated relationship to others who are difficult to confront in person. But the notion that such mediation can fully substitute for a more interpersonal engagement is problematic, if not unusual. As Edward Said observes, "It seems a common human failing to prefer the schematic authority of a text to the disorientations of direct encounters with the human" (93).

Moreover, if models for characters can become trapped by fiction, so too can authors become trapped by a fascination with their intimates. Although writing fiction can be an attempt to detach oneself from relationships and gain authority over them through narrativization, this process can involve rehearsing stories of those relationships over and over, not just in the writing of the fiction but in the promoting of it, such that authors risk becoming identified with the very experiences from which they were trying to gain critical distance. That much is clear from the case of Elizabeth Smart discussed in chapter 2; almost forty years after the publication of her novel *By Grand Central Station I Sat Down and Wept,* Smart still found herself facing questions from interviewers about the youthful affair with George Barker that had provided material for the novel. And in *The Game,* although Julia believes she will free herself from Cassandra by writing about her, she becomes only more haunted by her sister, something she realizes when she says to herself: "We think . . . that we are releasing ourselves by plotting what traps us, by laying it all out to look at it—but in fact all we do is show the trap up for real" (208). After Cassandra's suicide, Julia worries that her sister will continue to "gnaw intolerably at her imagination," and the final image in *The Game* is of Cassandra's private papers, now in Julia's possession and already possessing her in turn, such that she recognizes she will eventually be compelled to read them (237). With the sisters' alienation from each other complete in a physical sense, in another way their mutual inextricability has only deepened.

Perhaps no story represents an author's compulsion to return in fiction to intimate moments better than Raymond Carver's short story "Intimacy." The confession of an unnamed narrator who recalls dropping in unexpectedly on his ex-wife and being berated by her for having written about their marriage, "Intimacy" ostensibly focuses on giving voice to the ex-wife's feelings of having been "exposed and humiliated" (363). At the same time, "Intimacy" stands as the narrator's implicit admission of his writing's psychological investments, which become clear when his ex-wife asks if he is paying attention to her. He replies: "I'm listening. . . . I'm all ears" (364). The response reminds readers that he is recording the entire encounter on paper retrospectively, and that during the actual moment of confrontation, even while his ex-wife condemned him, he was mentally taking notes, preparing to transform the very scene of condemnation into a further written narrative. The ex-wife turns out to have been at least partially correct in her belief that he was visiting her because he was "hunting for *material*": even her castigation of him for doing so becomes fodder for his writing (365). Carver further emphasizes the appropriative character of the narrator's writing by staging the encounter in a minimalist prose that is constituted almost entirely by dialogue, giving it the quality of a transcript and suggesting that if the narrator's work is at all artful, the artfulness is in the creation of words that seem directly taken from reality. The narrator appears exquisitely detached from his situation, impassively recording what he hears and sees. At the same time, his seeming ability to record the encounter with such fidelity bespeaks a different sort of closeness to his ex-wife. She remembers: "We were so *intimate* once upon a time I can't believe it now. I think that's the strangest thing of all now" (364). The possibility that haunts the story is that the narrator has been capable of such intimacy in part, paradoxically, because of his authorial attention to her words and feelings.

"Intimacy" hints that the narrator's close attention is paralleled and perhaps even driven by a compulsive need to record what is experienced, suggesting that the production of fiction can be symptomatic of unconscious drives. At first the narrator's ex-wife implies that he is coldly calculating in his writing about their relationship, but his eventual prostration before her with her sleeve in his fingers is a gesture signaling more complex motivations. He says of the sleeve: "I won't let it go. I'm like a terrier, and it's like I'm stuck to the floor. It's like I can't move" (369). Finally, disconcerted, his ex-wife forgives him, saying: "You just tell it like you have to, I guess, and forget the rest. Like always. You been doing that for so long now anyway it shouldn't be hard for you. . . . There, I've done it. You're free, aren't you? At least you think you are anyway" (369). Her last sentence is striking; Carver implies that the writer's transgression is against not only the other person but also his own psyche. Like Julia in *The Game,* the narrator's writing about an intimate relationship traps him in an unhealthy attachment to it. In that respect, it is notable that he admits to having previously sent his stories to his ex-wife, claiming: "I don't know what I had in mind except I thought she might be interested" (363). More honestly, he might confess that sending the texts was a way of maintaining his intimacy with her, as well as a way of admitting to guilty behavior without apologizing for it. In that respect, it is notable that Carver's story ends with the narrator departing from his ex-wife's house, noticing the leaves scattered on the ground, and observing: "Somebody ought to get a rake and take care of this" (370). The leaves, suggesting leaves of paper, symbolize the fact that the story the narrator has told retrospectively does not offer the ethical, psychological, and interpersonal tidiness—nor the "care"—he might wish. He is detached enough to write about his ex-wife but not enough to stop writing about her, and while his narrative of their encounter is an admission of a discomfiting compulsion, it rehearses that compulsion more than working through it.

It seems easy enough but too superficial merely to condemn such an impulse in writers. For example, in Roth's novel *The Anatomy Lesson*, Nathan Zuckerman at once derides and expresses a certain fatalism about his own desire to fictionalize experience, declaring:

> Monstrous that all the world's suffering is good to me inasmuch as it's grist to my mill—that all I can do, when confronted with anyone's story, is to wish to turn it into *material*, but if that's the way one is possessed, that is the way one is possessed. There's a demonic side to this business that the Nobel Prize committee doesn't talk much about. (133–34)

Zuckerman's invocation of demonic possession recognizes that the uncanny doubling which intimates experience when confronted with their fictional alter egos is a feeling also experienced by authors. They can become preoccupied by the partly referential fictions they create at the expense of interrelational engagement; they are also liable to apprehend in their own preoccupation the presence of frightening unconscious motives. However, one need not be quite so demonizing of this preoccupation as Zuckerman is. There is nothing intrinsically immoral in writing about one's intimates. As *The Game* suggests, such writing might even express a genuinely ethical impulse to understand loved ones better. It may also manifest an intuition on the author's part that something in an intimate relationship needs addressing. In that regard, the fiction might stand as a catalyst for change, a statement that the status quo in a relationship is untenable and that some kind of dialogue is necessary. Accordingly, *The Game* serves as a reminder that many of the ethical issues involved in the writing of autobiographical fiction are ones that pertain likewise to close relationships more generally. As Julia recognizes, to imagine the thoughts and emotions of one's intimates is not something only writers do; rather, it is "simply another part of that structure of our thought about another person which we do not admit to, and therefore do not have to justify, or stand by" (216). Authors are unusual only in the extent to which they publicize such imaginings.

METAFICTION'S TURN OF THE SCREW

Part of the ethical difficulty for authors as they publish autobiographical fiction lies in anticipating what a text's ramifications will be. Authors cannot be certain as to what identifications readers will make between characters and real people, and authors also cannot know how widely these identifications will be publicized. What is more, no matter how careful authors are to disguise their models, and no matter what state of denial or silence they maintain about their writing's referentiality, they are largely unable to discourage a biographical hermeneutics. Given the conventional ironies of authorial claims about fiction's referentiality observed in chapter 1, authors who insist that their fiction is not autobiographical are liable to be greeted with skepticism. Consequently, for authors who wish to engage in an authentic public dialogue about autobiographical fiction, a more promising option has been to write metafiction on the topic: stories that dramatize fictive responses to invented texts. Metafiction about life-writing issues is not new. As early a novel as Laurence Sterne's *Tristram Shandy* includes self-reflexive meditations on the process of writing autobiographically. What is more, in the first decades of the twentieth century there was a certain amount of fiction published about authors drawing on their own and others' lives, such as O. Henry's "Confessions of a Humorist," Thomas Wolfe's *You Can't Go Home Again*, and Randall Jarrell's *Pictures from an Institution*. However, it was in the 1960s that narratives treating the ethics of fiction began to be more common. Byatt's *The Game*, Doris Lessing's *The Golden Notebook*, and Ingmar Bergman's film *Through a Glass Darkly* are examples of texts that dramatize situations in which authors confront the ethics of fictionalizing their intimate relations. These texts follow the example of confessional poetry from the period, which was often self-reflexive about its apparent betrayals of intimacy, thus anticipating the third-party public debates it catalyzed. Indeed, the growth of paratextual production and candor in the 1960s helps to explain the proliferation of metafiction in the same decade. Both literature and a commentary on literature, metafiction is fiction approaching the status of paratext.

More recently, authors such as Kureishi, Carver, and Roth have followed Byatt in producing metafictional texts concerned not just with the ethics of writing autobiographical literature but also with its reception by authors' intimates.[6] One might view the turn to this subject matter as part

---

6. These texts support Linda Hutcheon's contention that postmodern metafiction de-

of a cultural shift in views of authorship: Lee T. Lemon, for one, argues that while early modernists depicted artists as "isolated rebels," novelists of the postmodern era have tended to present the artist as "primarily an ordinary human being trying to live in a world peopled with individuals as important as himself" (xiii). If this is true, it makes sense that contemporary metafiction would attend to readers as much as to authors. At the same time, the confessional imperatives of the mass media have rendered authors more accessible and susceptible to public scrutiny than in the past. In that light, it is not surprising that some authors have turned toward assessing their profession ethically in fiction as well. Metafiction about autobiographical fiction demonstrates to readers that authors are conscientious about the ethics of their work and the public perception thereof. Furthermore, metafiction promises to grant its audience a glimpse of the personal conflicts that fiction can create in authors' lives; in other words, metafiction also exploits readers' biographical desire.

More particularly, authors' dramatization in metafiction of characters responding to literature draws the authors into a closer relationship with their audience, insofar as the fiction mirrors for readers their own interpretative processes. Brian Stonehill observes this audience-oriented quality of metafiction in general, asserting: "By dramatizing within its pages a version of its own reader, the self-conscious novel welds a bond of intimacy with its actual readers that is beyond the means of naturalistic, non-self-conscious novels" (7). In the more specific case of metafiction about autobiographical fiction, the texts foster an even greater intimacy by anticipating and identifying readers' desire for closeness with the author. Indeed, it is authors' felt need to address this desire—even if only to dismiss it as a reductive way of reading fiction—that often seems to have sparked the writing of the metafiction in the first place. This possibility heightens the reader's sense of intimacy with the author insofar as the metafiction is then effectively the author's response to the reader's desire. By acknowledging readers in this way, metafiction satisfies their wish not only to know authors but also to be recognized and even desired by them in turn.

Meanwhile, metafiction offers authors a unique opportunity to engage with issues confronting them as writers. For instance, a book like Byatt's *The Game* makes a significant contribution by examining ethical questions more rigorously and honestly than might be possible for an author

---

parts from its antecedents in that it accounts for the reading process as well as the writing process (*Narcissistic* 27).

in nonfictional commentary. If writers believe strongly in protecting their own or others' privacy, then answers to questions such as "Are your characters based on real people?" are sometimes impossible to answer publicly without evasions or lies. It is no wonder, then, if most writers' responses in interviews are often clichéd, enigmatic, or pointedly disingenuous. For instance, when Kurt Vonnegut was asked where his characters came from, he replied: "Cincinnati" (qtd. in T. Jones 18). In metafiction, authors have more control over the conversation. They can dwell on examples and complexities while avoiding the explicitly personal. What is more, they can encourage readers to focus on complexities as well. By presenting characters who practice a biographical hermeneutics, metafiction often encourages its audience to recognize the reductiveness of such an approach and develop alternative modes of reading.[7]

If metafiction can be didactic, it also allows authors to explore a diversity of perspectives on the ethics of their art. *The Game,* for one, presents an assiduously dialogical debate, sympathetically depicting both Cassandra's and Julia's points of view in a nuanced manner. Cassandra may be the novel's chief prosecutor of autobiographical fiction and Julia its most prominent apologist, but Cassandra is usually sensitive to her sister's position and Julia is conflicted about her own choices, admitting that although she has tried to "tug" her novel away from Cassandra, she has "perhaps . . . not tugged it far enough" (145). The manner in which a metafiction dramatizes such issues inevitably sways readers in favor of certain positions over others, but if a dialogic story as Mikhail Bakhtin defines it is one in which there is "one point of view opposed to another, one evaluation opposed to another, one accent opposed to another," then *The Game* fits the bill: free indirect discourse gives readers access to the thoughts of both sisters, while other characters offer supplementary views about authorial ethics (314). For example, Julia's lover, Ivan, is the mouthpiece for a particularly elitist, aestheticist perspective, claiming that authors are "both different from and the same as the common man," and telling Julia about her novel: "Publish and be damned. I don't think you can be scrupulous. A writer can't, with his good stuff. That overrides any other consideration" (49, 145). In contrast, one of Cassandra's colleagues attacks Julia by asserting: "There are moral obligations that come before self-expression" (220). In presenting both sides of the debate,

---

7. Hutcheon makes this point about metafiction more generally when she observes that its "parody and self-reflection . . . work to prevent the reader's identification with any character and to force a new, more active, thinking relationship upon him" (*Narcissistic* 49).

The Game functions ethically by elucidating the subtleties of the issues involved. Philip Roth has remarked that "one of the strongest motives for continuing to write fiction is an increasing distrust of 'positions,' my own included" (qtd. in Shostak 7). Metafiction permits authors to eschew an explicit stance in favor of putting a variety of perspectives under the microscope while remaining catholic in their sympathies, referees of arguments rather than antagonists in them.

However, the distinction between dialogism and appropriation is by no means always clear, especially if the metafiction in question uses material from the author's own experience of causing offense. Such fiction might be defended as giving a voice to the author's intimates; for example, one could view Roth's dramatization in *Deception* of an author named Philip being castigated by his wife as Roth's way of attending earnestly to the protests of his partner at the time, Claire Bloom, against being fictionalized—protests she subsequently recounted herself in her memoir *Leaving a Doll's House*. Alternatively, Roth's metafiction may suggest not only that he has appropriated the experiences of his significant other, but also that he has become caught up in a vicious circle of representation by appropriating her protests about being appropriated. From the perspective of intimates such as Bloom, this metafiction can be doubly mortifying, presenting them with another instance of theft while seeming to preempt further criticism by criticizing itself first. Metafiction thus conceived is an authorial mea culpa that recommits the very crime to which it confesses.

Metafiction about the ethics of autobiographical writing risks committing a similar appropriation in its relationship to the general reader by presenting a self-critique to forestall external condemnations. Marie A. Danziger argues that by occupying the hermeneutic space normally reserved for readers, the author of metafiction "shoots himself (or some lesser, alternate version of himself) in the foot rather than run the risk of a more lethal blow from his well-placed audience" (12). Roth's fiction often leaves itself open to such accusations. Several of his writer-protagonists are excruciatingly self-conscious and self-interpreting: they tell stories and then recognize those stories' weaknesses, presenting criticisms of those weaknesses as well as rebuttals of the criticisms. For example, Roth's novel *My Life as a Man* begins with two "Useful Fictions," short stories purportedly written by Peter Tarnopol about Tarnopol's alter ego, Nathan Zuckerman. The second half of Roth's novel is constituted by what Tarnopol calls "My True Story," and this narrative includes various responses to the Zuckerman stories, giving Roth an opportunity to comment metafictionally on the poetics and ethics of autobiographical fiction. At one point Tarnopol states his fear that he has turned his art into "camouflage for self-vindication," and he also imagines his dead ex-wife telling him sarcastically: "Of course you know best how to exploit my memory for high artistic purposes" (231, 227). We know from Roth's autobiography, *The Facts,* that in fictions such as *My Life as a Man,* Roth himself likewise created alter egos of his first wife and dramatized aspects of their marriage (107). Accordingly, although within the frame of *My Life as a Man* it is Tarnopol who has generated the Zuckerman stories, in a sense they have generated him: Tarnopol, not Zuckerman, is the "useful fiction" who provides Roth with a means of anticipatory self-critique. Echoing Danziger, Mark Shechner calls such metacommentary "Roth's way of getting to the shortcomings in his writing before the critics do and softening the blows by striking them himself" (*Up* 61). In chapter 2, I have argued that such a complicated blending of referentiality and invention cannot simply be taken as a manner of self-defense on Roth's part; instead, a key effect of such narrative complications is to exhaust the reader's biographical hermeneutic drive. Still, to exhaust readers is also to master them in a way that is at once intimate and combative.

What is more, metafictions can court the same sorts of biographical readings that they dramatize and seem to repudiate, and authors discussing such metafictions may end up complicating their writing's ostensible message by further stimulating biographical desire. For instance, although Byatt has declared with regard to *The Game* that her inspiration for the Corbetts was "taken from the family of a friend," some critics might consider that claim to sound suspiciously vague and generic (qtd. in Dusinberre 188). Kathleen Coyne Kelly, for one, writes that "it is difficult to approach *The Game,* a tale of two sisters, without being conscious of the rivalry—real, imagined, or exaggerated by the literary press—between Byatt and her novelist sister Margaret Drabble" (25). Even more particularly, Joanne Creighton believes that "it is impossible not to think of Julia Corbett as an unflattering and hostile portrait of Drabble" ("Sisterly" 24). After all, Drabble, like Julia, is the younger sister as well a novelist, and her first book, *A Summer Bird-Cage,* which also focuses on the competitive relationship between two sisters, was published four years before *The Game,* making it attractive to read the latter novel as Byatt's response to Drabble's publication. Complicating the matter, Byatt has shown affinities with Cassandra in statements aggressively defending her privacy. With regard to her relationship with Drabble, she has said: "I have an absolute rule not to be interviewed on that topic" (qtd. in Creighton, "Sisterly" 15). And when she has in fact spoken about the subject, she has described a process of artistic development mirroring that of the Corbetts in *The Game,* identifying her own move toward authorship with an attempt to delineate her identity, in contrast with a childhood of joint experiences, saying that is it "hard to have shared memories with another writer. So much of art is a transmutation of memory, and this needs to be private, not communal, or it is in danger of being destroyed" (qtd. in Dusinberre 190). This affinity between Byatt's opinion and her fictional scenario in *The Game* abets those who would prefer to read her metafiction biographically.

In both refusing to discuss autobiographical aspects of her fiction and suggesting them, Byatt is not dissimilar to many authors in the confessional age, when the mass media have changed the stakes with regard to authorial confessions. *The Game* demonstrates a consciousness of this transformation, not least when Julia appears on a television talk show and discusses the connections between her fiction and her life as a stay-at-home mother, an action which, according to one viewer, amounts to Julia publicly "hacking away at [her] husband's character" (116). *The Game* suggests the conventionality of such confessions in the mass media through its representation of Simon, the man whom Cassandra and Julia have both desired. Simon hosts a television nature show and becomes well-known for his introspective musings. Julia's husband thinks of him as an exhibitionist, calling him somebody who "bares his soul for other people," and this self-exposure is clearly one part of Simon's public appeal (88). *The Game* suggests that television in particular has invested interactions between producers and consumers of cultural commodities with a new immediacy—what the critic Richard Schickel calls an "illusion of intimacy" (13)—while creating expectations that other art forms will likewise provide such closeness. In this regard, metafiction's increasing presence through the 1960s and 1970s can be viewed not just as a response to the growth of biographical desire, with such texts providing another form of authorial public commentary of the sort expected by a confessional culture, but also as more particularly prompted by literature's position in an evolving constellation of mass media. Metafiction gains an impetus from the appetite for spectacles of personal confrontation that televisual media have helped to create. As we saw in chapter 1, fiction has long traded on its cachet as a transgressive form, and one way authors have sought to prove their fiction's worth in this regard has been to provoke condemnations of their work. Although the fiction itself is not always sufficient to prompt such condemnations—whether by critics or outraged intimates—authors in the twentieth century had unprecedented opportunities to prompt them through paratextual confessions, as in the case of Julia's appearance on the television show. And one more way for authors to stage confrontations has been through dramatizations of them in metafiction, which allows authors to confirm their writing's aura of transgression without relinquishing control over the script of accusation and self-defense.

HANIF KUREISHI AND THE TROUBLE WITH INTIMACY

In both metafiction and nonfictional commentary, certain authors have moved beyond dramatizing fiction's betrayals to take up the project of defending them. They have done so by insisting on literature's role in combating social norms such as privacy and interpersonal intimacy that, they say, are often upheld in a manner stifling free expression. Few authors have made this case so forcefully and controversially as the British writer Hanif Kureishi. Andrew Billen observes that "Kureishi enjoys a reputation as a perpetrator of artistic hate crimes"; his mother and sister were upset by the portrayal of their fictional equivalents in his novel *The Buddha of Suburbia,* and an ex-girlfriend referred to his film *Sammy and Rosie Get Laid* as "Hanif Gets Paid, Sally Gets Exploited" (8). Perhaps the most notorious of Kureishi's alleged misdeeds came in 1998 with his novel *Intimacy*. It is narrated by Jay, a middle-aged, London-based, Oscar-nominated writer in the process of leaving his two sons and wife to be with his lover, a younger woman. Jay says and thinks various unkind things about his wife, and he is generally unsympathetic to her. Reviewers of *Intimacy* did not fail to notice that Kureishi himself was a middle-aged, London-based, Oscar-nominated writer who had recently left his two sons and his partner, Tracey Scoffield, and that shortly thereafter he had moved in with his lover, a younger woman. Moreover, they perceived little ironic distance between Kureishi and the voice of his misogynistic narrator. *Intimacy* only ever presents Jay's perspective, and his opinions go largely unchallenged by himself or other characters. However, in real life Kureishi was taken to task by several critics, including Scoffield, who protested in a newspaper interview that the novel was much less fictive than he had publicly implied and that mutual friends agreed it was a disguised "hate letter" to her. She also declared: "There are sections and sequences in that book which are intended for me only and only I can understand them" (qtd. in Johnston 8). In return, Kureishi insisted: "The only thing that occurred to me in *Intimacy* is a bloke leaving his wife. . . . It is a mistake to believe I experience everything I write about" (qtd. in Ramesh 2). However, Kureishi also claimed to be suffering from cryptomnesia about the source of his material, saying: "Some stuff came from me, lots from other people. I can't remember which was which" (qtd. in Higgins).

If Kureishi sometimes sounded unconvincing when defending *Intimacy,* at other times he has presented a more compelling case for the salutary social effects of fiction's betrayals. For example, in his essay "Loose Tongues and Liberty" he rejects censorship of any sort by characterizing art as a "place where the speaking of the darkest and most dangerous things has always gone on, which we might call a form of lay therapy." In an interview he has similarly avowed:

> I think it would dangerous for writers to have too much of a sense of responsibility. And I would say, in so far as a writer has any responsibility, it's to their own imagination, which is important, but also the responsibility of being sceptical, of asking questions, of being provocative, of looking at things.
>
> What writers do, if writing has any value, is for us to have a conversation with ourselves and with each other, about the kind of men and women we are. About the relationships we have, about the society we live in. (qtd. in MacCabe 53)

Fiction so conceived is a form in which, among other things, readers may consider whether public reticence as a value associated with intimacy might actually harm the relationships it is supposed to protect. A similar debate about norms of privacy has taken place among philosophers and legal scholars. Every society has some concept and practice of privacy, but these concepts and practices differ significantly across cultures. For instance, contemporary Western prohibitions of public excretion, nudity, and sexual acts have not been held by all peoples.[8] Even more germane is the increase in privacy accorded the companionate couple and nuclear family in the modern era, which strengthens their respective intimacies but also makes significant demands of them in terms of mutual loyalty and responsibility. Accordingly, it is debatable whether current norms of intimacy do more harm than good.

Those who support a strongly protected sphere of intimacy often argue from a psychological perspective, claiming that mental health depends on the existence of a space in which one feels secure and unobserved. Stanley

---

8. See Rosenberg 73–74 and Westin 59–60.

Benn writes: "To remain sane, we need a closed environment, open only to those we trust, with whom we have an unspoken understanding that whatever is revealed goes no farther" (241). Such an environment protects numerous interests. Not least, it allows one to discuss with a limited number of intimates certain secrets that, if publicly known, might damage one's reputation. Also, most people need privacy in order to enjoy activities such as sex, in part because public exposure while engaging in them would involve too much self-consciousness. Indeed, most people require such activities to remain private not only in the doing but also in the telling. For example, a video of a couple having sex that found its way online might be humiliating to them even if the video disclosed nothing particularly unusual. Meanwhile, intimate relations allow likewise for the reduction of anxiety with regard to more prosaic activities. For many people, life in public involves varying performances of self in response to changing circumstances. As Adam Phillips remarks, "We are daunted by other people making us up, by the number of people we seem to be. We become frantic trying to keep the numbers down, trying to keep the true story of who we are really in circulation" (*Monogamy* 7). The private sphere allows people to try out and test ideas, opinions, and so forth, that they would be hesitant to voice in public; privacy also permits them to let down their guard and settle into a more limited number of social roles. They can put aside the multiple masks of identity that public social interactions demand in favor of less self-conscious performances. Accordingly, intimacy is attractive not least for the narrative security it provides, as partners become collaborators in privileged stories of personal identity. In that light, it is an especially cruel betrayal when, rather than helping to reduce versions of their intimates' identity, authors begin instead to proliferate them in fiction, while putting into public circulation stories with sexual or other personal content that some readers will take to be drawn from intimate experience.

At the same time, such fiction can draw attention to the psychological and social costs that come with a privileging of privacy and intimacy. For instance, if the exposure of private life sometimes makes people injuriously self-conscious, it is likewise true that human beings are always already not only participants in moments of intimacy but also observers of themselves in those moments, even if they do not identify themselves as such. However, when authors write about intimate experiences, they are often reneging on a tacit compact among the participants not to admit their own detachment from those experiences. It is understandable if that reneging is taken as a betrayal, but authors such as Kureishi might argue it is a necessary one drawing attention to aspects of human experience which otherwise can become dangerously shielded from public discourse by an overvaluation of privacy and secrecy. For instance, the very reduction of selves that Phillips identifies as one of intimacy's attractions can be harmful in forcing people always to play a consistent, static role to avoid disappointing their intimates. Phillips himself recognizes that "we can suffer most as adults from not being able to let people down. And one lets people down—or 'deceives' them—when one refuses to be only one version of oneself" (*Flirtation* 169). Autobiographical fiction can create precisely such disappointment on the part of intimates by revealing alternate versions of the author that may surprise and discomfit them but that are nevertheless no less real or true than the authorial self with whom they are most familiar and comfortable. Likewise, such fiction may reveal disconcerting versions of their own identities that they did not realize the author apprehended, or ones they did not apprehend themselves. By creating fictional alter egos, authors unsettlingly reclaim some of their own and others' possibilities. Lauren Berlant calls intimacy "a relation associated with tacit fantasies, tacit rules, and tacit obligations to remain unproblematic" ("Intimacy" 7). Fiction that explores these aspects of intimacy while foregrounding the plural nature of identity might seem painful, even treacherous, but it might also lead to more authentic, sustainable relationships.

Autobiographical fiction can similarly challenge intimacy by presenting scripts of intimate relations that have not been jointly authorized, that do not circulate exclusively among the intimates involved, and that testify to illicit desires. In this regard, autobiographical fiction can constitute a textual equivalent to adultery and a form of resistance to a demand for what might be called narrative monogamy. For example, in Philip Roth's novel *Deception,* Philip's wife confronts him after discovering a notebook that contains his recorded conversations with a lover. Philip reassures her that the relationship depicted is only an imagined one and that the notes are preparatory to a novel. Nevertheless, his wife takes his very fabrication as signaling his desire to escape their marriage, even if solely through the solitary pastime of imagining. She tells him: "I suppose I ought to interpret what I've read here as a measure of my terrific failure. Whether I believe she exists or whether I believe she doesn't exist, certainly the love for her exists, the desire for her *to* exist exists. And that is even more wounding" (181–82). Philip accepts her rationale, admitting that he is "guilty of a sort of perverse betrayal" (179). However, his insistence that most married men indulge in such fantasies points to a failure in monogamy more generally to accommodate the role of fantasy in psychic life and the persistence of polymorphous desire.

In that light, fiction and adultery seem to go hand in hand, channeling a need to tell new stories about the self. Not least, the narratives that adulterers invent to cover their tracks and make affairs possible are strongly reminiscent of fiction: fabrications are blended seamlessly with actual events, while lovers' identities are masked by invented or ambiguously referential ones in the stories that are told: for example, "I'm having lunch with a friend." Indeed, Louise DeSalvo asserts that narrativization is not just analogous to adultery but also foundational to it, and not only in terms of the lies that lovers invent in order to meet. She claims that one of the great pleasures of adultery can be "*the talking about sex,*" with all the anticipation, desire, and performances of new selves such talk involves (*Adultery* 21). When Laura Kipnis describes adultery's attractions, she similarly pays attention to the rebellious recreations of identity permitted by it and draws a comparison to "aesthetic transgression," suggesting that "in many respects they are not dissimilar. Don't both make you see something differently—at least temporarily?" ("Adultery" 31). Elsewhere, Kipnis echoes Roth's and others' celebration of fiction as a subjunctive space of experimentation and performance when she calls adultery "a way to have a hypothesis, to be improvisational" (*Against* 9). This conception of fiction and adultery posits them as responses to intimacy's unrealistic demands for discretion and exclusive desire. It suggests that a life lived in compliance destroys autonomy and that sometimes people betray their intimates simply to prove—to others and to themselves—that they possess the freedom to do so. But although fiction and adultery have affinities, fiction might function alternatively as Philip claims in *Deception* that it does for him: namely, as a way of exploring desire and fantasy without actually resorting to sexual infidelity. Indeed, given a characterization of ethics as "a process of formulation and self-questioning that continually rearticulates boundaries, norms, selves, and 'others,'" autobiographical fiction might be considered a staunchly ethical project (Garber, Hanssen, and Walkowitz viii).

In that regard, it is notable that autobiographical fiction makes its interventions through publication. As it does so, it challenges the implicit or explicit demand for silence that can attend intimacy—a demand that can be harmful in preventing public awareness, debate, and action with regard to personal issues. Patricia Boling observes that such a strict emphasis on privacy "shuts off parts of our lives from public debates and prevents us from taking political action to improve those parts of our lives" (xi). Sissela Bok notes that secrecy in particular can cause people to be "mired down in stereotyped, unexamined, often erroneous beliefs and ways of thinking. Neither their perception of a problem nor their reasoning about it then receives the benefit of challenge and exposure" (25). Likewise, a privileging of privacy breeds a shame culture in which people keep things from the public eye due to a fear of embarrassment. As Richard Wasserstrom puts it, "We have made ourselves excessively vulnerable . . . because we have accepted the idea that many things are shameful unless done in private" (330). The branding of various acts, statements, or beliefs as shameful leads to a society in which people devote enormous amounts of energy to dubious acts of self-discipline and self-concealment, as well as to the surveillance and disciplining of others, from governmental policing to gossip.

In terms of literature, censorship laws and book bans have their intimate correlatives in unwritten rules of propriety that act as explicit or implicit shaming devices, often before an author has written a word. Erica Jong points out that such mechanisms have affected female writers in particular, asserting: "Every woman artist has to kill her own grandmother. She perches on our shoulder whispering: 'Write nice things. Don't embarrass the family" ("Grandmother" 106, 109). But if autobiographical fiction can seem like an indiscreet infidelity, authors such as Jong, Kureishi, and Roth have claimed loyalty instead to the combating of secrecy and shame. Roth argues: "Fiction has an obligation to be about those things that we're too ashamed to talk about with those we trust the most" (qtd. in Danziger 96). Standing against reticence, authors of autobiographical fiction argue that their writing exposes the conservatism, stresses, and inevitable failures produced by an overvaluation of intimacy. Their stance receives an equivalent articulation in creative writing manuals, which sometimes configure writing as a battle for self-expression against family members who are externalizations of the superego. For instance, Anne Lamott advises aspiring authors in her book *Bird by Bird*: "Write as if your parents are dead" (199). Indeed, Lamott advocates a poetics that explicitly draws on antisocial impulses, claiming: "I tell my students that they should *always* write out of vengeance, as long as they do so nicely. If someone has crossed them, if someone has treated them too roughly, I urge them to write about it" (226). However, books such as Lamott's are often silent about what one should avoid writing. This is not surprising, when their audience includes would-be authors who are desperate to confess, to be told it is all right, even necessary, to do so. As a result, the imperative to "write what you know" is also often unapologetically one to "write about those you know."

THE PROBLEM OF REBEL PRIVILEGE

Taking themselves to be among the cultural vanguard in challenging privacy and reticence, fiction writers sometimes propose that they should not be held to ordinary ethical standards in conducting interpersonal relations. Philip Roth asserts in his novel *Operation Shylock:* "I hadn't chosen to be a writer . . . only to be told by others what was permissible to write. The writer redefined the permissible. *That* was the responsibility" (377). Likewise, Hanif Kureishi has articulated a rebellious authorial ethics in which "the job of the writer is to create argument and create dissent. That's one's integrity and it's an integrity that involves letting other people down" (qtd. in Billen 9). Both authors find an ally in Jacques Derrida, who says that the writer

> must sometimes demand a certain irresponsibility, at least as regards ideological powers . . . which try to call him back to extremely determinate responsibilities before socio-political or ideological bodies. This duty of irresponsibility, of refusing to reply for one's thought or writing to constituted powers, is perhaps the highest form of responsibility. (38)

Given such claims, should writing that offends the author's intimate relations be excused because it aims to effect social change? Anne Roiphe goes some way toward making this case when she states that authors "are rather like those ruthless explorers who kill off the natives, maltreat their own men, go to the ends of the earth for personal glory and riches. But if they've charted new territory, retrieved a few treasures, expanded our horizons, well perhaps they may be forgiven" (30). Roiphe's ambivalence is clear, and forgiving authors is not the same as exculpating them. Still, her comment opens the door for an ethicality of authorial rebellion premised upon weighing private harm against public good. In Roth's novel *Deception*, the protagonist Philip goes further by suggesting that when loved ones feel betrayed, their unwarranted expectations of authors are to blame. After writing about his ex-lover, he tells her: "I am a thief and a thief is not to be trusted" (201). Philip's declaration implicitly characterizes authors as a Promethean class constitutionally predisposed to betrayal.

The figure of the rebel author has been conventional at least since the Romantics, and it remains a popular persona—especially, it must be said, for male authors, who have generally been more prominent than women in assuming the posture of the obstreperous aestheticist or subversive contrarian. Meanwhile, in cases such as Roth's and Kureishi's, those who have complained publicly about fiction's betrayals have tended to be female lovers and family members. Accordingly, one might ask whether the mantle of rebel authorship serves to rehearse the dynamics of patriarchal gender relations, in which men have more broadly claimed a prerogative to be unfaithful.[9] Moreover, male authors who identify themselves as rebelling against norms of intimacy might be seen to depend on the alignment of conventional morality with femininity in order to define their own daring and gender identity simultaneously. The narrator of Alice Munro's short story "Five Points" has just such a suspicion about men's habits when she finds her husband arguing with her in favor of taboo-breaking practices that she suspects he does not really support. "Men wanted you to make a fuss, . . . and why was that?" she asks. "So they could have your marshmallow sissy goodness to preen against, with their hard showoff badness?" (*Friend* 46–47). From this perspective, authors of autobiographical fiction are not so much exceptional as exemplary of a broader social dynamic, and their ethical situation does not exempt them from a need to consider the unconscious impulses and social advantages that might be directing their self-assertions.

Male or female, authors of transgressively autobiographical fiction also secure for themselves the cultural capital of what has been called "rebel chic" (Heath and Potter 4). Laura Kipnis observes that "when stamped with the imprimatur of Art and the Romantic myth of talent, all sorts of violations—aesthetic and social—can be regarded as their own sphere of inventiveness; rebellion and bad behavior much admired as privileged domains of truth and insight" (*Against* 113). Given this celebration of artistic transgression, it is not surprising that authors of fiction defend their betrayals as socially remedial ones. Indeed, it makes sense if they are intentionally courting controversy and censure. Seldom are these things injurious to an author's public stature or pocketbook. Rather the opposite: as the proliferation of cultural products means that literature receives an ever-diminishing share of the public's attention, a scandal remains a reliable way for a new book to garner headlines and a prominent space

---

9. With regard to the claim that defenses of sexual infidelity serve patriarchy, see Kipnis, "Adultery" 27.

in stores. What is more, a controversial work of fiction is more liable to appeal to a particular niche of consumers: those who, as Angela McRobbie and Sarah L. Thornton put it, "see themselves as alternative, avant-garde, rebellious, or simply young" (572). If authors say what others cannot or will not say, it may be for ethical reasons, but it is also because there is a market for such utterances.

Consequently, although autobiographical fiction challenges norms of privacy and intimacy, it profits from the existence of those norms. Authors require a culture of reticence against which to define their fiction as candid, even while they make strategic use of reticence in commentary to deny their texts' referentiality and foster biographical desire. In that light, authors who take up the role of social contrarians might be regarded as rebels rather than revolutionaries, in keeping with Jean-Paul Sartre's distinction between the two: "The revolutionary wants to change the world; he transcends it and moves toward the future, towards an order of values which he himself invents. The rebel is careful to preserve the abuses from which he suffers so that he can go on rebelling against them" (*Baudelaire* 50–51). In other words, by positioning their fiction as transgressive, authors reinforce social conventions even while they defy them. Here there is another parallel between autobiographical fiction and adultery. As Kipnis puts it, the prevalence of the latter does not necessarily suggest an insurrection against monogamy so much as it signals that "the system needs propping up with these secret forms of enjoyment" (*Against* 188). Likewise, autobiographical fiction may function as a social coping mechanism, adding to the public sphere a certain indiscreet discourse that gives pleasure and, insofar as it is condemned, confirms conventional morality.

If authors have more self-interest and less sociotransformative efficacy in their writing than they admit, one might question the rhetoric of necessary transgression they use to legitimize their actions. In particular, those whose fiction has caused offense to their intimates might ask themselves Judith Butler's question: "If there is no becoming ethical save through a certain violence, then how are we to gauge the value of such an ethics?" ("Ethical" 26). To ignore the question is to risk indulging in self-justifications that are exercises in egoistic sophistry, especially given the money and fame writing can bring. Authors also may not be admitting the degree to which there is a satisfaction in betrayal that has nothing to do with ethics. Roth suggests as much in his novel *I Married a Communist* when he has a character claim that people betray not least "for the *pleasure* in it. The pleasure of manifesting one's latent power. The pleasure of dominating others.... You're surprising them. Isn't that the pleasure of betrayal?

The pleasure of tricking somebody" (262). Because fiction can transform lives even while its authors deny the referentiality of their work, they can enjoy unique feelings of control. What is more, an intimate's sense that an author's betrayal might have been pleasurable for the author potentially adds to the betrayal. In the same way, authors' self-justifications may strike intimates as further treacheries, exercises in bad faith from which authors take satisfaction as they invent publicly laudable reasons for their private transgressions.

Should this possibility make rebel authors seem callous, even malevolent, it must be said that Kureishi, for one, is self-conscious about the personal consequences of the offense that authors give, acknowledging that "people can be formed and also deranged by the stories others tell about them" ("Loose"). He is almost painfully attentive to those aspects of intimacy most people cherish. This attention is no more evident than in the last paragraph of *Intimacy,* which is apparently a stand-alone coda to the novel with no transition from what came before. It reads:

> We walked together, lost in our own thoughts. I forget where we were, or even when it was. Then you moved closer, stroked my hair and took my hand; I know you were holding my hand and talking to me softly. Suddenly I had the feeling that everything was as it should be and nothing could add to this happiness or contentment. This was all that there was, and all that could be. The best of everything had accumulated in this moment. It could only have been love. (155)

The paragraph is striking for readers of *Intimacy* not least because until this point the narrative has documented a stream of infidelities suggesting anything but intimacy between Jay and his wife. However, this last paragraph implies that Jay is mourning a profound loss of connection. At the same time, readers cannot be certain that the "you" and "I" described in the passage are Jay and his wife. They might very well be Jay and his young lover. Readers might also see themselves in this paragraph, locked in their own intimacy with Jay and, phantasmatically, with Kureishi. The paragraph might even depict Kureishi stepping out of the fiction's frame and addressing Tracey Scoffield directly, in a way that is both intimate and excruciatingly public. In this last paragraph, Kureishi implicitly connects all these relationships by suggesting they each bring together a self and another, a "you" and "I"—the relationship that is also arguably the fundamental one of ethics. At the same time, the text's indeterminacy in terms of identifying the "you" and "I" renders the paragraph flirtatiously uncommitted with regard to its apostrophic object of desire. If authors of fiction cannot be faithful to one person or cause without betraying another, the paragraph insinuates, then they might refuse to be strictly faithful to anyone. But because the addressee is undetermined, the paragraph also reminds readers that authors can never quite be sure who their audience will be, that readers as Others will not only differ from authors but also differ in unexpected ways, and that authors cannot always tell exactly what kinds of intimacies they will foster or what betrayals they will commit. The unpredictability of the relations created through literature presents a serious problem for those concerned with fiction's consequences. For that reason, as I argue in the next chapter, uncertainty must be at the center of ethical thinking about autobiographical fiction.

4

In Bed with an Author

> You're frightened for yourself, but especially for those you love. . . . You inscribe in shorthand their natures, their features, their habits, their histories; you change the names, of course, because you don't want to create evidence, you don't want to attract the wrong sort of attention to these loved ones of yours.
>
> —Margaret Atwood, "The Tent" 80

> You can never feel comfortable with a novelist, never be sure that he will not put you into bed one day, quite naked, between the pages of a book.
>
> —Guy de Maupassant (qtd. in Kureishi, "Something")

Atwood's and Maupassant's identifications of discomfort on the part of authors and their intimates, respectively, emerge from fiction's potential to produce an uncanny sense of exposure. If Gaston Bachelard is right about the house's preeminent function being that it "allows one to dream in peace," then the bed—the quintessential site of dreaming—is the heart of the home, but those people who find themselves transmogrified in a novel or story can discover the bed they have literally or figuratively shared with the author has become mortifyingly *unheimlich*, a deathbed instead of a dream space (6). For these people, the author appears to have affinities with those who, in the middle of lovemaking, secretly record the proceedings or imagine their partners to be someone else. The most private and proximate acts are suddenly alienating; vulnerability begets injury; intimacy becomes indecency. In the previous chapter, it emerged that at least some authors reject their intimates' expectations and insist they have professional obligations to their art that trump the demands of intimacy. Moreover, there is the possibility that great literature is sometimes the product of immoral motivations; as Jonathan Dollimore puts it, art's "dangerous insights and painful beauty often derive from tendencies both disreputable and deeply anti-social" (xi). One of the characters in Philip Roth's novel *I Married a Communist* is blunter about the matter, saying there is "nothing so ruthlessly creative in even the most refined of the refined as the workings of betrayal" (184). For some authors, it may be that only the pleasures of infidelity are an adequate muse and that to produce satisfactory fiction they must rebel against their intimate relations or at least approach those relations instrumentally. For such authors, ethics considered at the interpersonal level is a nonstarter, and this chapter is probably not for them.

It is, however, for those who think that if the fountainhead of the imagination lies in betrayal, this fact provides all the greater impetus for ethics, and authors would do well to supplement their antisocial impulses with an attention to the needs and desires of their closest relations. One can recognize the immoral and amoral motivations behind much fiction but still take this recognition as a foundation for relations that are more ethical. This is not to suggest that authors' professional ambitions and their intimates' preferences can always be easily allied. Granted, it would be convenient if one could accept the argument that aesthetics and ethics are interdependent, that unethical autobiographical fiction can never be aesthetically superior, and that great literature cannot be blamed when intimates take offense at it. Claudia Mills argues in this vein, claiming that "exaggerated villainous portraits of the kind that cause pain to their models in fact compromise a work's artistic greatness" ("Appropriating" 202). But much of literature's history does not support her. For instance, most critics have not taken distortions of Leigh Hunt's character in Charles Dickens's depiction of Harold Skimpole to detract from the "greatness" of *Bleak House*. One could point to any number of other authors, including many discussed in this book, who have managed to carry out literary assassinations and reach the heart of canons.[1] In fact, "great" fiction—and here, acknowledging the contingencies of literary value, I mean nothing more than texts recognized as "great" by those who embrace that valuation—is often more, not less, likely to give offense to intimates, because it

---

1. Berys Gaut observes that even if one's ethical judgment of an artwork affects one's aesthetic evaluation of it—and Gaut thinks such an influence can be legitimate—there is still a "plurality of aesthetic values, of which the ethical values of artworks are but a single kind" (183). Accordingly, a reader can despise an author's betrayal of intimates in a novel but still admire the text for its other merits.

disseminates the offensive portrait widely, it is often aggressively defended by third parties, and it promises centuries of infamy to the models for its characters.

Still, one need not embrace a zero-sum model of ethics in which artistic success always competes with interpersonal harmony. One might believe that the social objectives of the rebel author described in the previous chapter are valid yet think they can be met without sacrificing valuable aspects of interpersonal intimacy. Consequently, while the previous chapter focused on the problems that fiction causes, the present one turns to the question of how those problems might be solved through unilateral and collaborative actions by authors and their intimates. How might autobiographical fiction be a game they could play with, not against, each other? Given the inherently transgressive nature of such fiction, to imagine it being written ethically might seem akin to imagining ethical adultery. But then, as I have argued, the analogy is more than metaphorical, and fundamental challenges pertaining to the one activity also pertain to the other. For example, both involve the intransigent complications of the unconscious and fantasy life. As well, both express people's simultaneous desires for intimacy and for independence. In this chapter, I investigate how authors and their loved ones might manage to be unfaithful together in ways that enhance rather than threaten intimacy. The strategies I explore are for writers who recognize ethical commitments to their intimates even as they want to pursue public rebellion.

First to be considered are intimates' options in terms of replying to injurious fiction. As noted in the previous chapter, Cassandra Corbett's reaction to such fiction in A. S. Byatt's novel *The Game* is to commit suicide. In this chapter, I examine two other case studies featuring more attractive possibilities: Alice Munro's short story "Material," which presents the scenario of a woman responding to her ex-husband's writing, and a real-life situation from the 1990s involving Philip Roth and his ex-wife Claire Bloom. These examples demonstrate that responding to fiction by publishing further texts is subject to the same ethical complications as the offending fiction, and that such action often leads to unanticipated, unwanted consequences. It is also clear in these cases that part of fiction's affront lies in its authors' assertion of the power and distance necessary to tell a story and to change it—power and distance that become only starker in the wake of an intimate's public response.

Next, I consider various strategies authors have employed to write fiction ethically. Although authors often seem to disregard their intimates' sensitivities as they write, many are intensely aware of them and go to great lengths to protect them. Sometimes authors even use their fiction as a vehicle for positive engagement with their intimates. Recognizing the limitations of such individual actions, I also imagine how intimates might join authors in their role as social rebels. While heeding the objections to norms of intimacy raised in the previous chapter, I consider the question of how both intimate relations and the writing of fiction might be renegotiated by those who hope to enjoy both. In this regard, I recognize that fiction's ambiguous referentiality means its authors face unique ethical challenges. However, I argue that it also allows them unique opportunities for ethical engagement with their loved ones, and I propose an ethics of responsible indiscretion that authors and their intimates might hold together. Such a shared ethics involves respecting but reconfiguring the notion of literary authorship as a radically individualist practice. In suggesting such a reconfiguration, I return to a lesson offered by the metafictional and real-life examples discussed in this book: namely, that ethical prescription for fiction writing should not be universalizing or inflexible. Rather, what is called for is an ethics built upon specificity, improvisation, and doubt, not least about one's own motivations and the possible consequences of one's writing. Accordingly, rather than scripting rules, in this chapter I identify possible ethical approaches to autobiographical fiction.

ALICE MUNRO AND THE HAZARDS OF PROTEST

In the previous chapter, I observed that fiction's power to mortify lies partly in the difficulty of protesting a text that does not claim to be entirely referential. Aggrieved parties risk being told that they have mistakenly recognized themselves as the model for a character or that they have misunderstood the very nature of fiction. If they respond to the fiction publicly, they also risk further attracting the public spotlight that the fiction threatens to turn on them. In Philip Roth's novel *Deception*, the protagonist-writer recognizes as much, counseling his lover that if she is upset about being represented in his fiction, she should simply stay quiet. "However much you may have served as a model," he says, "the great British public happens to be ignorant of it and you only have not to tell them for them to remain ignorant" (201). In contrast, once a text has been identified publicly as referring to a real person, it becomes difficult for those discussing it to avoid acknowledging the identification.[2] As a result, it makes

---

2. Brian Busby refers to an unsurprising fear "that once the connection has been

sense that those affronted by their fictional doppelgängers might simply keep quiet and hope the text passes into obscurity. Indeed, given that often it takes a scandal for the mass media to pay attention to literary fiction at all, to protest in public not only puts intimates under greater scrutiny but also provides the authors in question with free publicity and consolidates their status as rebels. Deborah Nelson notes with regard to contemporary talk shows: "It is no longer sufficient to simply tell your shocking story.... You must tell your story to an intimate in front of an audience. The witness's shock becomes the audience's gauge of transgression" (72). In an age where, as I have argued, fiction's traditional cachet in representing the private sphere has been eroded by a proliferation of texts preoccupied by exposés and confessions, fiction increasingly follows nonfictional forms in depending upon such reactions to gain publicity. Authors' intimates' are drafted into the field of commentary and promotion, where the story of their conflicts with authors over fictional texts becomes another narrative to be consumed.

Offensive autobiographical fiction offers intimates the dilemma of either remaining silently humiliated or imperiling themselves by identifying publicly as the originals for characters with whom they do not want to be associated. In that regard, it is remarkable that when the writer Peter Carey's ex-wife, Alison Summers, felt she had been defamed as an unlikable character in his 2006 novel *Theft,* she chose to protest in the British newspaper *The Guardian.* Summers said she did so because she wanted her dissent on record for the sake of posterity, stating: "This is a book that will have a shelf-life. This is a book my grandchildren will know about so that is why I felt I couldn't stay in the cave. I had to step out of the cave, and I had to defend myself" (qtd. in Goldenberg). Even as Summers's choice was hazardous for the reasons adumbrated above, she articulates clearly the calculus according to which she made it: she judged her exposure already to be significant and irrevocable, such that to remain silent would have ceded the representational ground wholly to Carey. Instead, Summers embraced her ability, as a party with a grievance against a well-known figure, to attract media attention and marshal public opinion to her side.

To those people like Summers for whom remaining quiet about such fiction seems like an untenable further injury, a few options present themselves. Litigation, for one, offers more tangible forms of redress than mere

---

made, the work in question will forever be affected; that the reader will not be capable of divorcing the character from the original or, worse, will refuse to recognize the character as a creation" (2).

protest in a newspaper, and occasionally people have gone so far as to sue novelists for defamation or invasion of privacy. Given that the courtroom is commonly taken as a place to establish truth, it promises not only monetary compensation but also the possibility of speculative gossip being halted by an authoritative confirmation that the offensive representation was indeed of the plaintiff. However, for plaintiffs to win such suits has proven complicated. In American law, those claiming to have had their privacy invaded must demonstrate that the fictional character in question is a representation of them, that the representation caused emotional or financial damages, and that it would be considered offensive by any reasonable person. The question of what constitutes reasonable grounds is not straightforward though. As the judgment in the 1993 case *Haynes v. Alfred Knopf* notes: "Even people who have nothing rationally to be ashamed of can be mortified by the publication of intimate details of their life" (1229). Meanwhile, plaintiffs in defamation suits face the paradoxical situation whereby they must identify themselves with unattractive characters through certain points of affinity at the same time as they declare other points to be untruthful and defamatory. Judges have it no easier: in both privacy and defamation cases, they confront the significant challenge of weighing the harm done to plaintiffs against the harm that would be done by censoring authors and chilling free speech. What is more, given the transgressive hermeneutic habits of readers, who are liable to read fiction as biographical even when its authors insist it is not, to condemn authors alone for such identifications might be considered a punishment of one for the trespasses of the many.

Another choice for intimates is to respond by writing themselves. This alternative poses its own problems, as is clear from the case of Sheila Munro, the daughter of the short-story writer Alice Munro. For Sheila, a longstanding ambition was to become an author of fiction too, but in 2001 she published her memoir *Lives of Mothers and Daughters* instead. In it, she discusses having grown up in her mother's literary shadow, admitting that her view of the world has been deeply informed by Alice's fiction. Sheila writes: "So much of what I think and I know, and I think I know more about my mother's life than almost any daughter could know, is refracted through the prism of her writing. So unassailable is the truth of her fiction that sometimes I even feel as though I'm living inside an Alice Munro story" (11). Sheila's perspective appears to be sufficiently infused with her mother's fiction that even her phrasing at the outset of this passage echoes a moment in Alice's story "Material" when the narrator declares: "Hugo's is a very good story, *as far as I can tell, and I think I can tell"* (*Something* 35, emphasis added). Such careful qualifying remarks and self-doubt are a hallmark of the elder Munro's fiction, especially when articulated by author figures who agonize over the possible misrepresentations and ill effects of their writing. Accordingly, even as Sheila attempts in her memoir to establish an identity independent of her mother, she declares her connections to Alice's fiction both explicitly and through her use of language. By choosing to tell her story in nonfiction, Sheila distances herself from the senior Munro, perhaps even trumping her by telling the "real" story of Alice's life, but implicitly she is also admitting an inability to produce fiction equal to her mother's.

By writing her memoir, Sheila would seem to be living inside an Alice Munro story in another way too, because the possibility that an author's intimate might end up aligning herself with the author even while meaning to individuate herself is also examined in "Material," the very text Sheila echoes. First collected in Alice Munro's 1974 book *Something I've Been Meaning to Tell You,* "Material" features a narrator who is the ex-wife of an author named Hugo. As such, she is in a position not dissimilar to Sheila Munro's, especially in that she considers the author's fiction to be based on shared experience. "Material" takes the form of the narrator's response to Hugo when, two decades after he treated their neighbor callously, she finds he has written a story about the woman. Upset by this action, the narrator adjudicates the ethicality of his fiction while telling her own story of his misbehavior during their marriage. But the story is not merely about Hugo's ethical shortcomings. It is equally about his ex-wife's challenges in articulating her sense of victimization, expressing her anger with him, and making him understand his failures. As she does these things, she risks committing the very transgressions for which she holds him accountable.

From the narrator's perspective, Hugo was the quintessence of chauvinist egoism when they lived together as newlyweds in an apartment above their neighbor, Dotty. Not least he was unable to bear the sounds of Dotty's piano playing when he was busy writing a verse play, and he bullied the narrator into asking Dotty to be quiet on his behalf. Emmanuel Levinas characterizes the ethical moment as occurring in the sight of "the face of a neighbor," but Hugo failed even to turn and face his neighbor literally (*Otherwise* 12). This failure recurred when Hugo turned off a water pump in their building's basement, even though the pump had been preventing Dotty's apartment from flooding, because he was being kept awake by the mechanism's noise. Although the narrator castigates him for this behavior, her judgment is complicated by the existence of his later short story, which she says is "about Dotty," even though the woman "has been changed in some unimportant ways and the main incident concerning her has been invented, or grafted on from some other reality." It is, the narrator says, "a very good story, as far as I can tell." Hugo has managed to distill something of Dotty in fiction, so that she is "lifted out of life and held in light." The narrator goes so far as to call this representation of Dotty an act of "unsparing, unsentimental love" on Hugo's part, perhaps implying that the aesthetic merit of his fiction redeems him in some way, atoning for his neglect of Dotty with regard to the water pump by showing that he was paying attention to her after all (35). However, the narrator's attribution to him of "a fine and lucky benevolence," along with her praise of his story, is shot through with irony: for instance, her observation that Dotty has been "lifted" from life carries the connotation of theft, while it is not clear that an "unsparing" love is a very attractive one. Furthermore, when the narrator states that Dotty "was lucky to live in that basement for a few months and eventually to *have this done to her*," her phrasing implies that Hugo's aesthetic achievement might perpetuate his earlier victimization of their neighbor (35, emphasis added).

The narrator's ironic praise betrays an ambivalence that says as much about her as it does about Hugo's fiction. In particular, it speaks to a complicity with his actions that dates back at least to her own refusal to restart the water pump after Hugo turned it off. When she later criticizes men who are "cosseted" by the "literary life" and by women, the remark hangs over her past role in the marriage, during which the couple functioned dyadically, with the two people defined as one unit sharing identical interests and with all loyalty directed toward each other (20). In this dyad, the narrator and Hugo played creatively with one another, acting as co-conspirators against the world. The narrator observes: "All our life together, the successful part of our life together, was games" (30). She strove to maintain a collaboration with him, whether playing instrumental duets or reporting details to him about Dotty's possessions and telling him that "he ought to pay more attention to Dotty if he wanted to be a writer" (27). In bed, he and the narrator created scenes together, taking on the roles of Mellors and Lady Chatterley, and the two of them improvised shocking conversations in public. One such scene involved Hugo sitting with the narrator in a bar and berating her loudly for fictive infidelities. Afterward, the narrator says, the two of them laughed at the reactions of people nearby until they had to "hold each other up" (30). By rehearsing infidelities in this way, the two of them were in fact able to affirm their allegiance to one another, figuratively as well as literally supporting each other, enjoying the intimacy of the public charade and defining themselves in opposition to their audience, whose alienation from them was a point of the exercise. The game suggests that intimacy does not necessarily require privacy. For Hugo and the narrator, such playing doubly cemented their exclusive relationship by allying them against the outside world and by symbolically relegating infidelity to the status of a mutually enjoyed fantasy.

If "Material" illustrates the role that collaborative creativity can play in strengthening relationships, it also suggests that collaborators feel betrayed when creative pursuits are taken up without them. That much is evident from the scrutiny to which the narrator subjects Hugo's fiction and its paratexts: for instance, she chastises him for claiming in the biographical blurb accompanying his short story that he grew up *"in the bush"* and was once a lumberjack (24). Her attention to that particular detail is notable because in her and Hugo's public enactment of infidelity during their marriage, he played a worker whose employment was "in the bush" (30). For this reason, the extent to which she has the moral high ground in damning his blurb seems dubious. Even if he is making things up, his deceptions are very similar to those in which she happily participated during their marriage. Hugo's treacherous infidelity, then, is not so much to the truth as to the narrator in his having gone on to tell autobiographical lies without her. By staging the narrator's outrage at this fact, Munro hints that the fundamental betrayal of autobiographical fiction lies less in its revelations or fabrications than in its association with an individualist model of authorship, one that celebrates solitary genius while insufficiently recognizing how, in one way or another, the production of literature almost inevitably involves more than one person. Even as the individualist model turns authors into clearly delineated, marketable commodities, it facilitates antagonism between authors and their intimates by isolating the authors and making their profession an intrinsically appropriative one.

Munro's story also insists that authors' instrumentalization of others has correlatives in everyday social practices. For instance, although the narrator seems to condemn Hugo for appropriating Dotty in his story, during their marriage she joined him in playing games that similarly made use of the woman. Not least, after noticing a series of men visiting Dotty's apartment, the narrator and Hugo "named her the harlot-in-residence and began to brag about her" to their friends (28). Through such details, "Material" reminds its readers that if fiction caricatures and misrepresents people, these are common practices for many people, not just authors. The ambiguously referential characters that fiction presents are foils for the ones created and circulated in other forms of social discourse, from email and gossip to job applications. With loved ones as well as coworkers and strangers, people are narrating each other all the time, and inevitably these stories have fictive components: lies and misremembering, suppositions and improvisations.

Munro's attention to the fictive quality of everyday social discourse signals that the narrator's story is not an innocent, objective attempt at remedial narration. Rather, it may be significant that she is silent about whether Hugo has ever written about *her*. If he has not, one might view "Material" as her attempt to write herself back into a story from which she has been omitted, giving herself a narrative prominence she may covet. Her adroit storytelling as she does so would support a reading in which she emerges as another author in the family, one who has been effaced and oppressed by Hugo's ambition. Indeed, the assumption that she is writing underpins Magdalene Redekop's contention that the narrator has "appropriated some of the power invested in Hugo the writer" by going public with her own narrative (31). The possibility that the narrator has been an aspiring author all along is supported by her detailed observations of Dotty's possessions, along with her suggestions to Hugo that these sorts of details are important to writing. Moreover, her later criticisms of his story and paratexts carry a note of competitiveness.

Tied up with this latent rivalry is a lingering investment in her relationship with Hugo that she does not explicitly recognize but that becomes manifest through her repeated attempts to address him. Although she abandons a letter to him after only a few sentences, her apostrophes to him in the course of her narrative imply that what we are reading functions in part as an extension of her attempted correspondence. For instance, she harangues him about his book's author blurb:

> Look at you, Hugo, your image is not only fake but out-of-date. You should have said you'd meditated for a year in the mountains of Uttar Pradesh; you should have said you'd taught Creative Drama to autistic children; you should have shaved your head, shaved your beard, put on a monk's cowl; you should have shut up, Hugo. (25)

In telling him to shut up, the narrator is creating space for her own voice, but the fact that she is apostrophizing him and still suggesting subject matter for his writing also reveals that in some sense she remains bound by the intimacy that characterized their marriage, even as she seems to be committing her own infidelity by transforming him from an interlocutor into the subject of her narrative. In this respect, significantly it is never clear whether she is writing, speaking, or only mentally narrating her story. She observes that because Hugo is an author, he can work "daringly out in the public eye," just as he did with her during their marriage, but through the indeterminacy of her narrative mode, "Material" suggests an ambivalence in the narrator about such self-exposure when she is acting alone (23). It is as though a published rebuke of Hugo would be a final surrender of the collaborative intimacy she once enjoyed with him, in the same way that he has abandoned it himself by writing about Dotty. "Material" demonstrates that a challenge for intimates who wish to respond publicly to fiction is that they must emerge from the narrative monogamy they have valued and, paradoxically, join authors in being unfaithful through the act of writing about their relationships. One infidelity seems to necessitate another.

Meanwhile, if the narrator takes Hugo to task for the ethical failings of his story, her own storytelling's ethics is open to question. Not least, she demonstrates a tendency toward abridgements, elisions, and the deployment of stereotypes. For example, after presenting what appears to be a direct quotation from Dotty, she admits: "I am condensing" (26). She offers a similar caveat when describing the present-day Hugo after viewing a photograph of him on his book's cover: "I have no proof. I construct somebody from this one smudgy picture, I am content with such clichés. I have not the imagination or good will to proceed differently" (24). Paratextual materials, which ostensibly help readers know an author better, draw attention in this case to the narrator's troubled distance from Hugo. Given these reminders of her emotional investments and fabrications, her motivations and silences are somewhat suspect. For instance, she says virtually nothing about the content of Hugo's story, so readers must take her at her word when she asserts that he has used Dotty as material at all, to say nothing of whether he has rendered her in a way that is "honest" and "lovely" as the narrator claims (25). Her elliptical descriptions of the story make it difficult for readers to have any opinion of it other than her own, even as her perspective begins to seem less trustworthy. The narrator's unreliability reminds Munro's audience that stories are always subjective and therefore partial and that one should not take any one account—whether fictional or nonfictional—to be telling the whole truth or equipping them adequately for ethical judgments of the people involved. By drawing attention to the question of the narrator's reliability, "Material" also serves as a warning that writing back leaves intimates open to the same ethical dangers as the authors who have offended them. They risk multiplying the misrepresentations of the first, offensive fiction while exposing their own prejudices through their testimony.

Despite these risks, "Material" and other writings by Munro depict such responses as important in calling fiction to account. Common in her stories are figures who articulate skepticism about the adequacy of the narratives they construct. For instance, in "Who Do You Think You Are?" the actor Rose becomes aware of her tendency to caricature people onstage: "The thing she was ashamed of, in acting, was that she might have been paying attention to the wrong things, reporting antics, when there was always something further, a tone, a depth, a light, that she couldn't get and wouldn't get" (*Who* 254). For Rose, as for many of Munro's narrators, the challenge is to render what is real, but to do so with complete verisimilitude is impossible, so that every narrative seems to be a failure, and potentially an unethical one. The narrator of "Meneseteung" worries that she "may have got it wrong" in telling her story (*Friend* 73), and in "Home," when the narrator thinks of her own representation of reality, she declares: "*I can't get it, I can't quite bring it out. . . . I feel a bit treacherous and artificial*" (142). Munro herself has said in an essay: "I am a little afraid that the work with words may turn out to be a questionable trick, an evasion (and never more so than when it is most dazzling, apt and striking), an unavoidable lie" ("Colonel's" 182). For Munro, all writing is potentially a betrayal, something indiscreet. At the same time, she has asserted her right to use real-world material in fiction, saying: "I need it there and it belongs there" ("What" 226). Evidently for her there is a sense in which fiction, as much as nonfiction, is tied to the real: the original title for her novel *Lives of Girls and Women* was "Real Life," and the manuscript title for "Material" was "Real People." Munro's anxiety about the real in her fiction bespeaks a poetics in which fiction and nonfiction are vitally connected to one another, in which each is held to the same standards of verisimilitude, if not of referentiality, and in which each has a fraught relationship to reality.

But just as my discussion of Philip Roth in chapter 2 presented him as making the case for fiction's role in admitting the presence of fantasy, fragmentation, and theatricality into conceptions of personal identity, Munro's writing insists that reality is more complex than positivist accounts recognize. Her fiction gestures toward what is unknown or only dreamed; her stories open a seam in the everyday to explore the "deep caves paved with kitchen linoleum" that are people's lives (*Lives* 249). She has commented in an interview:

> I want to move away from what happened, to the possibility of this happening, or that happening, and a kind of idea that life is not just made up of the facts, the things that happened. . . . [b]ut all the things that happen in fantasy, the things that might have happened, the kind of alternate life that can almost seem to be accompanying what we call our real lives. (qtd. in Thacker 450)

An implication here is that because fiction is not bound by juridical standards of verification, it can explore more fully than nonfiction the presence of fantasy in the real. An ethical framework emerges in which fiction and nonfiction exist in a dialectical, even antiphonal, relationship to one another, each providing compelling but insufficient versions of reality, each responding to and correcting the other. Any story, Munro suggests, requires a supplement, even if that supplement will be just as provisional, subjective, and suspect as the one that catalyzed it.

CLAIRE BLOOM AND THE PUBLIC MACHINE

Alice Munro may posit an antiphonal relationship between fiction and nonfiction, but she also recognizes that not all authors have an equal voice in answering one another. She has written with regard to the romantic couple in particular: "There is more than one truth about most lives and most marriages. The famous person's 'truth' gets broadcast and believed, and the obscure person's 'truth' doesn't" (Letter 38). Munro's observation should give one pause when considering suggestions by certain authors that injured intimates should simply publish their own narratives as a *quid pro quo,* as though there is a free marketplace of narratives. For example, having offended his friend Dave Peltz by publishing fiction that borrowed from Peltz's privately shared stories, Saul Bellow enjoined him to make similar use of Bellow's own anecdotes, telling him: "You are welcome to my facts. You know them, I give them to you. If you have the strength to pick them up, take them with my blessing" (qtd. in Wood). However, in practice the playing field is hardly level. Not everyone has the talent or opportunity to tell stories to a large audience, and an author's suggestion that an intimate write back can sound more like a taunt than a solution. This is the case not least when it is a male writer who has offended a woman, given that men have long enjoyed a greater license to write about their lives than women have. Maryann Burk Carver observes this gender imbalance with regard to her ex-husband Raymond Carver's representations of her in fiction:

> As I look back, I see Ray did not hesitate to portray himself either, in any position, humiliating or not. But he was a man and could get away with it better. He was also a star. He had a voice. . . . After all, what does it matter if Ray Carver humiliates himself? He doesn't really. He is Ray Carver. (qtd. in Halpert 144)

For people like Burk Carver, it is their intimate, not they, who has the cultural prerogative to make public use of private material and who may well have the last word in print about any privately contested issues.

The perils of entering a war of words with an established author are clear from the case of the actor Claire Bloom, who wrote about her relationship with Philip Roth after they divorced. Mark Shechner states: "We know little about that marriage or its dissolution, unless one is to take [Roth's] novel *Deception,* published in 1990, about a wife's discovery of her writer-husband's journal of adultery, as a window onto the trouble behind that relationship" (*Up* 25). But the public has also received Bloom's nonfictional version of what happened: in 1996 she published *Leaving a Doll's House,* a memoir that devotes considerable attention to her marriage with Roth and that she presents as an attempt to reclaim her life story by telling her own version of events instead of remaining in the sway of Roth's imagination. For Bloom, this reclamation entails revealing the intimate facts she sees lying behind Roth's fiction, so that she often discusses novels as though they were setting out to be referential. For instance, she says of *My Life as a Man:* "This work catalogues, in hilarious yet savage terms, Roth's marriage to Margaret Michaelson" (158). Bloom also writes herself back into narratives from which she has felt excluded, as when describing Roth's depression after knee surgery, which she says he documented in *Operation Shylock.* Bloom affirms that "it was just as he recorded it, with the added factor, unmentioned in the book, that I was dangerously close to going down with him" (196). And she notes her contributions to his texts; for instance, she claims to be the model for the wife of author E. I. Lonoff in *The Ghost Writer,* asserting that Roth asked her "to describe to him what it was like to live with a writer in the country" and that her words "appear almost verbatim in the book" (183–84). She also asserts that she forced Roth to alter *Deception* after she read his manuscript and found he had given her name to the protagonist's wife. Bloom writes: "I found the portrait nasty and insulting, and his use of my name completely unacceptable" (201).

The publication of *Leaving a Doll's House* seemed to hoist Roth on his own petard, as he was exposed in public by an intimate narrative for once not in his control.[3] Remarkably, he had foreseen just such an eventuality in *Deception,* having Philip's lover in that novel express her displeasure with his fictionalization of her by threatening to write her own book called *Kiss and Tell.* Philip replies by saying "Do what you like," telling her that he is himself working on another book about their relationship, implicitly *Deception* itself (200). By so replying, Philip reminds her that whether or not she manages to publish her story, he will simply be able to write yet another narrative himself. In real life, Roth seemed to follow his character's impulse by responding quickly to Bloom's memoir and, as Shechner says, "slicing her up neatly with a portrait of her as Eve Frame" in his 1998 novel of the McCarthy era, *I Married a Communist* (*Up* 26). In that text, Eve is described as a self-hating Jew with a faded film career who writes a book about her marriage to Ira Ringold and falsely claims he is a Soviet spy (242).

Meanwhile, not everyone in the media was sympathetic to Bloom. For instance, in a review of *I Married a Communist* for *Esquire,* Scott Raab calls her someone "who shirked a lifetime of adult responsibility," and he says he is unsurprised that she "would not only blame her failures as a wife and mother on her famous last ex but turn a profit doing it." Raab's comments make it clear that the media, rather than siding with intimates or seeking justice, can take an interest in their complaints that is voyeuristic and bent on trading in scandal. Raab, for one, exhorts his readers to buy *I Married a Communist* "for the whack job done upon Bloom." Such a review bolsters Catherine Bennett's claim that "once their stories are published, the betrayed may be judged just as sternly as they judge their own betrayers." With a certain irony, Roth reflects on this very

---

3. In fact, it was seemingly at least the second such occurrence for Roth. Jeffrey Berman observes that in 1967, the psychoanalyst Hans Kleinschmidt published an article in *American Imago* called "The Angry Act: The Role of Aggression in Creativity" about a patient whom he identified as a "successful Southern playwright" (qtd. in Berman 264). The article recounted three episodes from the patient's life very similar to episodes that later appeared in Roth's novel *Portnoy's Complaint.* Roth responded to the analyst's apparent use of his life story with what Debra Shostak calls "a reciprocal act of appropriation," borrowing Kleinschmidt's published words for a scene in Roth's 1974 novel *My Life as a Man* where Peter Tarnopol's analyst similarly writes about him in a psychoanalytic journal (163).

process in *I Married a Communist* when a character says of Eve's book: "The public machine she set in motion doesn't always go in the direction one wants. It takes its own direction. The public machine she wanted to destroy Ira begins to turn against her. . . . The moment you start this public machine, no other end is possible except a catastrophe for everybody" (306). We have seen in chapter 2 with regard to Elizabeth Smart how even as authors attempt through paratextual commentary to influence perspectives of themselves and their fiction, participation in the paratextual realm is at the same time a ceding of control and a surrender to other people who will inevitably create their own narratives. The case of Claire Bloom serves as a reminder that such dangers are even more prominent for authors' intimates, whose comments in public are often read through the lens of scandal, with their relationship to the authors construed in the most antagonistic, sensational ways. By responding publicly to an offensive fictional representation of them, they can inadvertently catalyze further offensive representations of them in nonfiction. Intimates may even lay themselves open to charges of desiring the very notoriety that the original fiction has imposed on them. Meanwhile, once the media turn the story into a scandal, intimates are liable to lose whatever chances for reconciliation they had with the author who has offended them. In the court of public opinion, the price of having one's voice heard is that the intimate relationship which has been violated is further attenuated, and the parties involved are pitted against each other in a zero-sum game, with spectators encouraged to take sides.

At this point, one might be tempted to say that authors who write autobiographically or wish to do so would be well served to look for intimate relations with people who do not mind finding versions of themselves in print, and that those who do mind being fictionalized should think twice about getting into bed with authors. In fact, the legal scholar Paul A. LeBel thinks people who share intimacy with authors should expect that their private lives might be made public. LeBel argues further that by entering into such relations voluntarily, authors' intimates are ceding certain privacy rights (306). Given the track record of writers such as Roth and Hanif Kureishi, it would certainly appear unwise for someone to share intimate relations with them and expect never to serve as the material for fiction. However, it is unrealistic and unnecessary to suggest as a general principle that the choice is to avoid close relations with authors entirely or to surrender privacy rights beyond the extent to which personal inviolacy is surrendered in any intimate relationship. Similarly, it would be understandable but implausible if someone were to recommend that authors look for intimacy only among other writers. It is true that fellow authors might better appreciate the complexities of creativity and its relation to intimacy; they might even serve as collaborators and coauthors.[4] However, the example of Zelda and F. Scott Fitzgerald demonstrates that there can be competition between writers as to which of them will use material from their lives first or better in fiction. Authors are also no less apt than anyone else to value their privacy and reputation.

HOW TO USE PEOPLE

I suspect that few authors are so intent on the pursuit of artistic immortality as to leave aside the question of interpersonal ethics altogether. Not all would agree with William Faulkner, who claimed: "If a writer has to rob his mother, he will not hesitate; the 'Ode on a Grecian Urn' is worth any number of old ladies" (qtd. in *Writers* 112). To be sure, some writers have had less than kind intentions with regard to those whom they have depicted in fiction, but usually even authors whose fictions militate against norms of intimacy are liable to show some consideration for their own intimates. It is worthwhile, then, to examine how authors have set out to avoid giving offense, to conciliate, and even to pay tribute to loved ones; how they have attempted to use people ethically in literature by writing, publishing, and discussing their fiction in ways meant to enhance rather than diminish intimacy.

The strategies and techniques for doing so speak to authors' assumptions about their intimates' values and reading habits, as well as to the authors' sense of their own obligations. For some writers, the very choice to label a book "fiction" is an ethical one. In Philip Roth's *The Facts*, Zuckerman suggests as much by arguing that when publishing fiction rather than nonfiction, an author "can be so much more truthful without worrying all the time about causing direct pain" (162). The implication is that fiction's combining of disguise and confession reaches toward an ideal compromise between interpersonal loyalty and public candor, offering a way to stage and advocate explicit discussions of intimate issues without wholly sacrificing others' privacy. However, in some cases the pain for intimates can be even more intense if they believe an author has chosen to call a book "fiction" merely to avoid taking responsibility for its

---

4. For discussions of literary collaboration, see Felber, Koestenbaum, Laird, and Stillinger.

referentiality. Accordingly, a transformation of source materials is often also necessary. It is unclear how radical such transformations must be in order to exculpate authors though. Giving characters a sex, nationality, or hair color different from that of their originals may be enough to protect an author for legal purposes, but it will not necessarily preclude people from noticing other resemblances.[5] A certain amount of disguise might even exacerbate the crime, since the fictionalized characteristics to which the author points in self-defense may be the same aspects that the intimate finds most defamatory. Attempts at disguise can also seem pathetically or even cruelly perfunctory, no matter how well-intentioned they actually are. And intimates can seem almost egomaniacally sensitive to the least offensive resemblances. The writer Lionel Shriver has recognized as much with regard to her novel *A Perfectly Good Family*. She claims that even though she took care to invent aspects of her characters and give them flattering attributes, her family still took offense at their doppelgängers. Shriver observes: "Even with the tough-skinned, you can write reams about how accomplished and charming they are, but if you include a *single sentence* that puts the knife in—that defies what they think of themselves, that hits a point of special sensitivity, if only by accident—that sentence will be *all they remember*."

As a result, some contemporary authors have followed their forbears and gone a step further to prevent identifications by disguising not merely their characters but also themselves, publishing anonymously or pseudonymously, as Sylvia Plath did with *The Bell Jar* in 1963, using the name "Victoria Lucas." However, the fact that the novel appeared under Plath's own name within the decade confirms Gérard Genette's assertion that "biographical renown eventually catches up with literary renown or surrounds it like a halo. Consequently no pseudonymous writer can dream of glory without foreseeing this disclosure" (50). The successful maintenance of anonymity requires considerable effort, skill, and luck on the part of authors, and still it is seldom entirely successful. By refusing direct participation in confessional culture, pseudonymous and anonymous authors force and even encourage the mass media to play a different biographical game by hunting after their true identities. Often the media are also spurred on to seek out the models for the fiction's characters as well, fol-

---

5. Such changes may not even be adequate from a legal perspective. In the 1979 California case *Bindrim v. Mitchell*, author Gwen Davis was held accountable for libel after the court decided that the psychiatrist in Davis's novel *Touching* was identifiable as Dr. Paul Bindrim, with whom Davis had undertaken group therapy, even though the fictional psychologist did not resemble Bindrim physically. See Anderson 388.

lowing the logic that if authors have chosen to disguise themselves, other names in their texts are likely to be disguises too.

For authors who wish to avoid offending their intimates, perhaps the most obvious choice is not to write about them at all. According to Erica Jong, this was Henry Miller's decision with regard to Anaïs Nin: he promised her that he would not write about their affair because he did not want to "jeopardize her marriage in print" (*Devil* 95). This choice also seems to be common with regard to authors' children, as though there is a felt imperative to honor what Axel Honneth calls "the notion that childhood represents a special phase of protected intimacy" (142). Hanif Kureishi is one of few writers to defend his right to fictionalize his children, claiming in an interview: "Children are durable. . . . They are tough. It's not as though I am killing them" (qtd. in Johnston 8). At the same time, the fact that he feels obliged to state the obvious—that he is not literally murdering them—suggests his recognition of the mortification that could befall them. Because of such a possibility, another common strategy on the part of authors, especially with regard to their parents, is to wait for people to die before writing about them. This decision seems expedient both practically—the object of representation is not around to feel wronged—and legally, since the dead have no rights against defamation or invasion of privacy. There may also be a narratological reason, insofar as a life can offer itself most clearly for representation when it has a determinate ending, thus allowing its entire trajectory to become clear in retrospect. And writing about people after their deaths may be a way for the author to mourn and memorialize them. However, for some authors, to write about intimates only in the wake of their deaths can feel like a discomforting claim of absolute power over them. To write about intimates when they are still alive at least offers them a chance to respond. In contrast, depicting them posthumously can seem like profiting from the death of another. In Proust's *In Search of Lost Time,* Marcel suggests as much; reflecting on those who have died and subsequently found their way into his writing, he remarks: "All those people . . . appeared to me to have lived lives which had profited only myself, and to have died for my benefit" (6: 211).

Authors who feel uncomfortable waiting for other people's deaths to write about them might instead seek their permission to depict them. For instance, when Timothy Findley wanted to use his friend Dorothy Warren as the model for a character in his novel *The Telling of Lies,* he asked for her approval first. Warren agreed on the condition "that her character not be involved in any bizarre sex scenes" (Roberts 94). However, the dilemma facing Findley should she have refused suggests the unattractiveness of such requests. If authors ask too early in the creative process, they may not yet know exactly what kind of representation they are seeking permission to create. They also risk having to contend with the model's suspicion for the duration of the compositional period, and they may seem to have granted the intimate a right to censor the text. Conversely, if they ask after having already drafted the fiction and the intimate refuses to allow the representation as it stands, it may be too late to change the character adequately to appease the original while still maintaining the integrity of the text. By that stage, the author also risks losing a significant investment of time and energy by not publishing. Accordingly, perhaps abiding by the adage that it is easier to obtain forgiveness than permission, other authors have simply gone ahead and published fiction with the hope that their intimates will not encounter it. For example, Alice Munro chose not to include her story "Home" in her collection *Something I've Been Meaning to Tell You* because she feared the text's portrait of her father and stepmother would seem unflattering to them. Instead, she allowed it to be published in an anthology of Canadian authors' stories that she thought neither of her relations would be likely to read.[6] Such a strategy is pragmatic but hazardous, potentially creating in intimates an even greater sense of betrayal should they discover the text, given that its publication will seem—and indeed will have been—intentionally surreptitious, suggesting the author's belief that the fiction is hurtful. Surreptitious publication may also suggest an ambivalent, even unconscious, desire in the author precisely for intimates to happen upon the text, instigating a confrontation.

When moments of discovery do take place, authors may attempt to protect their intimates through a certain amount of casuistry. For example, once Leigh Hunt realized that he was the model for Harold Skimpole in *Bleak House*, Charles Dickens responded in a letter: "The character is not you, for there are traits in it common to fifty thousand people besides, and I did not fancy you would ever recognise it. Under similar disguises my own father and mother are in my books, and you might as well see your likeness in Mr. Micawber" (qtd. in Paull 247). Dickens is self-contradictory in the course of a single sentence, both denying a correspondence and implying one by claiming that he has similarly represented his parents. It would seem that the need to mollify Hunt was more urgent than the need to supply a coherent self-defense. Perhaps unsurprisingly, to a third party Dickens remarked about Skimpole's relationship to Hunt: "I suppose he

---

6. See Thacker 244.

is the most exact portrait that was ever printed in words! . . . There is not an atom of exaggeration or suppression. It is an absolute reproduction of a real man" (qtd. in Alexander 42). In chapter 2, I discussed such self-contradictory commentary as a way for authors to flirt with audiences and stimulate their biographical desire. To intimates, though, authorial self-contradiction suggests dishonesty and manipulation. Meanwhile, Dickens's example also demonstrates that ethical or unethical action by authors takes place as much in paratexts as in the creation of fiction. Given the inevitable effects of paratexts and commentary on fiction's reception, it is crucial for authors concerned about ethics to attend to the possibility that paratexts provide chances both to appease intimates and to increase their sense of betrayal.

RESHAPING INTIMACY, REBELLING TOGETHER

My focus thus far has been on strategies employed unilaterally by authors to accommodate the demands of intimacy without sacrificing their fiction's integrity. However, as I observed in the previous chapter, some authors would say that the sanctity of intimate relationships should hardly be respected; rather, intimacy itself should better accommodate the need for self-expression, the interrelation of public and private selves, and the role of fantasy in everyday life. Accepting these points, one might still seek the possibility of joint action, such that authors and their intimates together might reconceptualize their relationships with regard to the creation and promotion of autobiographical fiction while allowing the authors to continue exploiting fiction's cachet as a transgressive, indiscreet form. How might relationships deal with the thoughts and fantasies that so often cause offense when they are expressed in fiction? How might authors who value close relationships along with the public roles of the rebel, trickster, confessant, and contrarian hope to reconcile the two? In the previous chapter, A. S. Byatt's novel *The Game* was seen to depict the writing of autobiographical fiction as an ambivalent act that both strains toward an impossible unity with another and defines the author against the other. Likewise, Alice Munro's story "Material" insists on the erotic component of make-believe, hinting that a frisson of adulterous trespass can be integral to story-making. The question of how authors and intimates might proceed together, then, is partly a question of how to incorporate ostensibly contradictory desires for intimacy and separateness, as well as how to create a space for transgression that can be mutually enjoyed rather than resented. When the protagonist of J. M. Coetzee's *Youth* is abandoned by his lover after she reads his harsh thoughts about her in his diary, he wonders: "Must it all be so cruel? Surely there is a form of cohabitation in which man and woman eat together, sleep together, live together, yet remain immersed in their respective inward explorations" (11). The same possibility remains to be explored with regard to intimate relationships more generally.

Perhaps Coetzee's protagonist is begging the question in his assumption that intimacy requires separate self-immersion and a lack of communication about authorial projects. In fact, the protagonist himself perceives that by leaving his diary in a conspicuous place he may have been subconsciously courting just such communication with his lover. He asks himself: "Was leaving his true thoughts lying around where she was bound to find them his way of telling her what he was too cowardly to say to her face?" (9). Like his diary, some autobiographical fiction might be viewed as its authors' oblique, partly unconscious attempts to commune with their intimates. But while fiction is often the cause for misunderstandings, it seldom produces understandings on its own. Instead, at once it potentially facilitates, forecloses, and procrastinates from the interpersonal dialogue that might lead to understanding. To be sure, even if reactions to a fiction are negative, it has at least succeeded in changing the tenor of relationships that otherwise might have remained paralyzed by silence, and this catalytic quality might be considered ethical. However, fiction alone is not sufficient in this regard, given that frequently it remains silent about key matters such as the writer's motives and intentions. Accordingly, some further author–intimate exchange is necessary. Barbara Johnson insists about psychoanalysis: "Perhaps a synonym for 'using people' would be, paradoxically, 'trusting people,' creating a space of play and risk that does not depend on maintaining intactness and separation" (62). One might say the same of writing. Certain authorial strategies such as asking for permission and post-hoc explanations of intention point the way toward a more harmonious poetics that involves dialogue and mutual participation in the life of fiction. It is true that sometimes authors and intimates do have incommensurate interests and values; the situation of authors confronting their ex-lovers, so common in metafiction, can be especially difficult. However, behind an optimism in the efficacy of dialogue lies a belief that often conflict emerges from a mere misunderstanding of the other's position.

As we have seen, misunderstanding is frequently autobiographical fiction's *métier*, but although an author might exploit misapprehensions productively in public with regard to a biographically desirous audience, such a lack of understanding in private is often corrosive. Fiction's manifold ambiguity leaves intimates feeling misrepresented, while authors are wont to reply that their intentions—and indeed the nature of fiction—have been misconstrued. For example, in Rohinton Mistry's short story "Swimming Lessons" a man laments his wife's response to their son's fiction:

> Don't you see, said Father, that you are confusing fiction with facts, fiction does not create facts, fiction can come from facts, it can grow out of facts by compounding, transposing, augmenting, diminishing, or altering them in any way; but you must not confuse cause and effect, you must not confuse what really happened with what the story says happened, you must not loose your grasp on reality, that way madness lies. (256)

The man's fear of fiction interpenetrating with reality is more symptomatic than instructive, expressive of a culture that is highly verificationist and not always eager to recognize the prevalence of metaphor and fantasy in human relations. Such a lack of recognition is part and parcel of a hermeneutics ill-suited to apprehending the insights about intimate relationships that fiction might provide. This is not to say that authors always offer legitimate views of their intimates in fiction. Rather, it is to suggest that when authors seem to get things wrong or appear to have fantasized in preposterous ways, outrage might not be the only response. Adam Phillips imagines just such a possibility in a broader context, writing: "Instead of the culture of complaint in which we are forever aggrieved about being misunderstood, we would think of misunderstanding as the name of the game" (*Promises* 144). Faced with the phantasmagoria of fiction, authors and their intimates might take Phillips's tip to heart and treat apparent misrepresentations as the starting point for discussions about their views of one another and of the authors' art, not to force their own narratives on the other or coerce each other into ever more exclusivity and silence but to understand better the other's point of view. This includes an understanding of each other's ways of reading. As we saw in chapter 2, autobiographical fiction tends to encourage a diversity of interpretive habits. Even when authors and their intimates cannot reach an agreement about how to read a text, they might benefit from better appreciating the other's approach.

Intimates might also aim to embrace a fiction's insights about them and their shared history with the author. Although the appearance of one's doppelgänger in fiction can be mortifying, there is something to be said for the possibilities that such self-confrontation creates. Geoffrey Galt

Harpham argues that one of the ethical functions of literature is precisely its "holding the mirror up to the community and the individual so they can judge themselves" (400). Gail Anderson-Dargatz articulates such a role for her fiction when she says that in writing her novel *A Recipe for Bees,* she tried to reveal to her parents something about themselves and each other. By her own account she succeeded remarkably, claiming: "My father, in particular, came to understand how isolating ranch life had been for my mother. Their romance rekindled, they eloped and got remarried. . . . There were many reasons they came back together, but it was obviously very satisfying to be one of those reasons" (qtd. in Busby 194). As the case of *The Game* made clear in the previous chapter, an authorial desire to understand intimates better by writing about them can be complicated by a desire to possess them and avoid facing them directly, but Anderson-Dargatz's example provides another model of engagement whereby fiction facilitates rather than replaces face-to-face encounters. It is a case in which fiction is not just about but partly for the other. In that regard, another way for fiction to be ethical is offered by Philip Roth, who in *Deception* gestures to the possibility that fiction might foster intimacy by including secret acts of devotion. In that book, Philip tells his lover he has "planted" things in his recent novel that he intended for her alone to notice and "be amused by" (202). This use of published fiction for private ends cleverly turns on its head the negative association of fiction with veiled secrets. The same ambiguous referentiality that makes fiction ethically complicated creates a unique opportunity for the intimate to become a privileged reader, as the familiar game of biographical sleuthing is transformed into a playful mode of interpersonal intimacy, one that gains an added, transgressive pleasure by being conducted through a public text.

Another option in terms of addressing fiction's unclear referentiality is for authors to talk with intimates before publication, not afterward when feelings of betrayal have already arisen, and to explain the rationales underlying their transformations of autobiographical material. Explanations are particularly attractive given that fiction's seeming orientation away from interpersonal intimacy and toward a public audience can be injurious in itself. In contrast, ethics requires a turning back toward the intimate other. Adriaan Peperzak suggests as much in explicating the philosophy of Levinas:

> I must let the Other criticize my spontaneous will to power, I must not flee from the face-to-face that accuses me. . . . If I talk or write a book *about* the Other (or about our relation), this can only be an appendix to

the truth of our face-to-face. The reduction of the Other to an element of my text about him/her can only be redeemed by offering this text to him/her. (139)

With regard to fiction in particular, authors and intimates may even find themselves needing to do something that adults only rarely undertake: reading together. As they do so, an untangling of the lines connecting words to reality might be necessary. In *Deception,* Philip proposes precisely such a conversation, telling his wife: "I will, if I have to, explain to you, line by line, if I have to, what I have been up to, as best I understand it" (178). Such an explicatory approach is apt to diminish the mortifyingly uncanny quality of fiction. It also offers intimates a glimpse into the author's compositional methods that is more personal and rigorous than the flirtatious, reticent commentary about fiction's referentiality usually offered to a general readership. The author's public flirtations will still leave intimates open to a sense of mortification should they be identified as the models for fiction, but if authors have drawn them into their confidence about their intentions, the models will be less prone to worry about what an audience thinks of a text and less likely to feel they have been turned into mere "material." Although accepting the publication of fictional texts about their intimate lives requires them to sacrifice narrative monogamy with the author, their privileged readings afford them a different kind of narrative intimacy. Authors may tell stories to others, but there is still room for unique and special attachments with their intimates in terms of shared reading practices. The intimate has the pleasure of seeing how the veils of fiction operate for the author and of being in on the secret—the same pleasure other readers seek when pursuing their biographical desire.

I do not mean to suggest that authorial explanations to intimates are intrinsically ethical. For good reasons, intimates may have a hard time accepting that authors are not proffering the kind of sophistical self-justifications Dickens offered Leigh Hunt. Authors' explanations may also be obscurantist or even self-deluded. After all, as Nadine Gordimer observes, the relationship between fiction and reality is "partly a mystery to writers themselves" (*Writing* 3). They may protest sincerely that their fiction is wholly invented when it is painfully clear to others that this is not the case. Authors' intentions may be multiple, self-contradictory, substantially unconscious, and not wholly innocent. As Jonathan Dollimore writes: "The creative imagination is inseparable from fantasy and where there is fantasy there is immorality and amorality. In fantasy the unconscious surfaces, and norms of morality, reason and humanity are violated" (xii). If one accepts the psychoanalytic claim that humans are incorrigibly ambivalent in their feelings even toward loved ones, it is hard to imagine a case in which an author did not express some iota of ill will toward intimates. Indeed, authors' recognition of this fact might be one reason they can be so quick to disavow their writing's referentiality. Better to insist it is all make-believe than argue about whether a portrait is malicious in some way. But given such blanket denials, it is unsurprising if intimates often find author's self-explanations unsatisfactory.

Accordingly, authors might consider a more counterintuitive alternative: namely, to embrace their fiction's potential confessional qualities and invite rather than discourage biographical interpretation by their intimates. Instead of unilaterally writing and then unilaterally explaining what it all means, authors might reject not only the notion of biographical heresy but also their own hermeneutic authority over their text. They might admit their limitations in terms of apprehending what their fiction says of their minds, and they might encourage discussion of their work's biographical inflections. This option requires humility, to be sure. It is also likely to produce readings that are uncomfortable for both authors and their intimates. It is liable to lay bare how the parties see each other and how they think the other sees them. Some intimate relationships may not be built on sufficiently strong foundations of care, sensitivity, mutual esteem, and clear communication to allow for such a practice. Indeed, the question of how to talk about the thorny personal matters evoked in a fiction may be as troubling as the fiction itself. Fiction may draw attention to feelings or situations that neither authors nor their intimates have been able to articulate consciously to themselves, much less to each other. However, dialogue has the potential to disarm the fiction in the eyes of intimates by transforming it from an authoritatively delivered judgment of them into a thing that can be scrutinized collaboratively, their perspective on it heard and validated. It might be read not just as something that has betrayed them but also as a text that has betrayed its author, despite the author's intentions, in ways that can be both hurtful and revelatory. Fiction so considered becomes an instrument for improving intimate relationships rather than an instrumentalization of them. Just as Alice Munro's fiction self-reflexively posits a dialectic between fiction and nonfiction in which each holds the other to account, there is the possibility for fiction to function in a similar manner with regard to intimate relations. Discussion of a fiction can draw attention to its symptomatic qualities as well as its insights, even while the fiction can help to recast the nature of the discussion.

While conversations about a fiction's biographical aspects are bound to be fraught, their collaborative nature may also carry with it a positive affective, if not erotic, charge. For instance, Maryann Burk Carver writes of the pleasures brought by her editorial discussions with Raymond Carver: "Nothing was as exciting for me as Ray saying, 'I've got a draft of a story to show you now, Maryann!' All the magic in the universe gathered in his study when we read and analyzed the first draft of a story or poem, our cups of hot coffee together on the floor beside us" (160). Similarly, there is the satisfaction that the narrator of Munro's "Material" takes in reporting details about her neighbor to her author-husband, reportage that constitutes a form of joint research for his writing. Intimates need not be outright collaborators in composition or editorial work to experience such closeness. Merely through discussion, they might join authors in the fiction-making process and enjoy the *jouissance* that has been associated with such self-estranging, imaginative activity.

Playful collaboration might also extend beyond private interpretive acts into the public sphere. As we have seen in chapter 2, it is generic in the present confessional age for authors to engage with their readers in a referentially flirtatious manner that can seem threatening to intimates. Should intimates wish to regain a sense of agency, they might join authors in playful public performances akin to those given by Hugo and the narrator in "Material": performances that provide creative opportunities for both parties and build intimacy. It should be noted that "Material" also demonstrates how such play can become tainted by competitiveness and jealousy, patriarchal gender dynamics, and unethical behavior toward people outside the sphere of intimacy. However, Munro's story still suggests that authors and their intimates might begin to think about rebelling together: for instance, by jointly flirting in public about texts' referentiality. Burk Carver, for one, reports that she played coy when people asked her whether Raymond Carver's stories were based on real life, only replying: "What is art without mystery?" (212). Evidently she enjoyed the same pleasures of veiled exposure that authors do. Intimates who engage in such public intimacy with authors are able to feel less like victims and more like partners in crime. They are acting in line with the notion of intimacy offered by Slavoj Žižek, who argues for the abandonment of dyadic relations in favor of shared public action. Žižek writes that "the way—the *only* way—to have an intense and fulfilling personal (sexual) relationship is not for the couple to look into each other's eyes, forgetting about the world around them, but, while holding hands, to look together outside, at a third point (the Cause for which both are fighting, in which both are engaged)" (85). One might extend this ideal from the domain of the romantic couple to encompass other kinds of intimate relationships as well. In each case, public acts of authorial rebellion can serve to augment rather than traduce relations with the intimate. Through joint participation in public commentary, the line between authorship and intimacy can blur in a salutary manner; authors and their intimates might newly apprehend that a relationship can be a work of art too, one that generates aesthetic as well as affective responses, public and private meanings, critics and fans. It can be collaboratively scripted and performed to include ironies and ambiguities, narrative arcs, motifs, and manipulations of genre.

Then again, explanation, consultation, and collaboration arguably involve more effort and complexity than, say, silence, solitude, ultimatums, and submission. With regard to a more general discourse of "working" at relationships, Laura Kipnis asks: "When monogamy becomes labor, when desire is organized contractually, with accounts kept and fidelity extracted like labor from employees, . . . is this really what we mean by a 'good relationship'?" (*Against* 19). Consultation and work might seem distastefully businesslike to those who want their intimacy soft-lit and unspoken. Richard Wasserstrom has similar concerns about a demand that people always be forthright and candid, suspecting it would "make ordinary social interaction vastly more complex and time-consuming than it now is" (332). For some, one of the greatest attractions of intimacy is that allows them to be less self-conscious than in other relationships. Discussions of fiction that turn to addressing unspoken thoughts and desires might strike such people as veering too close to what Rochelle Gurstein calls "the brutality of full disclosure" (42).

Authors in particular are liable to resist full disclosure, preferring to guard their intentions and understanding of their fiction in the belief that the intimacy of writing requires its own silences. No doubt for some authors, writing fiction necessitates precisely the kind of megalomaniacal control and distance of which they sometimes stand accused. Dialogue before publication would risk destroying their own relationship with their work. In chapter 2, I argued that Philip Roth's fiction makes a case for the liberating aspects of fiction's veiled referentiality, and I pointed out that because authors of fiction do not expect to be held accountable for the truthfulness of their stories, they can afford to let down their psychic guards when they write, channeling fantasy and unconscious life more directly into their narratives. To write with the expectation of having to explain their work's referential nuances might make it impossible to produce in the first place. Franz Kafka, for one, saw writing as a manner of confession that requires utter isolation, avowing in a letter:

> Writing means revealing oneself to excess; that utmost of self-revelation and surrender, in which a human being, when involved with others, would feel he was losing himself, and from which, therefore, he will always shrink as long as he is in his right mind.... That is why one can never be alone enough when one writes, why there can never be enough silence around one when one writes, why even night is not night enough. (271–72)

Just as intimate relations sometimes require a lack of self-consciousness, so can writing demand self-abandonment and the absence of the other whose perspective would destabilize the artistic vision. It would thus take a considerable toll on some writers to explain their fiction when in fact many do not fully understand their own procedures, fewer still are able to articulate them, and many are loath to interrogate them, lest in the process they poison the well of their creative powers.

Perhaps it is the fate of some authors to live alone. That much is implied by the ending of Woody Allen's film *Deconstructing Harry,* where the eponymous novelist seems to have driven away everyone in his life by writing about them. Yet as Ruth Perry points out, intimates help "to create the conditions for another's creativity," and the fact that Harry ends up suffering from writer's block in his solitude similarly underscores an author's need of company, if only to provide material for further fiction (3). As a consequence, accommodations of the other have a pragmatic impetus: namely, to furnish authors with the support and inspiration they need. But it would also be hypocritical for authors who rail against the oppressiveness of silence to write and publish silently themselves, leaving their closest relations to encounter their fiction in a most nonintimate way. Instead of rejecting social obligations outright, then, authors might aim to use their fiction as a means to reshape their relationships. Rebelling against oppressive norms of intimacy need not always mean rebelling against one's intimates too.

AN ETHICS OF UNCERTAINTY

Even for those authors who prioritize responsible relations with their intimates, no single strategy for ethical action is certain to be effective. A recognition of that fact is likely one reason why literary critics have been reluctant to postulate ethical guidelines for writers similar to those governing medicine or law. The ethical codes for psychotherapists in particular might seem attractive as a model, given that therapists, too, sometimes seek to publish texts drawing on intimate confessions that were predicated on the expectation of confidentiality. Therapists are obliged to obtain consent from their patients if they write about them, or they must disguise the subjects sufficiently that the patients would not recognize themselves. However, the appropriateness of such rules to fiction based on nontherapeutic encounters is limited. Psychotherapy is a professional undertaking with clear expectations and boundaries from the outset of the relationship. In contrast, authors of fiction are involved in wide varieties of intimacy with diverse, changing expectations and contexts, from casual encounters to lifelong forms of devotion. It would be impossible to create a set of rules that apply usefully to all situations. Claudia Mills's article on the ethics of fiction does propose one overarching precept: namely, that when an author "treats someone else's story at length, and gained access to that story only through intimacy, she should ask before she appropriates" ("Appropriating" 203). However, while Mills is careful here to define precise conditions in which writing requires permission, she seems to forget that she is talking about fiction, where the "treatment" of a story may involve significant transformations of it. The kind of consideration that authors should extend to their sources surely depends not only on how the story was obtained and how much of it was used but also on what changes were made to it. It depends further on how the fiction will circulate, what paratexts will accompany it, and how it will be promoted. My sense here that ethical deliberation about fiction must pay attention to each case's context emerges from the previous chapters' identification of the various cultural forces affecting fiction's reception and of the role that third parties play in fiction's transgressions.

The need for a particularist ethics also follows from the distinctiveness and opacity of each person's psyche. Richard Rorty points out that in giving us "the equipment to construct our own private vocabulary of moral deliberation," Sigmund Freud facilitated the telling of "a narrative of our own development, our idiosyncratic moral struggle, which is far more finely textured, far more custom-tailored to our individual case, than the moral vocabulary which the philosophical tradition offered us" (32). Not least, Freud's attention to the role of the unconscious has implications for the ethics of autobiographical fiction. A recognition of unconscious motives and desires requires writers to put aside the assumption that they have authority over a text's meaning simply because they wrote it, and to acknowledge that they may have forged unintentional links between life and art. The value of skepticism about one's interpretations also applies to intimates. In the eyes of authors who have meant no harm and even intended no portraiture, the offense their intimates take at fictional characters must seem exasperating; sometimes it must appear as though the person has fixated upon certain negative aspects of a character and is determined to be a victim. Somerset Maugham writes: "So colossal is human egotism that people who have met an author are constantly on the look out for portraits of themselves in his works" (141–42). Likewise, James Wood observes that people who see their own reflections in the glass of fiction "miss the very handsome window displays that have nothing to do with them." Authors feel betrayed when their intimates have not engaged with their work as impersonally as they would have wished, and they might rightly insist that a text is not unethical simply because an intimate is offended by it. G. Thomas Couser asserts that "if life writing were considered unethical whenever it caused its subjects any sort of discomfort or pain, it would be the end of life writing as we know it" (30). In some cases, intimates' sensitivity might be something to challenge, not accommodate. Intimates might recognize that their own faulty assumptions and self-conceptions are responsible for the injury they feel. Rather than jumping to conclusions about authors' intentions, they might follow Adam Phillips's suggestion and view the representations or misrepresentations of them in fiction as potentially interesting, not merely injurious. Fiction could be taken as a kind of dream that, through sensitive joint interpretation, can lead to better interrelations.

The need for a particularist ethics of autobiographical fiction also emerges from the insights of metafictions by Roth, Munro, Carver, Byatt, and others. As these texts dramatize ethical debates, they insist that there are any number of ways to have a relationship and that each relationship is significantly unique. Behavior that in one case constitutes a gross ethical violation might in another be precisely what ethics demands. Defamation law recognizes this diversity at the level of community, taking into account that, as Lawrence McNamara puts it, "any given jurisdiction will contain numerous communities and sub-communities that will, by definition, have different and sometimes conflicting moral taxonomies" (9). The same principle holds true at the individual level: one person's betrayal is another's tribute. An ethical intimacy must respect such pluralism while attempting to reconcile the disparate needs of those sharing a relationship. Phillips asserts: "The only sane foregone conclusion about any relationship is that it is an experiment; and that exactly what it is an experiment in will never be clear to the participants" (*Going* 187). In that light, the ethical complications introduced by autobiographical fiction are no less varied or surprising than other complications arising from everyday intimacy. In fact, the impracticality of formulating universal rules says something about the nature of ethics itself. Laws must be predictable in their application, but as Derek Attridge argues, ethical matters "always involve unpredictability and risk" (28). Ethical engagement means being sensitive to the diversity of otherness and cognizant of the challenges in getting on better together while remaining committed to the possibility of doing so.

Near the outset of this book, I characterized the work of talking about ethics as treacherous; the same can be said of ethical practice itself. Not least, it is difficult to identify a clear-cut calculus whereby one might weigh fiction's public good against its private harm when one seems to come at the expense of the other. I have identified autobiographical fiction as having numerous reader-oriented ethical functions: among them, it articulates otherwise-unspeakable truths, it foregrounds the role of fantasy in the everyday, and it tests audiences' abilities to distinguish truth from falsehood while allowing them to explore the multiplicity and performative aspects of identity. It can also give authors a therapeutic distance from themselves and their intimates. Nevertheless, an accurate assessment of the extent to which any single text has these effects is impossible given the multiple contingencies of a text's reception. Simply put, one cannot know who will read the text or how they will interpret and discuss it. The same uncertainties make it difficult to calculate in advance the harm a text may do to a person's reputation, privacy, and closest relationships. It is not even self-evident that certain kinds of personal content should always be protected against fictionalization or, conversely, considered fair game. The more-or-less factual representation of sexual relations is perhaps the most obvious candidate for being declared unethical outright, given that sex has been considered the epitome of the private. Indeed, Mills thinks such representations should be out of bounds not only for that reason but also because narratives about sex are "inherently uninteresting" ("Friendship" 112). However, if there was any one shared project among writers of autobiographical fiction in the twentieth century, it was to follow Freud in asserting that stories about sex can be among the most interesting and important stories people tell. This assertion serves as a reminder that one ethical role authors of fiction have played is to challenge conventional notions of what counts as interesting and what can be discussed publicly. The history of literature demonstrates that whatever the rules set out to govern fiction, authors have responded by shifting their practices in order to continue operating on the boundaries of the permissible. Accordingly, proscription is difficult to enforce and also perhaps misconceived insofar as it is catalytic rather than effectively disciplinary.

Still, it is understandable that authors should be nervous about ethics, fearful of its threat to their art's very possibility. A requirement that they inspect their own methods and intentions, to say nothing of changing them, might smack of censorship. Acceding to such a demand might seem especially unappealing given that, as Freud saw it, one of fiction writers' great achievements is to foil their own internal censors through the use of metaphor and seemingly nonautobiographical scenarios, thereby allowing them to tell a more complete truth about themselves than they could through nonfiction. Yet if it is consequently fiction writers' role to be indiscrete and indiscreet—to blur borders between realities, say the unsayable, and explore hypotheticals as nonfiction cannot—indiscretion need not be entirely irresponsible. Rather, authors might be more open-minded about what ethics requires of them. It could be that a turning back to intimates to speak about fiction does not always entail the silencing writers fear. In fact, if they do not turn back in this way, their antipathy to conversation is liable to breed a different kind of silence in them: that of the autonomous, alienated creator who cannot tolerate challenges to his or her narratives. Alternatively, authors might open themselves up to the uncertainties of discussion. The same argument that Hanif Kureishi has made against censorship equally underscores the possibilities inherent in dialogue between authors and their intimates about fiction's ethics. Kureishi writes: "You can never know what your words might turn out to mean for yourself or for someone else; or what the world they make will be like. Anything could happen. The problem with silence is that we know exactly what it will be like" ("Loose"). For authors to find a path of responsible indiscretion while engaging reciprocally with their intimate others is integral to an ethics of autobiographical fiction.

Conclusion

> I came upstairs from the scene between Tommy and Molly and instantly began to turn it into a short story. It struck me that my doing this—turning everything into fiction—must be an evasion. Why not write down, simply, what happened between Molly and her son today? Why do I never write down, simply, what happens?
>
> —Doris Lessing, *The Golden Notebook* 232
>
> *I want to do this with honour, if I possibly can.*
>
> —Alice Munro, "Home" 153

As Munro's narrator in "Home" attempts to describe a visit with her father and his second wife, she is simultaneously bent on producing an ethical narrative and doubtful that the dictates of writing truthfully will allow her to complete her story without causing harm. It is no wonder that authors such as Doris Lessing's protagonist in *The Golden Notebook* turn to writing fiction instead. But because fiction has a flirtatious relationship to facts, it too must also flirt with ethical failure: not least, a failure to fulfill whatever obligations its authors might have to depict or protect their intimates' lives. I draw this inference from the metafictions considered in this book, few of which seek to depict a satisfying rapprochement, never mind a full-blown concord, between authors and their intimates. In A. S. Byatt's *The Game*, Cassandra kills herself after her sister writes about her, and although in Raymond Carver's "Intimacy" the narrator's ex-wife tells him that he will have to go on writing about their shared past, she seems to do so with resignation rather than approval. In that regard, metafiction about the ethics of writing one's life seems consonant with Anton Chekhov's precept that it is fiction's job only to ask questions, not to provide solutions.[1] In terms of autobiographical fiction's function in confessional culture, though, one might respond to Chekhov by saying that fiction is not asking or answering questions so much as it is both an intervention and a symptom. On the one hand, its ambiguous referentiality frustrates desires to reduce its narratives to the factual, and it encourages readers to embrace metaphor. It rejects the reticence and propriety of intimacy norms even while breeding intimacy of a different kind with its audience. As a site of play for authors and readers alike, autobiographical fiction problematizes identity, and it models for people an alternative to the limited selves they are able to perform in interpersonal relationships. On the other hand, authors often pander to an audience's desire for scandalous personal narratives, traducing intimates in the process. A form of cultural dream-space, fiction is a provocation and a balm, a way for society to rehearse and also to examine its ambivalence around privacy and confession, verificationism and fantasy, iconoclasm and conformism, free speech and reputation. It is by attending to the complexities of this ambivalence that one might locate autobiographical fiction's ethical impetus at the cultural level.

Because the ethics of autobiographical fiction is bound up with literature's public life as much as its private reception, I have argued that authors cannot be solely blamed for their fiction's misdeeds. Publicity material, journalistic commentary, and readers' preexisting biographical desire contribute to the offense fiction gives. Especially in the mass media, authors are assigned the role of *poètes maudits,* condemned and scapegoated for transgressing social norms most people find difficult to embrace. What is more, nowadays it is inevitable that many intimates of authors not only find their alter egos lurking in fiction but are also drawn into the public sphere themselves and urged to express their reactions to putatively offensive texts. If I have paid considerable attention to the role of paratexts and commentary in the life of fiction, it is with a sense that intimates and authors alike face a relatively new challenge in working out how to participate ethically in the promotion of literature through the mass media, and that any account of literary ethics needs to attend to this challenge.

---

1. Chekhov writes in a letter to Alexei Suvorin: "You are right to demand that an author take conscious stock of what he is doing, but you are confusing two concepts: *answering the questions* and *formulating them correctly.* Only the latter is required of an author" (117).

But I have argued further that if paratextual performance creates ethical complications, it also opens up possibilities for ethical action. As Pierre Bourdieu points out, although what people "can or cannot do is largely determined by the structure in which they are placed and by the positions they occupy within that structure," that is not to deny the possibility of individual responsibility or efficacy (54). Likewise, Charles Taylor accepts the insight that "much of our motivation—our desires, aspirations, evaluation—is not simply given" but insists that people are still responsible insofar as "it is always possible that fresh insight might alter my evaluations and hence even myself for the better" (36, 39). At the same time that this conception of agency complicates ethics, it provides further grounds for an ethics attuned to cultural contexts as well as personal motives.

Although the love triangle that autobiographical fiction creates between authors, intimates, and other readers is a precarious one, I have suggested that it is not without its rewards and possible successes for all, such that intimacy between any two of the parties involved need not come at the expense of the third. In particular, authors and their loved ones need not maintain narrative monogamy—an insistence on telling a static story about themselves, and only to each other—to enjoy narrative intimacy. This is especially true if authors and intimates can bring to fiction the same sense of playful collaboration that authors often share with their general readership. Certainly the metafictions I have discussed in this book confirm that fiction seldom ruins intimacy on its own; rather, the trouble fiction seems to cause is often already lurking in the practice of intimacy. At its best, fiction is a unique vehicle for redeeming the past, paying tribute to loved ones, and engaging with their complexity and otherness as well as one's own. Still, a recurring theme of this book has been that infidelity is pleasurable and intrinsic to creativity and that autobiographical fiction has always gone hand in hand with trespass. It might be said that at a fundamental level, any act of remaking of the world is a betrayal of the world as it is, and so fiction based on intimate relations is bound to betray another person's facts. Moreover, misrepresentations of others seem unavoidable because it is not quite clear what a "correct" representation in fiction would look like. And if fiction is a space of hypotheticals and suppositions, then it is sometimes a space in which authors try out not only new ways of being people but also new ways of hurting people, however tentatively, ambivalently, and indirectly.

To the extent that autobiographical fiction insists people pay attention to the complexities of their various selves, it has provided a model for this present book, in which I have sought to foster a greater consciousness about the ethical issues fiction raises. For instance, I have drawn attention to biographical desire in readers and authors alike with the hope that when this desire draws them toward certain approaches to—and judgments of—fiction, they may be more cognizant of what is happening. Bourdieu believes that "if people became aware of them, conscious action aimed at controlling the structural mechanisms that engender moral failure would be possible" (56). Similarly, authors and intimates who are more self-conscious and more articulate about fiction's problems are more likely to forestall or resolve conflicts. The problems of writing metafiction identified in chapter 3 make it clear that self-consciousness is not enough and that public self-reflexive discourse on the part of authors can in fact exacerbate rather than alleviate their trespasses. But at least for some authors, self-consciousness can be more ethical if articulated within the intimate sphere, before the mutual alienation, power imbalances, and unpredictable consequences of publication. Having said that, in this book I have argued that universalized prescription is of little use. Instead, I have presented historical and cultural contexts in which autobiographical fiction's dilemmas can be situated, a vocabulary for discussing these dilemmas, and a variety of possible approaches to solving them. I have done so with the hope that as a result, individual cases might be considered with greater sophistication, nuance, and sensitivity. Often the feelings of uncertainty and intense, sometimes excruciating intimacy that autobiographical fiction can create are bound up with a sense of betrayal, but they also constitute fertile ground for a reexamination of intimate relations, as well as of the stories we tell in and about those relations. Autobiographical fiction holds the capacity both to harm and to help people in unique ways, and the same referential ambiguity that is its most vexing characteristic is also a potentially ethical one. The space of uncertainty that fiction creates is also a space of potentiality, a space where nothing has been decided and so everything might be discussed.

Works Cited

Abbott, H. Porter. "Autobiography, Autography, Fiction: Groundwork for a Taxonomy of Textual Categories." *New Literary History* 19.3 (1988): 597–615.
Abrams, M. H. *The Mirror and the Lamp: Romantic Theory and the Critical Tradition.* 1953. New York: Norton, 1958.
Adachi, Ken. "'Conformist' Was Years Ahead of Her Time." *Toronto Star* 4 Dec. 1982: 17.
Adams, Timothy Dow. *Telling Lies in Modern American Autobiography.* London: University of North Carolina Press, 2000.
Aelian. *Historical Miscellany.* Trans. and ed. N. G. Wilson. Cambridge, MA: Harvard University Press, 1997.
Alexander, Doris. *Creating Characters with Charles Dickens.* University Park: Pennsylvania State University Press, 1991.
Ali, Monica. *Brick Lane.* New York: Scribner, 2003.
Alighieri, Dante. *The Divine Comedy.* Trans. John D. Sinclair. New York: Oxford University Press, 1961.
Amos, William. *The Originals: An A–Z of Fiction's Real-Life Characters.* Boston: Little, Brown, 1985.
Anderson, David A. "Avoiding Defamation Problems in Fiction." *Brooklyn Law Review* 51.1 (1986): 383–99.
Aristotle. *Poetics.* Trans. Malcolm Heath. London: Penguin, 1996.
Attridge, Derek. "Innovation, Literature, Ethics: Relating to the Other." *PMLA* 114.1 (1999): 20–31.

Atwood, Margaret. "The Tent." *Harper's Magazine* Oct. 2005: 80.
Axelrod, Steven Gould, ed. *The Critical Responses to Robert Lowell*. Westport, CT: Greenwood, 1999.
Bachelard, Gaston. *The Poetics of Space*. Trans. Maria Jolas. Boston: Beacon, 1994.
Bakhtin, M. M. *The Dialogic Imagination: Four Essays*. Trans. Caryl Emerson and Michael Holquist. Ed. Holquist. Austin: University of Texas Press, 1990.
Bal, Mieke. "Allo-Portraits." *Mirror or Mask? Self-Representation in the Modern Age*. Ed. David Blostein and Pia Kleber. Berlin: Vistas, 2003. 11–44.
Barbour, John D. *The Conscience of the Autobiographer: Ethical and Religious Dimensions of Autobiography*. New York: St. Martin's, 1992.
Bardwell, Leland. "The Language of Love." Rev. of *By Grand Central Station I Saw Down and Wept* and *A Bonus*, by Elizabeth Smart. *Hibernia* 22 July 1977: 20.
Barker, George. *The Dead Seagull*. London: Lehmann, 1950.
Barnes, Julian. *Flaubert's Parrot*. 1984. London: Picador, 1985.
Barthes, Roland. *Camera Lucida: Reflections on Photography*. Trans. Richard Howard. New York: Noonday, 1991.
———. *A Lover's Discourse: Fragments*. Trans. Richard Howard. New York: Hill & Wang, 1978.
———. *The Pleasure of the Text*. Trans. Richard Miller. New York: Hill & Wang, 1975.
Belsey, Catherine. *Desire: Love Stories in Western Culture*. Oxford: Blackwell, 1994.
Benedetti, Carla. *The Empty Cage: Inquiry into the Mysterious Disappearance of the Artist*. Trans. William J. Hartley. Ithaca: Cornell University Press, 2005.
Benn, Stanley. "Privacy, Freedom, and Respect for Persons." Schoeman, *Philosophical* 223–44.
Bennett, Arnold. *How to Become an Author: A Practical Guide*. London: Pearson, 1903.
Bennett, Catherine. "The Ex-Rated Confessionals." *The Guardian*. The Guardian, 25 Mar. 1999. Web. 26 Jan. 2004.
Berlant, Lauren, ed. *Intimacy*. Chicago: University of Chicago Press, 2000.
———. "Intimacy: A Special Issue." Berlant, *Intimacy* 1–8.
Berman, Jeffrey. *The Talking Cure: Literary Representations of Psychoanalysis*. New York: New York University Press, 1985.
Bernard, André. *Madame Bovary, C'est Moi! The Great Characters of Literature and Where They Came From*. New York: Norton, 2004.
Billen, Andrew. "Love: Not the End of Your Problems, the Beginning." *The Times* 6 Sept. 2005: times2 8–9.
Bloom, Claire. *Leaving a Doll's House*. London: Virago, 1996.
Bok, Sissela. *Secrets: On the Ethics of Concealment and Revelation*. New York: Pantheon, 1982.
Boling, Patricia. *Privacy and the Politics of Intimate Life*. Ithaca: Cornell University Press, 1996.
Boorstin, Daniel. *The Image: A Guide to Pseudo-Events in America*. New York: Atheneum, 1982.
Booth, Wayne C. *The Company We Keep: An Ethics of Fiction*. Berkeley: University of California Press, 1988.

———. *The Rhetoric of Fiction*. 2nd ed. Chicago: University of Chicago Press, 1983.
Bourdieu, Pierre. *On Television*. Trans. Priscilla Parkhurst Ferguson. New York: New Press, 1998.
Brennan, Timothy. *At Home in the World: Cosmopolitanism Now*. Cambridge, MA: Harvard University Press, 1997.
Brooks, Peter. *Body Work: Objects of Desire in Modern Narrative*. Cambridge, MA: Harvard University Press, 1993.
Brown, Andrew. "Fragments of a Conversation with Elizabeth Smart." *Festival Times* 29 Aug. 1980: 2.
Bruccoli, Matthew J., Scottie Fitzgerald Smith, and Joan P. Kerr, eds. *The Romantic Egoists*. New York: Scribner's, 1974.
Bruner, Jerome. *Actual Minds, Possible Worlds*. Cambridge, MA: Harvard University Press, 1986.
Bruss, Elizabeth W. *Autobiographical Acts: The Changing Situation of a Literary Genre*. Baltimore: Johns Hopkins University Press, 1976.
Buell, Lawrence. "Introduction: In Pursuit of Ethics." *PMLA* 114.1 (1999): 7–19.
———. "What We Talk about When We Talk about Ethics." Garber, Hanssen, and Walkowitz 1–13.
Busby, Brian. *Character Parts: Who's Really Who in CanLit*. Toronto: Vintage, 2003.
Butler, Judith. *Antigone's Claim: Kinship between Life and Death*. New York: Columbia University Press, 2000.
———. "Desire." Lentricchia and McLaughlin 369–86.
———. "Ethical Ambivalence." Garber, Hanssen, and Walkowitz 15–28.
———. *The Judith Butler Reader*. Ed. Sara Salih. Oxford: Blackwell, 2004.
Rev. of *By Grand Central Station I Sat Down and Wept*, by Elizabeth Smart. *Evening Standard* 19 July 1966. Box 4, folder 1. Alice Van Wart Collection. National Library of Canada, Ottawa.
Byatt, A. S. *The Game*. 1967. London: Vintage, 1999.
———. *Portraits in Fiction*. London: Chatto & Windus, 2001.
Carrell, Jennifer Lee. "A Pack of Lies in a Looking Glass: Lady Mary Wroth's *Urania* and the Magic Mirror of Romance." *ELH: Studies in English Literature 1500–1900* 34 (1997): 79–107.
Carver, Maryann Burk. *What It Used to Be Like: A Portrait of My Marriage to Raymond Carver*. New York: St. Martin's, 2006.
Carver, Raymond. *Where I'm Calling From: The Selected Stories*. London: Harvill, 1993.
Chase, Karen and Michael Levenson. *The Spectacle of Intimacy: A Public Life for the Victorian Family*. Princeton: Princeton University Press, 2000.
Chaucer, Geoffrey. *The Canterbury Tales*. Ed. Jill Mann. New York: Penguin, 2005.
Chekhov, Anton. "To Alexei Suvorin." 27 Oct. 1888. *Letters of Anton Chekhov*. Trans. Michael Henry Heim and Simon Karlinsky. Ed. Karlinsky. New York: Harper & Row, 1973. 116–20.
Coetzee, J. M. *Doubling the Point: Essays and Interviews*. Ed. David Attwell. London: Harvard University Press, 1992.
———. *Elizabeth Costello: Eight Lessons*. London: Secker & Warburg, 2003.

———. *Youth*. 2002. London: Vintage, 2003.
Cohen, William A. *Sex Scandal: The Private Parts of Victorian Fiction*. Durham: Duke University Press, 1996.
Cohn, Dorrit. *Transparent Minds: Narrative Modes for Presenting Consciousness in Fiction*. Princeton: Princeton University Press, 1978.
Couser, G. Thomas. *Vulnerable Subjects: Ethics and Life Writing*. Ithaca: Cornell University Press, 2004.
Creighton, Joanne. "An Interview with Margaret Drabble." *Margaret Drabble: Golden Realms*. Ed. Dorey Schmidt. Edinburg, TX: Pan American University Press, 1982. 18–31.
———. "Sisterly Symbiosis: Margaret Drabble's *The Waterfall* and A. S. Byatt's *The Game*." *Mosaic* 20.1 (1987): 15–29.
Danziger, Marie A. *Text-Countertext: Postmodern Paranoia in Samuel Beckett, Doris Lessing, and Philip Roth*. New York: Lang, 1996.
de la Durantaye, Leland. "How to Read Philip Roth, or the Ethics of Fiction and the Aesthetics of Fact." *The Cambridge Quarterly* 39.4 (2010): 303–30.
de Staël, Madame. "Essay on Fiction." Trans. Morroe Berger. *The Critical Tradition: Classic Texts and Contemporary Trends*. Ed. David H. Richter. Boston: Bedford, 1989. 279–82.
Deconstructing Harry. Dir. Woody Allen. New Line, 1997.
Defoe, Daniel. *The Life and Adventures of Robinson Crusoe*. 1719. Ed. Angus Ross. London: Penguin, 1988.
Derrida, Jacques. *Acts of Literature*. Ed. Derek Attridge. New York: Routledge, 1992.
DeSalvo, Louise. *Adultery*. Boston: Beacon, 1999.
———. *Conceived with Malice*. New York: Dutton, 1994.
Dollimore, Jonathan. *Sex, Literature and Censorship*. Cambridge: Polity, 2001.
Doubrovsky, Serge. *Fils: Roman*. Paris: Galilée, 1997.
———. *Le Libre brisé: Roman*. Paris: Grasset, 1989.
Drabble, Margaret. *A Summer Bird-Cage*. 1963. London: Penguin, n.d.
Durrell, Lawrence. *The Black Book*. 1938. New York: Dutton, 1960.
———. "To Henry Miller." Aug. 1935. *The Durrell-Miller Letters 1935–80*. Ed. Ian S. MacNiven. London: Faber/Haag, 1988. 2–3.
Dusinberre, Juliet A. "A. S. Byatt." Interview with Byatt. *Women Writers Talking*. Ed. Janet Todd. New York: Holmes & Meier, 1983. 181–95.
Eakin, Paul John, ed. *The Ethics of Life Writing*. Ithaca: Cornell University Press, 2004.
———. *Fictions in Autobiography: Studies in the Art of Self-Invention*. Princeton: Princeton University Press, 1985.
———. "The Unseemly Profession: Privacy, Inviolate Personality, and the Ethics of Life Writing." *Renegotiating Ethics in Literature, Philosophy, and Theory*. Ed. Jane Adamson et al. Cambridge: Cambridge University Press, 1998. 161–80.
Eliot, T. S. *The Sacred Wood: Essays on Poetry and Criticism*. 1920. London: Methuen, 1972.
Epstein, Joseph. "What Does Philip Roth Want?" *Commentary* 77.1 (1984): 62–67.
Felber, Lynette. *Literary Liaisons: Auto/biographical Appropriations in Modernist Women's Fiction*. DeKalb: Northern Illinois University Press, 2002.

Feuer, Alan. "At Trial, Writer Recalls an Alter Ego that Took Over." *New York Times*. New York Times, 21 June 2007. Web. 25 June 2007.
Fitzgerald, F. Scott. *The Beautiful and the Damned*. 1922. Ed. James L. W. West III. Cambridge: Cambridge University Press, 2008.
Fitzgerald, Zelda. *Collected Writings*. Ed. Matthew J. Bruccoli. New York: Scribner's, 1991.
———. *Save Me the Waltz*. 1932. New York: New American Library, 1968.
Fleming, David A. "Barclay's *Satyricon*: The First Satirical Roman à Clef." *Modern Philology* 65.2 (1967): 95–102.
Foucault, Michel. *The Foucault Reader*. Trans. Josué V. Harari et al. Ed. Paul Rabinow. London: Penguin, 1991.
———. *The History of Sexuality: Volume 1, An Introduction*. Trans. Robert Hurley. London: Penguin, 1990.
———. "Of Other Spaces." Trans. Jay Miskowiec. *Diacritics* 16.1 (1986): 22–27.
Franta, Andrew. *Romanticism and the Rise of the Mass Public*. Cambridge: Cambridge University Press, 2007.
Freud, Sigmund. *Art and Literature*. Trans. James Strachey. Ed. Albert Dickson. Penguin Freud Library 14. London: Penguin, 1990.
Frey, James. *A Million Little Pieces*. New York: Doubleday, 2003.
Gallagher, Catherine. *Nobody's Story: The Vanishing Acts of Women Writers in the Marketplace, 1670–1820*. 1994. Berkeley: University of California Press, 1995.
Garber, Marjorie, Beatrice Hanssen, and Rebecca L. Walkowitz. "Introduction: The Turn to Ethics." Garber, Hanssen, and Walkowitz vii–xii.
———, eds. *The Turn to Ethics*. New York: Routledge, 2000.
Gates, David. "Portnoy's Payback." Rev. of *I Married a Communist*, by Philip Roth. *Newsweek* 5 Oct. 1998: 84–85.
Gaut, Berys. "The Ethical Criticism of Art." *Aesthetics and Ethics: Essays at the Intersection*. Ed. Jerrold Levinson. Cambridge: Cambridge University Press, 1998. 182–203.
Genette, Gérard. *Paratexts: Thresholds of Interpretation*. Trans. Jane E. Lewin. Cambridge: Cambridge University Press, 1997.
Gibbons, Fiachra. "A. L. Kennedy Laments the Cheapening of Fiction." *The Guardian*. The Guardian, 13 Aug. 2001. Web. 26 Jan. 2004.
Gildon, Charles. *Robinson Crusoe Examin'd and Criticis'd*. 1719. Ed. Paul Dottin. London: Dent, 1923.
Girard, René. *Deceit, Desire, and the Novel: Self and Other in Literary Structure*. Trans. Yvonne Freccero. Baltimore: Johns Hopkins University Press, 1965.
Glass, Loren. *Authors Inc.: Literary Celebrity in the Modern United States, 1880–1980*. New York: New York University Press, 2004.
Goffman, Erving. *The Presentation of Self in Everyday Life*. 2nd ed. Garden City: Doubleday Anchor, 1959.
Goldenberg, Suzanne. "Two Scribes Go to War." *The Guardian*. The Guardian, 9 May 2006. Web. 8 May 2006.
Gordimer, Nadine. *Selected Stories*. London: Bloomsbury, 2000.
———. *Writing and Being*. Cambridge, MA: Harvard University Press, 1995.

Grant, Linda. "Spinning in the Family Plot." *The Guardian* 1 Mar. 1998: 3.

Gudmundsdottir, Gunnthorunn. *Borderlines: Autobiography and Fiction in Postmodern Life Writing*. New York: Rodopi, 2003.

Gurko, Leo. *Thomas Wolfe: Beyond the Romantic Ego*. New York: Crowell, 1975.

Gurstein, Rochelle. *The Repeal of Reticence: A History of America's Cultural and Legal Struggles over Free Speech, Obscenity, Sexual Liberation, and Modern Art*. New York: Hill & Wang, 1996.

Gust, Geoffrey W. *Constructing Chaucer: Author and Autofiction in the Critical Tradition*. New York: Palgrave, 2009.

H.D. *Bid Me to Live*. 1960. London: Virago, 1984.

Habermas, Jürgen. *The Structural Transformation of the Public Sphere: An Inquiry into a Category of Bourgeois Society*. Trans. Thomas Burger. Cambridge, MA: MIT Press, 1989.

Hall, Donald. "Knock, Knock." Rev. of *The Dolphin*, by Robert Lowell. *American Poetry Review* 2 (1973): 44.

Halpert, Sam. *Raymond Carver: An Oral Biography*. Iowa City: University of Iowa Press, 1995.

Hamilton, Ian. *Keepers of the Flame: Literary Estates and the Rise of Biography*. London: Hutchinson, 1992.

Harpham, Geoffrey Galt. "Ethics." Lentricchia and McLaughlin 387–405.

Haynes v. Alfred Knopf. No. 1222. 8 Fed. 3d. 7th circuit. 1993.

Heath, Joseph and Andrew Potter. *The Rebel Sell: Why the Culture Can't Be Jammed*. 2004. Toronto: HarperPerennial, 2005.

Helmholz, R. H., ed. *Select Cases on Defamation to 1600*. London: Seldon Society, 1985.

Henry, O. *Waifs and Strays*. 1917. New York: Doubleday, 1925.

Higgins, Rita Ann. "No Rhyme or Reason." *Sunday Times*. Sunday Times, 3 June 2001. Web. 14 Jan. 2004.

Hite, Molly. *The Other Side of the Story: Structures and Strategies of Contemporary Feminist Narrative*. Ithaca: Cornell University Press, 1989.

Honneth, Axel. "Between Justice and Affection: The Family as Field of Moral Disputes." *Privacies: Philosophical Evaluations*. Ed. Beate Rössler. Stanford: Stanford University Press, 2004. 142–62.

Hutcheon, Linda. *Narcissistic Narrative: The Metafictional Paradox*. 1980. New York: Methuen, 1984.

———. *A Poetics of Postmodernism*. New York: Routledge, 1988.

Huxley, Aldous. *Those Barren Leaves*. London: Chatto & Windus, 1925.

Jacobus, Mary. Rev. of *The Madwoman in the Attic*, by Sandra M. Gilbert and Susan Gubar, and *Shakespeare's Sisters*, ed. Gilbert and Gubar. *Signs: Journal of Women in Culture and Society* 6.3 (1981): 517–23.

Jaffe, Aaron. *Modernism and the Culture of Celebrity*. Cambridge: Cambridge University Press, 2005.

James, Henry. *Collected Stories*. 5 vols. New York: Everyman, 1999.

———. *Literary Criticism*. Ed. Leon Edel. Vol. 1. New York: Library of America, 1984.

Jarrell, Randall. *Pictures from an Institution: A Comedy.* 1952. Chicago: University of Chicago Press, 1986.
Johnson, Barbara. "Using People: Kant with Winnicott." Garber, Hanssen, and Walkowitz 47–63.
Johnson, Samuel. *Lives of the English Poets.* Ed. George Bickbeck Hill. Vol. 3. New York: Octagon, 1967.
———. *The Yale Edition of the Works of Samuel Johnson.* Ed. W. J. Bate and Albrecht B. Strauss. Vol. 3. New Haven: Yale University Press, 1969.
Johnston, Lucy. "Hanif and the Spurned Women." *The Observer* 10 May 1998: 8.
Jones, Ann. "Looking Back on Falling in Love." Interview with Elizabeth Smart. *East Anglian Daily Times* 21 July 1977: 5.
Jones, Elizabeth H. "Serge Doubrovsky: Life, Writing, Legacy." *L'Esprit Créateur* 49.3 (2009): 1–7.
Jones, Thomas. "Short Cuts." *London Review of Books* 5 Feb. 2004: 18.
Jong, Erica. *The Devil at Large: Erica Jong on Henry Miller.* New York: Turtle Bay, 1993.
———. *Fear of Flying.* 1973. New York: Signet, 2003.
———. "My Grandmother on My Shoulder." *Writers on Writing.* Ed. Robert Pack and Jay Parini. Hanover: University Press of New England, 1991. 105–11.
Jourde, Pierre. *Pays Perdu.* Paris: Balland, 2003.
Joyce, James. *Ulysses.* 1922. Ed. Jeri Johnson. Oxford: Oxford University Press, 1998.
Kafka, Franz. "To Felice Bauer." 14–15 Jan. 1913. *Letters to Felice.* Trans. James Stern and Elizabeth Duckworth. Ed. Erich Heller and Jürgen Born. Harmondsworth, UK: Penguin, 1978. 271–72.
Kelly, Kathleen Coyne. *A. S. Byatt.* New York: Twayne, 1996.
Kingston, Maxine Hong. *The Woman Warrior.* 1977. London: Picador, 1981.
Kipnis, Laura. "Adultery." Berlant, *Intimacy* 9–47.
———. *Against Love: A Polemic.* New York: Vintage, 2003.
Koestenbaum, Wayne. *Double Talk: The Erotics of Male Literary Collaboration.* New York: Routledge, 1989.
Kropf, C. R. "Libel and Satire in the Eighteenth Century." *Eighteenth-Century Studies* 8.2 (1974–75): 153–68.
Kureishi, Hanif. *The Buddha of Suburbia.* 1990. London: Penguin, 1991.
———. *Intimacy.* London: Faber, 1998.
———. "Loose Tongues and Liberty." *The Guardian.* The Guardian, 7 June 2003. Web. 26 June 2006.
———. *Midnight All Day.* London: Faber, 1999.
———. *Sammy and Rosie Get Laid: The Script and the Diary.* London: Faber, 1988.
———. "Something Given: Reflections on Writing." *Hanifkureishi.com.* Web. 29 May 2006.
———. "That Was Then." *Midnight All Day.* London: Faber, 1999. 64–91.
Lacan, Jacques. *The Four Fundamental Concepts of Psychoanalysis. The Seminar of Jacques Lacan, Book XI.* Trans. Alan Sheridan. Ed. Jacques-Alain Miller. New York: Norton, 1998.

Laird, Holly A. *Women Coauthors*. Champaign: University of Illinois Press, 2000.
Lamarque, Peter and Stein Haugom Olsen. *Truth, Fiction, and Literature: A Philosophical Perspective*. Oxford: Clarendon, 1994.
Lamb, Caroline. *Glenarvon*. London: Colburn, 1816.
Lamott, Anne. *Bird by Bird: Some Instructions on Writing and Life*. 1994. New York: Anchor, 1995.
Larsson, Stieg. *The Girl with the Dragon Tattoo*. Trans. Reg Keeland. New York: Knopf, 2009.
Lasch, Christopher. *The Culture of Narcissism: American Life in an Age of Diminishing Expectations*. New York: Norton, 1978.
Latham, Sean. *The Art of Scandal: Modernism, Libel Law, and the Roman à Clef*. Oxford: Oxford University Press, 2009.
Layton, Aviva. "After 40 Years Away, Smart's Not Ready for Canada." *Montreal Gazette* 21 April 1984: Books 1–2.
LeBel, Paul A. "The Infliction of Harm through the Publication of Fiction: Fashioning a Theory of Liability." *Brooklyn Law Review* 51.1 (1986): 281–354.
Lejeune, Philippe. *On Autobiography*. Trans. Katherine Leary. Ed. Paul John Eakin. Minneapolis: University of Minnesota Press, 1989.
Lemon, Lee T. *Portraits of the Artist in Contemporary Fiction*. Lincoln: University of Nebraska Press, 1985.
Lentricchia, Frank and Thomas McLaughlin, eds. *Critical Terms for Literary Study*. 2nd ed. Chicago: University of Chicago Press, 1995.
Lessing, Doris. *The Golden Notebook*. 1962. London: Grafton, 1989.
Levinas, Emmanuel. *Otherwise Than Being or Beyond Essence*. Trans. Alphonso Lingis. Pittsburgh: Duquesne University Press, 2004.
———. *Totality and Infinity: An Essay on Exteriority*. Trans. Alphonso Lingis. Pittsburgh: Duquesne University Press, 1969.
Lewis, Wyndham. *The Apes of God*. London: Arthur, 1930.
Lorde, Audre. *Zami: A New Spelling of My Name*. Berkeley: Crossing, 1982.
Lowell, Robert. *Collected Poems*. Ed. Frank Bidart and David Gewanter. New York: Farrar, 2003.
MacCabe, Colin. "Interview: Hanif Kureishi on London." *Critical Quarterly* 41.3 (1999): 37–56.
Mailer, Norman. *Advertisements for Myself*. London: Deutsch, 1959.
Malcolm, Janet. *The Silent Woman: Sylvia Plath and Ted Hughes*. 1993. London: Picador, 1994.
Manley, Delarivier. *The Adventures of Rivella*. London, 1714. Chadwyck-Healey. Web. 10 Jan. 2010.
———. *The New Atalantis*. 1709. Ed. Ros Ballaster. New York: New York University Press, 1992.
Marías, Javier. *All Souls*. Trans. Margaret Jull Costa. New York: New Directions, 2000.
———. *Dark Back of Time*. Trans. Esther Allen. New York: New Directions, 2001.
Massie, Allan. "No Heroic Confrontation." *The Scotsman* 28 Aug. 1980. Box 1, folder 5. Alice Van Wart Collection. National Library of Canada, Ottawa.
Maugham, W. Somerset. *Cakes and Ale*. London: Heinemann, 1930.

———. *The Summing Up*. 1938. London: Penguin, 1988.
McCormick, Peter J. *Fictions, Philosophies, and the Problems of Poetics*. Ithaca: Cornell University Press, 1988.
McEwan, Ian. *Atonement*. 2001. Toronto: Vintage, 2002.
McGill, Robert. "Biographical Desire and the Archives of Living Authors." *a/b: Auto/Biography* 24.1 (2009): 129–45.
———. *The Mysteries*. Toronto: McClelland & Stewart, 2004.
McGurl, Mark. *The Program Era: Postwar Fiction and the Rise of Creative Writing*. Cambridge, MA: Harvard University Press, 2009.
McKeon, Michael. *The Origins of the English Novel, 1600–1740*. 1987. Baltimore: Johns Hopkins University Press, 1988.
McNamara, Lawrence. *Reputation and Defamation*. Oxford: Oxford University Press, 2007.
McRobbie, Angela and Sarah L. Thornton. "Rethinking 'Moral Panic' for Multi-Mediated Social Worlds." *British Journal of Sociology* 46.4 (1995): 559–74.
Meyers, Jeffrey. *Manic Power: Robert Lowell and His Circle*. London: Macmillan, 1987.
Middlebrook, Diane Wood. "What Was Confessional Poetry?" *The Columbia History of American Poetry*. Ed. Jay Parini and Brett C. Miller. New York: Columbia University Press, 1993. 632–49.
Miller, Henry. *The Books in My Life*. Norfolk, CT: New Directions, n.d.
———. *Tropic of Cancer*. 1934. New York: Grove Weidenfeld, 1980.
Millet, Catherine. *The Sexual Life of Catherine M*. Trans. Adriana Hunter. London: Serpent's Tail, 2002.
Mills, Claudia. "Appropriating Others' Stories: Some Questions about the Ethics of Writing Fiction." *Journal of Social Philosophy* 31.2 (2000): 195–206.
———. "Friendship, Fiction, and Memoir: Trust and Betrayal in Writing from One's Own Life." *The Ethics of Life Writing*. Ed. Paul John Eakin. Ithaca: Cornell University Press, 2004. 101–20.
Mistry, Rohinton. *Tales from Firozsha Baag*. 1987. Toronto: McClelland & Stewart, 1997.
Moran, Joe. *Star Authors: Literary Celebrity in America*. Sterling, VA: Pluto, 2000.
Morrison, Jago and Susan Watkins. "Introduction: The Twentieth-Century Novel in the Public Sphere." *Scandalous Fictions: The Twentieth-Century Novel in the Public Sphere*. Ed. Morrison and Watkins. Houndmills, UK: Palgrave, 2006. 1–26.
Munro, Alice. "The Colonel's Hash Resettled." *The Narrative Voice*. Ed. John Metcalf. Toronto: McGraw-Hill Ryerson, 1972. 181–83.
———. *Friend of My Youth*. 1990. Toronto: Penguin, 1991.
———. "Home." *74: New Canadian Stories*. Ed. David Helwig and Joan Harcourt. Ottawa: Oberon, 1974. 133–53.
———. Letter. *Books in Canada* Aug.–Sept. 1987: 38–39.
———. *Lives of Girls and Women*. 1971. London: Penguin, 1982.
———. *Something I've Been Meaning to Tell You*. 1974. Scarborough, ON: Signet, 1975.
———. "What Is Real?" *Making It New: Contemporary Canadian Stories*. Ed. John Metcalf. Toronto: Methuen, 1982. 223–26.

———. *Who Do You Think You Are?* 1978. Toronto: Penguin, 1995.
Munro, Sheila. *Lives of Mothers & Daughters: Growing up with Alice Munro*. Toronto: McClelland & Stewart, 2001.
Nelson, Deborah. *Pursuing Privacy in Cold War America*. New York: Columbia University Press, 2002.
Nelson, William. *Fact or Fiction: The Dilemma of the Renaissance Storyteller*. Cambridge, MA: Harvard University Press, 1973.
Nettels, Elsa. "Henry James and the Art of Biography." *South Atlantic Bulletin* 43 (1978): 107–24.
Paull, H. M. *Literary Ethics: A Study in the Growth of the Literary Conscience*. London: Butterworth, 1928.
Peperzak, Adriaan. *To the Other: An Introduction to the Philosophy of Emmanuel Levinas*. West Lafayette, IN: Purdue University Press, 1993.
Perec, Georges. *W, or The Memory of Childhood*. Trans. David Bellos. London: Harvill, 1996.
Perry, Ruth. Introduction. *Mothering the Mind: Twelve Studies of Writers and Their Silent Partners*. Ed. Perry and Martine Watson Brownley. New York: Holmes & Meier, 1984. 3–24.
Petruso, Thomas F. *Life Made Real: Characterization in the Novel Since Proust and Joyce*. Ann Arbor: University of Michigan Press, 1991.
Phillips, Adam. *Going Sane: Maps of Happiness*. New York: Fourth Estate, 2005.
———. *Monogamy*. London: Faber, 1996.
———. *On Flirtation*. London: Faber, 1994.
———. *Promises, Promises: Essays on Literature and Psychoanalysis*. London: Faber, 2000.
Plath, Sylvia. *The Bell Jar*. 1963. London: Faber, 1986.
Proust, Marcel. *In Search of Lost Time*. Trans. Lydia Davis et al. Ed. Christopher Prendergast. 6 vols. London: Penguin, 2002–3.
Raab, Scott. "He Should Win a Prize for Evening It Up with Claire Bloom." Rev. of *I Married a Communist*, by Philip Roth. *Esquire* Oct. 1998: 46.
Ramesh, Randeep. "Interview: Hanif Kureishi." *The Independent* 3 May 1998: 2.
Redekop, Magdalene. *Mothers and Other Clowns: The Stories of Alice Munro*. London: Routledge, 1992.
Rhiel, Mary and David Suchoff, eds. *The Seductions of Biography*. New York: Routledge, 1996.
Rhys, Jean. *After Leaving Mr. Mackenzie*. 1930. New York: Vintage, 1974.
Rich, Adrienne. "On *History, For Lizzie and Harriet*, and *The Dolphin*." Axelrod 185–87.
Richardson, Samuel. *Clarissa*. 1747. Vol. 1. Oxford: Blackwell, 1930.
———. "To Anne Donellan." 22 Feb. 1752. *Selected Letters of Samuel Richardson*. Ed. John Carroll. Oxford: Clarendon, 1964. 196–97.
Roberts, Carol. *Timothy Findley: Stories from a Life*. Toronto: ECW, 1994.
Roiphe, Anne. "This Butcher, Imagination: Beware of Your Life When a Writer's at Work." *New York Times Book Review* 14 Feb. 1988: 3, 30.

Rollyson, Carl. *A Higher Form of Cannibalism? Adventures in the Art and Politics of Biography.* Chicago: Dee, 2005.

Rorty, Richard. *Contingency, Irony, and Solidarity.* 1989. Cambridge: Cambridge University Press, 2005.

Rosenberg, Alexander. "Privacy as a Matter of Taste and Right." *The Right to Privacy.* Ed. Ellen Frankel Paul et al. New York: Cambridge University Press, 2000. 68–90.

Rosenthal, M. L. *The New Poets: American and British Poetry since World War II.* New York: Oxford University Press, 1967.

———. "Poetry as Confession." Axelrod 64–68.

Roth, Philip. *The Anatomy Lesson.* 1983. New York: Vintage, 1996.

———. *The Counterlife.* 1986. New York: Vintage, 1996.

———. *Deception.* 1990. London: Vintage, 1997.

———. *Exit Ghost.* New York: Houghton Mifflin, 2007.

———. *The Facts: A Novelist's Autobiography.* 1988. New York: Penguin, 1989.

———. *The Ghost Writer.* 1979. New York: Vintage, 1995.

———. *I Married a Communist.* New York: Houghton Mifflin, 1998.

———. *My Life as a Man.* 1974. New York: Vintage, 1993.

———. National Book Critics Circle Award Acceptance Speech. *New York Times Book Review* 14 Feb. 1988: 3.

———. *Operation Shylock: A Confession.* 1993. New York: Vintage, 1994.

———. *Portnoy's Complaint.* 1969. New York: Bantam, 1972.

———. *Zuckerman Unbound.* 1981. New York: Vintage, 1995.

Rousseau, Jean-Jacques. *The Collected Writings of Rousseau.* Trans. Philip Stewart and Jean Vaché. Ed. Roger D. Masters and Christopher Kelly. Vol. 6. Hanover: University Press of New England, 1997.

———. *Confessions.* Trans. Angela Scholar. Ed. Patrick Coleman. New York: Oxford University Press, 2000.

Said, Edward W. *Orientalism: Western Conceptions of the Orient.* 1978. London: Penguin, 1995.

Salmon, Richard. *Henry James and the Culture of Publicity.* Cambridge: Cambridge University Press, 1997.

Sarsby, Jacqueline. *Romantic Love and Society.* Harmondsworth, UK: Penguin, 1983.

Sartre, Jean-Paul. *Baudelaire.* Trans. Martin Turnell. New York: New Directions, 1967.

———. *Being and Nothingness: A Phenomenological Essay on Ontology.* Trans. Hazel E. Barnes. New York: Washington Square, 1992.

Saunders, Max. *Self Impression: Life-Writing, Autobiografiction, and the Forms of Modern Literature.* Oxford: Oxford University Press, 2010.

Schickel, Richard. *Intimate Strangers: The Culture of Celebrity.* 1985. New York: Fromm, 1986.

Schoeman, Ferdinand David, ed. *Philosophical Dimensions of Privacy: An Anthology.* New York: Cambridge University Press, 1984.

———. *Privacy and Social Freedom.* Cambridge: Cambridge University Press, 1992.

Shechner, Mark. *Up Society's Ass, Copper: Rereading Philip Roth.* Madison: University of Wisconsin Press, 2003.

———. "Zuckerman's Travels." *American Literary History* 1.1 (1989): 219–30.
Shorter, Edward. *The Making of the Modern Family.* New York: Basic, 1975.
Shostak, Debra. *Philip Roth—Countertexts, Counterlives.* Columbia: University of South Carolina Press, 2004.
Shriver, Lionel. "I Sold My Family for a Novel." *The Guardian.* The Guardian, 17 Oct. 2009. Web. 17 Oct. 2009.
Shuger, Debora. "Life-Writing in Seventeenth-Century England." *Representations of the Self from the Renaissance to Romanticism.* Ed. Patrick Coleman, Jayne Lewis, and Jill Kowalik. Cambridge: Cambridge University Press, 2000. 63–78.
Sidney, Philip. *Astrophil and Stella.* 1591. Ed. Max Putzel. Garden City, NY: Anchor, 1967.
Smart, Elizabeth. *By Grand Central Station I Sat Down and Wept.* 1945. London: Flamingo, 1992.
———. "Fact and Emotional Truth." Interview with Bruce Meyer and Brian O'Riordan. *In Their Words: Interviews with Fourteen Canadian Writers.* Ed. Meyer and O'Riordan. Toronto: Anansi, 1984. 184–96.
———. *Necessary Secrets: The Journals of Elizabeth Smart.* Ed. Alice Van Wart. Toronto: Deneau, 1986.
Spenser, Edmund. *The Faerie Queene.* 1590–96. Ed. Thomas P. Roche, Jr. New York: Penguin, 1987.
Steedman, Carolyn. *Dust: The Archive and Cultural History.* New Brunswick: Rutgers University Press, 2002.
Sterne, Laurence. *The Life and Opinions of Tristram Shandy, Gentleman.* 1759–67. Ed. Ian Campbell Ross. Oxford: Oxford University Press, 1992.
Stillinger, Jack. *Multiple Authorship and the Myth of Solitary Genius.* New York: Oxford University Press, 1991.
Stone, Lawrence. *The Family, Sex, and Marriage in England 1500–1800.* New York: Harper & Row, 1977.
Stonehill, Brian. *The Self-Conscious Novel: Artifice in Fiction from Joyce to Pynchon.* Philadelphia: University of Pennsylvania Press, 1988.
Stott, Catherine. "Cosmo Reads the New Books." *Cosmopolitan (UK)* June 1977: 6.
Sullivan, Rosemary. *By Heart: Elizabeth Smart, a Life.* Toronto: Viking, 1991.
Sutton-Smith, Brian. *The Ambiguity of Play.* Cambridge, MA: Harvard University Press, 1997.
Taylor, Charles. *Human Agency and Language.* New York: Cambridge University Press, 1985.
Thacker, Robert. *Alice Munro: Writing Her Lives.* Toronto: McClelland & Stewart, 2005.
Through a Glass Darkly. Dir. Ingmar Bergman. Janus, 1961.
Todd, Richard. *A. S. Byatt.* Plymouth, UK: Northcote, 1997.
Tooby, John and Leda Cosmides. "Does Beauty Build Adapted Minds? Towards an Evolutionary Theory of Aesthetics, Fiction and the Arts." *SubStance* 94–95 (2001): 6–27.
Wachtel, Eleanor. Letter to Elizabeth Smart. 25 June 1980. Box 37. Elizabeth Smart Fonds. National Library of Canada, Ottawa.

———. "Stations of the Womb." *Books in Canada* Oct. 1978: 8–9.
Wakoski, Diane. "Reply to Adrienne Rich." Axelrod 187–88.
Waller, Philip. *Writers, Readers, and Reputations: Literary Life in Britain 1870–1918.* Oxford: Oxford University Press, 2006.
Walton, Kendall L. *Mimesis as Make-Believe: On the Foundations of the Representational Arts.* Cambridge, MA: Harvard University Press, 1990.
Warren, Samuel D. and Louis D. Brandeis. "The Right to Privacy." Schoeman, *Philosophical* 75–103.
Wasserstrom, Richard. "Privacy: Some Arguments and Assumptions." Schoeman, *Philosophical* 317–32.
Waugh, Patricia. *Metafiction: The Theory and Practice of Self-Conscious Fiction.* 1984. New York: Routledge, 2003.
West, Rebecca. *Sunflower.* London: Virago, 1986.
Westin, Alan. "The Origins of Modern Claims to Privacy." Schoeman, *Philosophical* 56–74.
Wilde, Oscar. *The Picture of Dorian Gray.* 1891. Ed. Robert Mighall. London: Penguin, 2003.
Williamson, Alan. *Introspection and Contemporary Poetry.* Cambridge, MA: Harvard University Press, 1984.
———. *Pity the Monsters: The Political Vision of Robert Lowell.* New Haven: Yale University Press, 1974.
Wimsatt, W. K. and Monroe C. Beardsley. *The Verbal Icon: Studies in the Meaning of Poetry.* Lexington: University of Kentucky Press, 1954.
Wolfe, Thomas. *You Can't Go Home Again.* 1940. New York: Perennial, 1989.
Wolff, Tobias. *Old School.* New York: Vintage, 2003.
Wood, James. "Give All." Rev. of *Bellow: A Biography*, by James Atlas. *The New Republic.* The New Republic, 13 Nov. 2000. Web. 21 Feb. 2005.
Woodmansee, Martha. *The Author, Art, and the Market: Rereading the History of Aesthetics.* New York: Columbia University Press, 1994.
Woolf, Virginia. *The Death of the Moth and Other Essays.* 1942. New York: Harcourt, 1974.
———. *A Room of One's Own.* 1929. London: Grafton, 1987.
Wordsworth, William. *The Prose Works of William Wordsworth.* Ed. W. J. B. Owen and Jane Worthington Smyser. Vol. 3. Oxford: Clarendon, 1974.
Writers at Work: The Paris Review Interviews. London: Secker & Warburg, 1958.
Wroth, Lady Mary. *The Countess of Mountgomeries Urania.* 2 vols. London: Mariott & Gismand, 1621.
Žižek, Slavoj. *Welcome to the Desert of the Real! Five Essays on September 11 and Related Dates.* London: Verso, 2002.

Index

Abbott, H. Porter, 8n6
Abrams, M. H., 22
Adachi, Ken, 59–60
Adams, Timothy Dow: *Telling Lies in Modern American Autobiography*, 5n2
adultery, 84, 86; attractions of, 110; autobiographical fiction as textual equivalent of, 109–10, 114; ethical, 119; language of, 4; narrativization as foundational to, 110
The Adventures of Rivella (Manley), 25–26
Advertisements for Myself (Mailer), 40–41
Aelian, 22
aestheticism, 37, 58, 102, 113, 144
aesthetics: and ethics, 118; of fiction, 48
aesthetic transgression, 110
After Leaving Mr. Mackenzie (Rhys), 37
agency: as complicating ethics, 152; lost, 89; regained by intimates, 143; removal of from authors, 52

Albert, Laura. *See* LeRoy, J. T
alcoholism, 42
Ali, Monica: *Brick Lane*, 9
alienation: of intimates, 96; mutual, 153; of private acts, 117
Allen, Woody: *Deconstructing Harry*, 145
All Souls (Marías), 10, 88–89
American Imago, 131n2
Amos, William: *The Originals*, 77
The Anatomy Lesson (Roth), 72, 99
Anderson-Dargatz, Gail: *A Recipe for Bees*, 140
anonymity, maintenance of, 134
anonymously published texts, 52, 134
antisocial impulses, 111
The Apes of God (Lewis), 37
apocryphal tales, medieval, 26
appropriation, 43, 131n3; of intimates' voices, 17; metafiction and, 85; of narrative control, 88; vs. dialogism, 103
Aristophanes, 35; *The Clouds*, 22

Aristotle, 22; *Poetics*, 72n3
artistic immortality, 133
artistic success, interpersonal harmony and, 119
artistic transgression, celebration of, 113
artists: as isolated rebels, 101; vs. subjects, 10
"The Aspern Papers" (James), 33
Astrophil and Stella (Sidney), 23
Atonement (McEwen), 20
Attridge, Derek, 148
Atwood, Margaret: "The Tent," 117
audience. *See* reader
authenticity vs. performance, 75
author(s): absent, intimacy with, 60–66; adoption of public personae, 81; association of with own fiction, 29; and authentic identity, 58; and biographical desire, 70; boundary between art and life of, 35; celebration of as dissenters and taboo-breakers, 80; celebrity of, 35; challenges for both commercial and critical success, 56; character relations as unclear to, 57; children of, 135; collaboration of with intimates, 119–20, 137–45, 152; and commentary as way of continuing to produce texts, 52; contesting authority of, 8; as creators of and servants to biographical desire, 50; death of (Barthes), 61; denials of autobiographical content by, 37, 52, 100, 115; desire to be sought out by readers, 47, 65; dismissal of aims and background of, 36; embodied, 62, 72; embodied vs. figure of, 61–62; enduring biographical speculation vs. providing confessions, 52–53; ethical difficulties for, 100; explanations to intimates, 141–42; fear of writing autobiography, 58; fiction creating personal conflicts in lives of, 101; as figuration, 61; flirting with readers, 4, 16, 48, 76, 81, 137, 141, 143; identified as "other," 80; impetus to focus on as hermeneutic and commercial, 51; *in propria persona*, 71, 73; installation of at center of literary discourse, 28; instrumentalization of others, 125; interiority of, 38; intimacy with, 43, 65, 101, 132, 143; intimates of, 46, 58, 76–77, 81, 82, 83, 85, 87–89, 94, 96–99, 100, 103, 114–15, 117–49, 150–53; motives of, 47, 84, 87, 138, 146, 152; name of as independent from person, 61; as performers and personalities, 51; and permission from intimates, 135–36, 138; as *poètes maudits*, 151; as Promethean class predisposed to betrayal, 112; protection of intimates by, 119–20, 136; psychology revealed by work, 30, 84; public vs. private identities of, 81; as rebel, 112–16, 119–20, 137–45; and reification of a subject, 51; as reinforcing social conventions while defying them, 114; relationally constituted identity of, 92; removal of agency from, 52; responsibility of to groups and nations, 9; right of to decide on autobiographical nature of work, 8; right of to use lives of others in work, 4; as scapegoats, 50, 79, 151; as sole creators of literature, 51; surreptitious publication by, 136; therapeutic distance from themselves and intimates, 148; unique experiences of, 81; usurpation of intimacy of personal relations of, 81; yoking of to texts, 51
authorial body: as plausible germinal site, 68; as site of desire, 68
authorial commentary, 52, 105; distrust of, 67; in mass media, 4
authorial confession, 30, 56, 105
authorial denials and disavowals, 37, 52, 100, 115
authorial detachment, 5, 95–99
authorial ethics, 102; rebellious, 112
authorial impositions, 95–99

authorial *mea culpa*, 103
authorial mind, writing as betrayal of, 3
authorial name, 61
authorial rebellion, 34; ethicality of, 112; public acts of, 144
authorial uncertainty, 57–58
author–reader relationship, 4, 15–16, 48–49; flirtatiousness in, 4, 16, 48, 76, 81, 137, 141, 143; phantasmatic nature of, 4
authorship: cultural shift in views of, 101; current understandings of, 21; as individualist practice, 120, 125; and intimacy, 144; rebel, 113; speculation about, 52; star system of, 31
autobiographical disclosure, anticipation of, 63–64
autobiographical fiction: as adultery, 109–10, 114; as authors' attempts to commune with intimates, 138; authors' desire to write, 85; authors of haunting their work, 87; betrayals of, 4, 85, 125, 153; as challenging assumptions and expectations of intimacy, 85, 109; commercial aspects of, 4; condemnation of, 29; definition of, 5–11; as encouraging diversity of interpretive habits, 139; as encouraging readers to embrace metaphor, 151; erotics of, 4, 84; as ethical project, 110; ethics of, 4, 13–14, 21, 34, 44, 99, 100, 110, 120, 146–48, 151; as expressing or disrupting desire, 4; as hermeneutic orientation toward a text, 8; as hyperbolizing anxieties about intimate relationships, 94; injurious, 94; and intersubjectivity of early family life, 89–90; as intervention and symptom, 151; and intimates, 83–85 (*see also* intimates); and intrinsic decline of culture, 50; and love triangle between authors, intimate and readers, 4, 152; ludic function of, 50, 66–70, 74, 76, 83, 84, 119, 143, 151; as making interventions through publication, 110; as metaphorical rape, 4, 84; and metaphors of vampirism and cannibalism, 87; misunderstanding as *métier* of, 138; need for complex account of production and reception of, 3; and occupation of heterotopic social space, 50; offense given by, 85–86, 121–22, 128; reader-oriented ethical functions of, 148; reasons for writing, 95; as recent coinage, 20; reductions of narratives to factual, 151; rejection of reticence and propriety of intimacy norms, 151; relationship of with readers, 76; as revelatory and coy, 79; role of in confessional culture, 151; as scandalous, 45–46, 78–79; and social constitution of identity, 91; as therapeutic, 70; as traducing authors' intimates, 81, 151; and trespass, 152; as unethical, 11, 118. *See also* fiction
autobiographical novel, definition of, 7
autobiographical pact, 6, 61, 63
autobiographical "phallacy," 58
autobiography, 5, 21; border between fiction and, 16, 29, 63, 71, 74; ethics of, 12; fiction as truer than, 39; fiction as veiled, 76; in fiction vs. nonfiction, 50; and invention, 45; and presentation of single subjectivity, 71; tell-all, 45; vs. autobiographical narrative, 6; women and, 58; writers' fear of writing, 58
autofiction, 6n5, 45–46; as paratextual phenomenon, 45–46
autonomy, intimacy and, 91

Bachelard, Gaston, 117
Bakhtin, Mikhail, 102
Barbour, John D.: *The Conscience of the Autobiographer*, 12n10
Barclay, John: *Euphormionis Lusinini Satyricon*, 24
Bardwell, Leland, 54
Barker, George, 53–55, 57, 59, 62, 66, 97; *The Dead Seagull*, 57

Barthes, Roland, 4, 61, 69; *Camera Lucida*, 86; *A Lover's Discourse*, 47
Beardsley, Monroe C., 36
Beat poets, 40
The Beautiful and Damned (Fitzgerald), 38
beds, as quintessential site of dreaming, 117
The Bell Jar (Plath), 7
Bellow, Saul, 129
Belsey, Catherine, 68–69
Benedetti, Carla, 51, 80
Benn, Stanley, 107–8
Bennett, Arnold: *How to Become an Author*, 34
Bennett, Catherine, 131
Bergman, Ingmar, 100
Berlant, Lauren, 109
Berman, Jeffrey, 131n2
Bernard, André: *Madame Bovary, C'est Moi!*, 77
betrayal: of adult individuation, 92; of autobiographical fiction, 4, 85, 125, 153; conflict and, 28; dramatization of fictional, 106–7; and family loyalty, 85; of fiction, 83–116; fountainhead of imagination in, 118; intimacy and, 34, 48, 100, 108–9, 136–37; meaning of, 3; media-disseminated spectacle of, 38; personal, 43; pleasure of, 114; of poetry, 30; politics of, 86; potential, 84; predisposition to, 112; reneging as, 108–9; as socially remediable, 113; vs. tribute, 147; of the world, 152; writing as, 3, 128
Bid Me to Live (H.D.), 39
bilateral contract, between author and reader, 8n6
Billen, Andrew, 106
Bindrim, Paul, 134n5
Bindrim v. Mitchell (1979), 134n5
biographical criticism, ethical complications of, 76
biographical curiosity, 24, 29, 33, 35–36, 38, 41

biographical desire, 4, 11, 18, 47–82, 83, 105, 114, 136, 151, 153; of authors, 70; in confessional age, 49; merits of, 80; metafiction and, 101, 104; as middlebrow taste for titillation, gossip, and scandal, 50; as reductive, 50, 68; as transgressive, 81; as thriving among *literati*, 66
biographical detection, 14, 55, 63, 76, 140; as crucial plot of fiction, 24
biographical flirtatiousness, 55–56
biographical heresy, 36, 52, 142
biographical hermeneutics, 36–37, 100; reductiveness of, 102
biographical reading: and denial of finality of text's reading, 69; as educative, 67; as expansion of reading experience, 69; interpersonal character of, 68; metafiction and, 104; as play, 66–70; and sexualization, 68; as transgressive, 67
biographical reductivism, 76
biography, 5, 21, 26, 51; ethics of, 12, 76
biomythography, 6n5
A Bird in the House (Laurence), 95
Birrell, Augustine, 34
The Black Book (Durrell), 39
Bleak House (Dickens), 32, 118, 136
blogs, 45
Bloom, Claire, 119, 129–33; *Leaving a Doll's House*, 18, 103, 130–31
Bok, Sissela, 67, 111
Boling, Patricia, 110–11
A Bonus (Smart), 54
book bans, 111
Boorstin, Daniel, 41n16
Booster magazine, 53
Booth, Wayne: *The Company We Keep*, 13–14, 48
borders, desire to cross vs. desire to patrol, 75
Bourdieu, Pierre, 152, 153
Brandeis, Louis D., 32–33, 36
Brennan, Timothy, 9–10
Brick Lane (Ali), 9

Bruner, Jerome, 72n3
The Buddha of Suburbia (Kureishi), 84, 106
Buell, Lawrence, 48
Burk Carver, Maryann, 130, 143
Burns, Robert, 30, 31
Busby, Brian, 120n2; Character Parts, 77
Butler, Judith, 65–66, 75, 114
Byatt, A. S., 86; The Game, 17, 84–85, 89–94, 95–99, 100, 101–5, 119, 137, 140, 147, 150; and discussion of autobiographical aspects of fiction, 105; relationship of with Drabble, 92, 104
By Grand Central Station I Sat Down and Wept (Smart), 16, 48–49, 53–60, 62–66, 75, 86, 97; as alternative to verificationist hermeneutics, 69; as anticipatory allegory of its own reception, 62; cover of 1977 edition, 55–56; as "cult" classic, 53; as fiction vs. as autobiography, 54; language in, 64–66; and love story between Smart and readers, 49; media commentary on, 49, 53–54; as metonym for Smart's vanished youth, 59–60; narrative of as catalyst for reader–author interactions, 49; narrator's name in, 54, 63; paratexts and, 49, 54–55, 57, 60; portrait of poet lover in, 64; public's wish for book to be confessional, 48; and reader expectations, 62–64; reception history of, 59–60, 62; reviews of, 54–55; screenplay of, 59; Smart's embracing and challenging biographical readings of, 54, 58–59; stage adaptation of, 59
Byron, Alfred Lord, 31

Cakes and Ale (Maugham), 37
Camera Lucida (Barthes), 86
cannibalism, metaphor of, 87
The Canterbury Tales (Chaucer), 22
capitalism, 11, 24
Carey, Peter, 121; Theft, 121
Carver, Maryann Burk. See Burk Carver, Maryann

Carver, Raymond, 100, 143, 147; "Errand," 7–8; "Intimacy," 88, 97–98, 150–51
casuistry, 136
CCTV, 45
celebrity: of authors, 31, 35; and confession, 78; creation of, 41n17, 80
cell-phone cameras, 45
censorship, 17, 107, 111, 149
Chase, Karen, 32
Chaucer, Geoffrey, 22–23; The Canterbury Tales, 22
Chekhov, Anton, 7, 151
Christie, Agatha, 6
Clarissa (Richardson), 27–28
The Clouds (Aristophanes), 22
Coetzee, J. M.: Elizabeth Costello, 7; Youth, 138
Cohen, William A., 32, 45
Cohn, Dorrit, 87n2
Cold War anxieties, 41
collaboration: between authors and intimates, 81, 108, 117–49, 152; in production of texts, 51
Commedia (Dante), 22
commentary: authorial, 4, 67, 105, 137; authors' intimates and, 121; collaboration and, 144; confessional, 44; distrust of, 67; journalistic, 151; literature as catalyst for production of, 51; literary, 29; in media, 4, 49; nonfictional, 102, 106; paratextual, 46, 49, 51, 74, 132; as prequels and sequels, 69; and promotion, 121; reticence in, 114, 141; Smart and, 53–54, 65; third-party, 44; as way for authors to continue producing texts, 52
commercialism, stereotype of U.S., 40–41
competitiveness, 143
confession: authorial, 3, 12n11, 21, 42, 105; celebrity and, 78; facilitation and dissemination of, 41; fiction as disguised, 39, 133; financial and cultural rewards of, 45; paratextual, 46, 106; preoccupation with, 11, 14–15, 42, 57, 121; proscribing vs. facilitating,

36–37; of psychoanalysis, 39; referential, 69; societal ambivalence around, 151; valuing acts of, 3; writing as, 145
confessional age, 35–41, 105, 143; biographical desire in, 49; contradictions of, 79–80
confessional candor, demands for, 79
confessional culture, 78, 101; intimacy and, 78; metafiction as symptom of, 85; moralizing of, 76–82; refusal of direct participation in, 134; role of autobiographical fiction in, 151; Smart and, 50–60
confessional poetry, 55, 100; scandal of, 41–46
Confessions (Rousseau), 30
"Confessions of a Humorist" (Henry), 34, 100
confidentiality: of friendship, family and erotic relations, 79; housing style and, 27
conformism, societal ambivalence around, 151
Cosmides, Leda, 66–67, 70
Cosmopolitan, 54
The Counterlife (Roth), 9, 71, 72–73, 75, 83, 88
The Countess of Montgomery's Urania (Wroth), 23
Couser, G. Thomas: *Vulnerable Subjects*, 12n10, 147
creative writing programs, 34, 41n16, 70
creativity: collaborative, 125; current understandings of, 21; demystification of, 67; infidelity as intrinsic to, 152; and intimacy, 133; privileging of, 80
Creighton, Joanne, 104
criticism. *See* literary criticism
Curll, Edmund, 28

Dante Alighieri, 22–23; *Commedia*, 22; self-representation of, 23
Danziger, Marie A., 75, 75n5, 103–4
Davis, Gwen: *Touching*, 134n5
The Dead Seagull (Barker), 57

death: of the author, 61; figurative, 86; of intimates, 135; language of, 89
"The Death of a Lion" (James), 33
Deception (Roth), 73, 82, 103, 109, 112, 120, 130–31, 140–41
Deconstructing Harry, 145
deconstruction, 78
decorum, 26; betrayals of, 79; erosion of, 32; ethics of, 86; flouting of, 42; norms of, 3, 30
defamation, 37, 79, 122; of dead, 55, 135; law, 24–25, 147
Defoe, Daniel: *Robinson Crusoe*, 28
de la Durantaye, Leland, 74
democratization, of literature, 34
Denny, Edward Lord, 23
Derrida, Jacques, 112
DeSalvo, Louise, 110; *Conceived with Malice*, 12
desire, 2, 84; authorial body as site of, 68; infidelity, fiction and, 3–5; persistence of polymorphous, 110; as psychical response to intimate relationships, 85; role and character of, 4; sexual, 39; unconscious, 39. *See also* biographical desire
dialogism, 102; vs. appropriation, 103
Dickens, Charles, 31–32, 35, 46, 141; *Bleak House*, 32, 118, 136–37
disguised self-portraits, 11
divorce, 42, 43
docudrama, 10
documentary fiction, 9, 10
Dollimore, Jonathan, 118, 141–42
The Dolphin (Lowell), 43
doppelgängers, 16, 61, 87, 134, 139. *See also* doubles
doubles, uncanny, 86–89, 99, 121
Doubrovsky, Serge: *Fils*, 45; *Le livre brisé*, 84n1
Drabble, Margaret, 92, 104; *A Summer Bird-Cage*, 104
Durrell, Lawrence, 40n15, 53–54; *The Black Book*, 39, 54; *The House of Incest*, 54
dyadic relations, abandonment of, 143

Eakin, Paul John, 10; *The Ethics of Life Writing*, 12n10; *Fictions in Autobiography*, 5n2
eavesdropping devices, 41
Edinburgh Festival, 57
editors, diminished role of, 51
education, universal elementary, 31
Eliot, T. S., 35; injunction of against biographical reading, 37; poetics of impersonality, 36–37; "Tradition and the Individual Talent," 36
Elizabethan poets, 23–24
Elizabeth Costello (Coetzee), 7
embodied author: as a back-formation, 62; as lost love object, 62; replacement of with ontologically ambiguous one, 72; vs. figure of, 61–62
empiricism, 26, 70; vs. fantasy, 21
empiricist discourse, privileging of, 11
epistolary novel, 28
Epstein, Joseph, 77
erotics: of autobiographical fiction, 4; of fiction, 16, 18, 46, 48, 143
"Errand" (Carver), 7–8
Esquire, 131
ethical adultery, 119
ethical functions of literature, 140
ethics, 2, 41; and aesthetics, 118; of autobiographical fiction, 4, 13–14, 21, 34, 44, 99, 100, 110, 120, 146–48, 151; of autobiography, 12; of biography, 12; built upon specificity, improvisation, and doubt, 120; cultural level of, 151–52; of fiction, 46, 85–86, 100, 119–20, 129, 133, 146; of hermeneutics, 14; impersonal, 133; of life writing, 12n10; literature as immune from, 37; literary, 13–14, 43; of nonfiction, 129; as a nonstarter, 118; normative code of, 12; of privacy, intimacy, and decorum, 86; rebellious authorial, 112, 120; of responsible indiscretion, 120, 149; treacherous, 11–19, 148; of uncertainty, 145–49; zero-sum model of, 119

Euphormionis Lusinini Satyricon (Barclay), 24
Evening Standard, 54
exclusivity, demands for, 79
Exit Ghost (Roth), 76
exposés, 31, 121
exposure: culture of, 32; drive toward vs. valorization of reticence, 30

fabrication: blending of with actual events, 110; boundary between fact and, 17, 66, 80; libelous nature of, 88
Facebook, 45
fact: boundary between fabrication and, 17, 66, 80; flirtatious relationship between fiction and, 150; and imagination, 21, 22; vs. falsity, 26; vs. fantasy, 10–11, 16–17, 58; vs. fiction, 22; vs. invention, 69
The Facts (Roth), 47, 57, 73, 104, 133
The Faerie Queene (Spenser), 23
family life: celebration of, 32; and desires and frustrations of childhood, 85; early, Freud and, 39; and fantasy, 89–94
fantasy: constitutive role of, 80; family and, 89–94; and fiction, 12, 76, 128–29; inevitable impositions of, 85; role of in everyday, 148; role of in psychic life, 110; societal ambivalence around, 151; subordination of, 75; vs. empiricism, 21; vs. fact, 10–11, 16–17, 58
fatalism, 90–91, 99
Faulkner, William, 133
Fear of Flying (Jong), 40, 44–45, 55, 96
Felber, Lynette, 72n4, 91n3
femininity, alignment of contemporary morality with, 113
fiction: and adultery, 110; aesthetics of, 48; antiphonal relationship with nonfiction, 129; as attempt to bridge chasm between authors and loved ones, 85; and authenticity of authors' unique experiences, 81; and auto-

rial detachment, 95; autobiographical dimensions of, 21; betrayal of, 83–116, 106–7, 113; as based on authors' lives, 50; biographical detection as crucial plot of, 24; biographical readings of as form of play, 50; border between autobiography and, 16, 29, 63, 71, 74; calling to account, 128; as caricaturing and misrepresenting, 125; as catalyst for change, 99; as causing offense, 2, 10, 12, 17, 82, 87, 103, 114–15, 118–19, 128, 137, 151; characters trapped by, 97; combination of disguise and confession, 133; confessional qualities of, 142; counterfactual license of, 71–72; as cultural dream-space, 151; definition of, 5–7; and desire, 3–5; as detachment, 97; dialectical relationship with nonfiction, 129, 142; dramatic license of, 87; educative role of in accepting uncertainty, 70; erotics of, 18, 46, 48, 143; and ethical failure, 150; ethics of, 46, 85–86, 100, 119–20, 129, 133, 146; evolution of conventions of, 11; expanding readership for, 24; and exploration of identity, 71; as facilitating face-to-face encounters, 140; failure of to provide referential certainty, 64; and fantasy, 12, 76, 128–29; flirtatious nature of, 4, 150; as gaining cultural capital through transgression, 81; "great," giving offense to intimates, 118–19; hypothetical elements of, 76; and illusion of authorial detachment, 5; immoral and amoral motivations behind, 118; impingements of on future, 89; inclusion of personal history in, 48; as independent of authors, 49; and infidelity, 3–5; inherently scandalous nature of, 15; injurious nature of, 18, 85, 86, 119, 147; as instrument for improving intimate relationships, 142; introduction of word, 20; job of to ask questions, 151; and juridical standards of verification, 129; labeling book as, 133; lack of commitment to referentiality, 86; as libelous in its fabrications, 88; license of to be nonreferential, 88; mapping and mastery of, 67; marketing of, 48; as mediator between author and audience, 4; mortification and, 86–89, 120; mortifyingly uncanny quality of, 141; multiple transgressions of, 14; narrow use of term, 6; and nonreferentiality, 24–25; as Pandarus mediating between separated lovers, 48; and personal conflicts in authors' lives, 101; phantasmagoria of, 139; poetics of vital connection with nonfiction, 128; portraits in, 86; as potentially metafictional, 63n1; preoccupation with factual basis of, 73; private life of, 26–31; and private sphere, 121; production and reception of, 21; and production of uncanny sense of exposure, 117; public intimations of, 4; as reader's friend, 48; and realism, 26; and reality, 68; referential character of, 8, 17, 47–51, 58, 88, 99, 120, 126, 133–34, 141–42, 144; relationship between life and, 2, 21; relationship of to reality, 4, 15; and reproduction, 68; and riddles, 24; scandalous nature of, 45–46, 55, 64; self-referentiality of, 8; self-reflexivity about, 85; self-revelatory nature of, 44; semantics of, 46; and sexuality, 39, 68; and social discourse, 126; as subjunctive space of experimentation and performance, 110; as sublimation of authors' unconscious desires, 39; as threat to personal relations, 32; transformative effect of, 2, 115; transgressive, 78; as a transgressive form, 33, 105, 119, 137; transgressively personal, 84; as truer than autobiography, 39; unique social role of, 70; as vehicle for redeeming the past, 152; as

veiled autobiography, 76; verisimilitude and incompleteness of, 68; vs. fact, 22; vs. history, 26–27; vs. nonfiction, 6, 8, 10, 14, 50, 70, 76, 121, 129, 133, 149; writing of as engaging with otherness, 95. *See also* autobiographical fiction
fictional, use of term, 6
fictional alter ego, 60, 75, 82, 87, 99, 121
fictional betrayal: complaints about, 113; dramatization of, 106; social effects of, 107
fictional pact, 8n6
fictional self-representation, 17
fictional selves, Roth's, 70–76
fictional stance, 8
fictional world: and analogue in author's life, 69; as radically incomplete, 68–69
fictive, use of term, 6
Fielding, Henry, 29
"The Figure in the Carpet" (James), 33n10
film, 10
Fils (Doubrovsky), 45
Findley, Timothy: *The Telling of Lies*, 135
Fitzgerald, F. Scott, 38, 133; *The Beautiful and Damned*, 38
Fitzgerald, Zelda, 38–39, 46, 133; *Save Me the Waltz*, 38
"Five Points" (Munro), 113
formalism, 80
Foucault, Michel, 35, 50, 51, 61, 75
free indirect discourse, 102
free speech, 34, 78, 79, 106; societal ambivalence around, 151; vs. libel, 21
Freud, Sigmund, 38–39, 42–43, 87, 146, 148–49
Frey, James: *A Million Little Pieces*, 6

Galignani's Messenger, 31
Gallagher, Catherine, 25
The Game (Byatt), 17, 84–85, 95–99, 100, 101–5, 119, 137, 140, 150; alienation in, 94, 97; family and fantasy in, 89–94; fatalism in, 90–91; idyllic imaginative play of childhood vs. betrayals of adult individuation in, 92; interpersonal motivations in, 95; interrelationality in, 93–94, 96; as metafiction, 85
game shows, 42
Gaut, Berys, 118n1
gender relations, dynamics of patriarchal, 113, 143
Genette, Gérard, 6, 8n6, 51, 52, 134
The Ghost Writer (Roth), 130
Gildon, Charles, 28
Girard, René, 62
The Girl with the Dragon Tattoo (Larsson), 6
Glass, Loren, 41, 77
Glenarvon (Lamb), 31
Goffman, Erving, 71
The Golden Notebook (Lessing), 72n4, 100, 150
Gordimer, Nadine, 77, 96, 141
gossip columns, 31
Grant, Linda, 89
Greece, classical, 21, 22; drama in, 22; fact vs. fiction in, 22
The Guardian, 121
Gudmundsdottir, Gunnthorunn: *Borderlines*, 5n2
Gurko, Leo, 58
Gurstein, Rochelle, 10n7, 144

Habermas, Jürgen, 27
Hall, Donald, 43
Hall, Radclyffe, 72n4
Hamilton, Ian, 28
Hardwick, Elizabeth, 43
Harold's End (LeRoy), 81
Harpham, Geoffrey Galt, 139–40
Harvard Law Review, 32
Haynes v. Alfred Knopf (1993), 122
H.D. [Hilda Doolittle]: *Bid Me to Live*, 39
The Heart Is Deceitful Above All Things (LeRoy), 81

Hemingway, Ernest, 48; resistance of to biographical criticism, 77
Henry, O.: "Confessions of a Humorist," 34, 100
Herder, Johann Gottfried, 29–30
hermeneutics, 8, 50, 61; biographical, 36–37, 100, 102; conventional order, 17; endless project of, 70; ethics of, 14; noncommittal, 76; of suspicion, 39, 48, 55, 76; transgressive, 122; verificationist, 69
heterotopia, 50, 75
Hibernia, 54
historical fiction, 9
history, fiction vs., 26–27
Hite, Molly, 80
Hollywood, 15, 35, 41, 44, 81
"Home" (Lowell), 83
"Home" (Munro), 128, 136, 150
Homer, epics of, 22
homicide, 86, 87
Honneth, Axel, 135
The House of Incest (Durrell), 54
houses: preeminent function of, 117; style of and connection to intimacy, 27
Hull, James, 78
human-interest stories, 31
Hunt, Leigh, 32, 118, 136, 141
Hutcheon, Linda, 63n1, 75n5, 100n6, 102n7
Huxley, Aldous: *Those Barren Leaves*, 37

iconoclasm, societal ambivalence around, 151
ideas, individual ownership of, 11
identity: authentic, 58; coming to terms with, 70; communal, 10; fiction as means of exploring, 71; fragmentation of over unity, 75, 128; Freudian narrative of, 43; gender, 113; independent, 123; literary transformation of, 72; multiplicity and performative aspects of, 148; personal, 49, 108, 128; plural nature of, 109; problematization of, 151; public performance of, 21, 29, 71, 81; public vs. private, 81; rebellious recreations of, 110; relationally constituted, 92; social constitution of, 91; static, 17, 86
imagination, fact and, 21, 22
I Married a Communist (Roth), 114–15, 118, 131–32
immorality, great literature as product of, 118
immortality, artistic, 133
impersonality, poetics of, 36–37
improvisations, 126
infidelity, 2, 111, 113, 124; fiction, desire and, 3–5; of fiction, 17; interpersonal, 86; pleasures of, 118, 152; sexual, 84, 110, 113n9
injuriousness, 18, 58, 85, 86, 94, 113, 119, 140, 147
injury: embarrassment and shame as, 33; intimates and, 12; and remaining quiet, 121; understanding, 85; vulnerability and, 117
inner life, concealment of vs. public performance of identity, 21
In Search of Lost Time (Proust), 39, 83, 135
intentional fallacy, 36
Internet, 51; hacking, 45
interpersonal ethics, 118, 133
interrelationality, 93–94, 96, 99
interviews, 51
intimacy, 2, 11, 12, 84, 98, 115, 132; with absent author, 60–66; ambivalence of, 43; attractiveness of, 108–9; with author, 43, 64–65, 69, 101, 132, 143; authorial, 38, 45–46, 144; autobiographical fiction as challenge to, 85, 109; autonomy and, 91; and betrayal, 17, 48, 79, 100; collaborative, 127; and confessional culture, 78; contemporary, 78–79; creativity and, 133; definition of, 10n7; and demand for silence, 110; demands, of, 118; erotic, 79; ethical, 147; ethics of,

86; and exclusivity, 4, 10; expected of authors, 30; and family, 43, 79; fiction as fostering, 140; and flirtation, 48; of friendships, 79; housing style and 27, 117; and indecency, 117; and individuation, 94; interpersonal, 106–8, 119, 140; mediated, 48; metafiction and, 101; monogamous sexual relations as paradigmatic of, 84; narrative, 141, 152; norms of, 78, 106–8, 113, 114, 120, 133, 145, 151; as not valuable, 86; overvaluing of, 111; of personal relations of author, 81; philosophical debates about, 80; and privileged stories of personal identity, 108; privileging of, 17, 79, 108–10; professional obligations trumping demands of, 117–18; public, 143; and public reticence, 107; with readers, 16, 101; rebellion against, 118; and reneging on tacit contract, 108–9; reshaping of, 137–45; self-reflexivity about, 85; and sense of loss, 48; spousal, 27; "tell-all" memoir and, 3; unclear norms around, 78; unrealistic demands of, 110; and vulnerability, 10
"Intimacy" (Carver), 88, 97–98, 150–51; appropriative character of writing, 98
Intimacy (Kureishi), 2, 8, 106–7, 115
intimate correspondence, dissemination of, 28
intimate obligations vs. personal advancement, 21
intimates: authors', 46, 58, 76–77, 81, 82, 83, 85, 87–89, 94, 96–99, 103, 114–15, 117–49, 150–53; biographical interpretation by, 142; collaborative actions by authors and, 119–20, 137–45; and commentary and promotion, 121; complaints of, 88, 121; explanations of authors to, 141–42; fictionalization of, 100; as implicated in and alienated from fiction, 96; litigation as response, 121–22; as offended by fiction, 17, 121–23, 135; options to correct available to, 18; paralysis of, 88; permission of requested by authors, 135–36, 138; poetic confession to, 42; protection of by authors, 119–20, 136; sense of future, 88; silence vs. protest as response, 121; therapeutic distance from authors, 148; vs. nonintimates, 10; writing back as response, 122–23, 128, 129–33
intratextuality, 6
invention: autobiography and, 45; referentiality and, 104; vs. fact, 69
inviolate personality, 32, 36

Jacobus, Mary, 58
James, Henry, 33, 52; "The Aspern Papers," 33; "The Death of a Lion," 33; "The Figure in the Carpet," 33n10; "The Lesson of the Master," 33n10; "The Middle Years," 33n10; "The Private Life," 33n10, 61; "The Real Right Thing," 33; "Sir Dominick Ferrand," 33n10
James VI, King of Scotland, 23
Jarrell, Randall: *Pictures from an Institution*, 100
jealousy, 143
Johnson, Barbara, 138
Johnson, Samuel, 26; "Life of Thomson," 29
Jones, Thomas, 55
Jong, Erica, 78, 79, 111, 135; *Fear of Flying*, 40, 44–45, 55, 96
jouissance, 4
Jourde, Pierre: *Pays Perdu*, 9
journalism, 41, 151; cultural, 76; hypocrisy of, 76
journalist–novelist relationship. *See* novelist–journalist relationship
Joyce, James, 37; *Ulysses*, 37
Julie, or The New Héloïse (Rousseau), 30
juridical discourse, privileging of, 11

Kafka, Franz, 145
Kelly, Kathleen Coyne, 104
Kennedy, A. L., 52
Kingston, Maxine Hong: *The Woman Warrior,* 6n5
Kipnis, Laura, 110, 113, 114, 144
Kleinschmidt, Hans: "The Angry Act," 131n2
Kureishi, Hanif, 13, 17, 86, 100, 106–12, 113, 115, 132, 135, 149; *The Buddha of Suburbia,* 84, 106; *Intimacy,* 2, 8, 106–7, 115; "Loose Tongues and Liberty," 107; *Midnight All Day,* 2; *Sammy and Rosie Get Laid,* 106; "That Was Then," 2, 3–4, 13, 84

Lacan, Jacques, 92
Lamarque, Peter, 8–9
Lamb, Lady Caroline: *Glenarvon,* 31
Lamott, Anne: *Bird by Bird,* 111
Larsson, Stieg: *The Girl with the Dragon Tattoo,* 6
Lasch, Christopher, 77–78, 80
Latham, Sean, 37–38
Laurence, Margaret: *A Bird in the House,* 95
Lawrence, D. H., 13
Leaving a Doll's House (Bloom), 18, 103, 130–31
LeBel, Paul A., 132
Lejeune, Philippe, 6, 6n5, 7, 8n6, 21, 54, 61
Lemon, Lee T., 72, 101
LeRoy, J. T., 81; *Harold's End,* 81; *The Heart Is Deceitful Above All Things,* 81; *Sarah,* 81
Lessing, Doris, 91; *The Golden Notebook,* 72n4, 100, 150
"The Lesson of the Master" (James), 33n10
Levenson, Michael, 32
Levinas, Emmanuel, 70–71, 123, 140
Lewis, Wyndham: *The Apes of God,* 37

libel, 13, 24–25, 46, 55, 78, 88, 89, 134n5; laws of, 25; vs. free speech, 21
library networks, growth of, 31
lies, 81, 102, 110, 125, 126
"Life of Thomson" (Johnson), 29
Life Stories (Lowell), 42
life writing: ethics of, 12n10; metafiction about, 100
Linerman, Stephen, 78
literacy rates, 31
literary canons, expansion of, 80
literary criticism, 22, 36, 42, 51, 146
literary culture, 34; changes in, 85; criticism of for biographical desire, 77; preoccupation of with de-fictionalization, 52; promotion of authors in, 40; shift in, 24, 46, 49, 85; simplistic notions of otherness in, 81; and yoking of authors to texts, 51
literary ethics, 13–14, 43, 151
literary originality, valuing of, 28
literary tourism, 31, 81
litigation, 121–22
Lives of Girls and Women (Munro), 128
Lives of Mothers and Daughters (S. Munro), 122–23
"Loose Tongues and Liberty" (Kureishi), 107
Lorde, Audre: *Zami,* 6n5
Lowell, Robert: *The Dolphin,* 43; "Home," 83; *Life Stories,* 42
loyalty: demands for, 79; housing style and, 27; interpersonal, and public candor, 133
Lucas, Victoria. *See* Plath, Sylvia
lyric poetry, 10

Mailer, Norman: *Advertisements for Myself,* 40–41; confession of ambition, 40
Malcolm, Janet: *The Silent Woman,* 12n10
Manley, Delarivier, 28; *The Adventures of Rivella,* 25–26; *The New Atalantis,* 25

Manners, George, 24
marginalized voices, expansion of canons to include, 80
Marías, Javier, 67; *All Souls*, 10, 88–89
marketing, of fiction, 48. *See also* promotion
marriage, 27; oppressiveness of, 86; terms of, 43
Mary, Queen of Scots, 23
Massie, Allan, 57
mass media: authorial commentary in, 4; authors as *poètes maudits* in, 151; and authors' private lives, 38, 40; and biographical desire, 74, 77–78, 134; biographical material in, 32; boundary between fact and fabrication in, 17; commentary in, 49; and confessional industry, 41, 53–54, 101, 105; growth of and relation to fiction, 21; position of literature in constellation of, 105; and scandal, 121, 132; Smart and, 48; thriving in environment of, 58
"Material" (Munro), 18, 119, 122–28, 137, 143; alienation in, 125; collaborative creativity in, 125; infidelity in, 125, 127; intimacy in, 125–27; narrative unreliability in, 127–28; paratexts in, 125–27
Maugham, Somerset, 147; *Cakes and Ale*, 37
Maupassant, Guy de, 117
McCormick, Peter, 6n3
McEwan, Ian: *Atonement*, 20
McGurl, Mark, 41n16
McNamara, Lawrence, 147
McRobbie, Angela, 114
media technology, innovations in, 31
medieval period, 22–23, 26
memoir, 5, 7; tell-all, 3
"Meneseteung" (Munro), 128
mental illness, 42
meta-ethical approach, 14
metafiction, 13, 15–17, 63n1, 74, 84, 85, 100–106, 120, 147, 150, 152–53; authorial control in, 102; about autobiographical fiction, 101; audience-oriented quality of, 101; as authorial mea culpa, 103; as author's response to reader's desire, 101; and biographical reading, 104; didactic nature of, 102; double mortification of, 103; about ethics of autobiographical writing, 103, 151; and exploitation of readers' desire, 101; and intimacy, 101; about life-writing issues, 100; as mode of writing ethically, 85; and paratext, 100; proliferation of, 100, 105; and reductiveness of biographical hermeneutics, 102; as self-scrutinizing, 85; as symptom of confessional culture, 85
Middlebrook, Diane Wood, 41, 42n18
"The Middle Years" (James), 33n10
Midnight All Day (Kureishi), 2
Miller, Henry, 40n15, 45, 53–54, 74, 135; *Tropic of Cancer*, 39–41
Millet, Catherine: *The Sexual Life of Catherine M.*, 45
A Million Little Pieces (Frey), 6
Mills, Claudia: "Appropriating Others' Stories," 11n9, 118, 146, 148
Mistry, Rohinton: "Swimming Lessons," 139
modernism, 35–41
Mona Lisa, 11
monogamy: failure of to accommodate role of fantasy, 110; insurrection against, 114; narrative, 4, 17, 109, 127, 141, 152
morality, conventional, 113–14
Moran, Joe, 31, 51, 52
Morrison, Jago, 21
mortification, 86–89, 103, 120, 135, 139, 141
Mukherjee, Bharati: *The Tiger's Daughter*, 83
Munro, Alice, 120–29, 142, 147; "Five Points," 113; "Home," 128, 136, 150; *Lives of Girls and Women*, 128; "Material," 18, 119, 122–28, 137,

143; "Meneseteung," 128; *Something I've Been Meaning to Tell You,* 123, 136; "What Is Real," 1; "Who Do You Think You Are?" 128
Munro, Sheila, 122–23; *Lives of Mothers and Daughters,* 122–23
My Life as a Man (Roth), 70–71, 72, 103–4, 130, 131n2

narcissism, culture of, 77
narrative control, appropriation of, 88
narrative intimacy, 141, 152
narrative monogamy, 4, 127, 141, 152; repudiation of, 17; resistance to, 109
narratives: as unethical failure, 128; of identity, 43; of individual difference and transformation, 27; individual ownership of, 11; of self, 78; of social discourse, 126
narrative unreliability, 127–28
narrativization: of experience, 96–97; as foundational to adultery, 110
native informants, 9–10
naturalism, 32
Nelson, Deborah, 121
Nelson, William, 26
Nettels, Elsa, 33n9
neurocognitive systems, 66–67, 69–70
The New Atalantis (Manley), 25
New Criticism, 35–36, 52, 56, 61, 78
New Journalism, 31
newspapers, illustrated, 31
New York Times, 76
New York Tribune, 38
Nin, Anaïs, 53–54, 72n4, 135
nonfiction, 5, 21, 45, 56, 102, 106, 123, 132; antiphonal and dialectical relationship with fiction, 129, 142; freeing from standards of, 95; poetics of vital connection with fiction, 128; sex and, 39; vs. fiction, 6, 8, 10, 14, 50, 70, 76, 121, 129, 133, 149; vs. *romans à clef,* 24
nonreferentiality, 24–25

novel: definition of, 27; and "ordinary people," 27; private life of, 26–31; vs. history, 27. *See also* fiction
novelist–journalist relationship, 56–57; symbiotic nature of, 56

Oedipus Rex (Sophocles), 22
Old School (Wolff), 47–48
Olsen, Stein Haugom, 8–9
Operation Shylock (Roth), 6, 73–74, 112, 130
otherness, 80–81, 95

painting, 10
paparazzi, 31
paratexts, 6–7, 16, 29, 44, 48–49, 54–55, 57, 69, 82, 125–27, 137, 146; autofiction as, 45–46; and biographical desire, 50–52; and control, 60; and fictive improvisations, 58; as intrinsic to fiction, 7; literary text as instrument of, 51; in mass media, 16; as mediated intimacy, 48; media through which disseminated, 46; metafiction as, 100; as performances, 55; as prequels and sequels, 69; proliferation of, 16; and *romans à clef,* 24; role of, 7, 16, 151; and shaping of texts' meaning, 51; as site for authorial reclaiming of authentic identity, 58; as sites of phantasmatic interpersonal relations, 48; as sort of fiction, 55
paratextual commentary, 46, 51, 74, 132
paratextual confession, 46, 106
paratextual performance, 46, 55, 58, 60, 74, 151
paratextual production, 11, 17, 31, 48–49, 82, 100
patriarchal gender relations, 113, 143
Paull, H. M.: *Literary Ethics,* 13
Pays Perdu (Jourde), 9
Peltz, Dave, 129
Peperzak, Adriaan, 140–41

Perec, Georges: *W, or the Memory of Childhood*, 6n5
A Perfectly Good Family (Shriver), 134
performance vs. authenticity, 75
Perry, Ruth, 145
personal advancement vs. intimate obligations, 21
personal boundaries, 84
personal identity, Roth and, 49–50
personal reputation, 35; overvaluation of, 12
Petruso, Thomas F., 6n4
phantasmatic, 6n5, 68; importance of, 76; paratexts and, 48; relationship between author and audience, 4
phantasmatic pact, 54, 63
Phillips, Adam, 108–9, 139, 147–48
photography, 10, 31; sepulchral character of, 86
Pictures from an Institution (Jarrell), 100
plagiarism, 13
Plath, Sylvia, 42; *The Bell Jar*, 7, 134
play: autobiographical fiction as site of, 151; biographical readings of fiction as form of, 50, 66–70; collaboration and, 143; hermeneutic, 84; practical and autotelic functions of, 76; referential, 74; self as layering of playful performances, 73
poète maudit: authors as, 151; Rousseau as precursor of, 30–31
poetics: of antisocial impulses, 111; of autobiographical fiction, 103; of confusion and exhaustion, 16, 74; of dialogue and mutual participation, 138; ethical, 14; of impersonality, 36–37; of responsible indiscretion, 18–19; Romantic, 36; of vital connection between fiction and nonfiction, 128
poetry: betrayals of, 30; confessional, 41–46, 55, 100; lyric, 10; Romantic, 15; self-revelatory nature of, 44
poets, as quasiprophetic figures, 36
Pontalis, J.-B., 71n2

Pope, Alexander: letters of, 28
Portnoy's Complaint (Roth), 44–45, 55, 72, 74, 131n2
portraiture, mass-produced, 31
possessiveness, 17; and creation of art, 95
postmodernism, 75, 101
poststructuralism, 80
prefatory disclaimers, 55; legal uselessness of, 55; as sensationalizing device, 55
print culture: and dissemination of intimate correspondence, 28; growth of, 24; and production of celebrities, 33
privacy, 32–33, 41; anxiety about, 33; current understandings of, 21; ethics of, 86; fiction as ill suited to, 32; fostering of, 42; housing style and, 27; increases in for couples and families, 107; invasion of, 13, 35, 77, 78, 88, 94, 122, 135; legal basis for rights of, 32; and mental health, 107; need for, 108; overvaluations of, 12, 109–11; philosophical debates about, 80; possibilities for vs. violation of, 79; preoccupation with, 11, 110–11; protection of, 102; psychological dimensions of, 33; rights of, 34, 132; social norm of, 106–8, 114; societal ambivalence around, 151; unclear norms around, 78; violation of, 42
"The Private Life" (James), 33n10, 61
profiles, 51
promotion, of fiction, 40, 50, 56, 137, 151; by authors, 40; of authors, 40; authors' intimates and, 121. *See also* marketing
Proust, Marcel, 45, 74; *In Search of Lost Time*, 39, 83, 135
proximate other, 10
pseudonymously published texts, 134
psychoanalysis, 3, 11, 38–39, 42–44, 80, 90, 138, 142; and sexuality, 39
psychotherapists, ethical codes for, 146
public vs. private, 11, 27–28
Pynchon, Thomas, 52

Raab, Scott, 131
radio, 51
The Rambler, 26
reader(s): authors' flirtatious behavior with, 136, 143; biographically curious vs. attentive to aesthetic matters, 56; desire of for embodied author vs. author figure, 61–62; desire to know author through text, 47, 65, 77; expectations of, 21, 30, 62–64; exploitation of curiosity of, 80; intimacy of with authors, 65, 101; mediation of desire of by texts, 62; and metafiction, 101–2; and participation in print culture, 33; preoccupation of with factual basis of fiction, 73; relationship of with author, 4, 15–16, 48–49, 81; transgressive hermeneutic habits of, 122; transgressive nature of biographical desire of, 81
reading: intrinsically exploitative nature of, 4; intrinsically sexual nature of, 4; understanding of ways of, 139
realism, 26, 32
reality, fiction vs., 4, 15
reality television, 45
real-life stories, penchant for, 80
"The Real Right Thing" (James), 33
rebel authors, 112–16, 137–45; and intimates, 120; social objectives of, 119–20
rebel chic, 113
rebel privilege, 112–16
rebels vs. revolutionaries, 114
A Recipe for Bees (Anderson-Dargatz), 140
Redekop, Magdalene, 126
referentiality, 7, 8, 30, 37, 41, 47–51, 54, 58, 75, 88, 99, 114, 128, 130, 133–34, 141–42; ambiguous, 17, 23, 45, 56, 64, 67–70, 73, 84, 87, 120, 126, 139–40, 151; appearance of, 74; controversial flirting with, 24; denials of, 24, 100, 115; evaluation of material with regard to, 67; fiction's lack of commitment to, 86; and invention, 104; nonfictional standards of, 95; play-space of indeterminate, 76; potential, 55; skepticism and curiosity of, 32; transgressions of, 21; veiled, 144
repression, 17
reputation: personal, 12, 35, 79; societal ambivalence around, 151
responsible indiscretion: ethics of, 120, 148–49; poetics of, 18–19
reticence: combating, 111; culture of, 17–18, 86, 114; standards of public, 32, 107; valorization of, 30
reviews, 51
Rhiel, Mary, 12n10
Rhys, Jean: *After Leaving Mr. Mackenzie*, 37
Rich, Adrienne, 43
Richardson, Samuel, 27–29; *Clarissa*, 27–28; condemnation of autobiographical fiction by, 29; letters of, 28–29; "To Anne Donellan," 29
"The Right to Privacy" (Warren and Brandeis), 32
Robinson Crusoe (Defoe), 28
Roiphe, Anne, 112
Rollyson, Carol: *A Higher Form of Cannibalism?* 12n10
roman à clef, 7, 13, 24, 55; proliferation of, 24, 37
Romanticism, 29, 36
A Room of One's Own (Woolf), 20
Rorty, Richard, 146
Rosenthal, M. L., 42, 42n18
rotary press, 31
Roth, Philip, 1, 16, 17, 18, 40, 49–50, 58, 76, 77, 95, 100, 103, 110, 111, 112, 128, 131–32, 144, 147; *The Anatomy Lesson*, 72, 99; and anticipatory self-critique, 104; *The Counterlife*, 9, 71, 72–73, 75, 83, 88; *Deception*, 73, 82, 103, 109, 120, 130–31, 140–41;

Exit Ghost, 76; *The Facts*, 47, 57, 73, 104, 133; fictional selves of, 70–76; *The Ghost Writer*, 130; marriage and relationship with Bloom, 18, 103, 119, 130–31; *I Married a Communist*, 114–15, 118, 131–32; melding of factual and invented selves, 58; metafiction of, 103–4; *My Life as a Man*, 70–71, 72, 103–4, 130, 131n2; *Operation Shylock*, 6, 73–74, 112, 130; *Portnoy's Complaint*, 44–45, 55, 72, 74, 131n2; resistance of to voyeuristic readings of work, 77; *Zuckerman Unbound*, 72

Rousseau, Jean-Jacques, 30–31; *Confessions*, 30; *Julie, or The New Héloïse*, 30; as precursor of *poète maudit*, 30–31

Said, Edward, 96–97
Salinger, J. D., 52
Salmon, Richard, 31
Sammy and Rosie Get Laid (Kureishi), 106
Sarah (LeRoy), 81
Sarsby, Jacqueline: *Romantic Love and Society*, 27n8
Sartre, Jean-Paul, 95, 114
satire, 37
Saunders, Max, 37n12
Save Me the Waltz (Z. Fitzgerald), 38
scandal, 26, 35; appetite for, 11, 14, 18, 151; of autobiographical fiction, 78–79; biographical desire as taste for, 50; of confessional poetry, 41–46; cultural preoccupation with, 46, 131; currency of in popular imagination, 64; of fiction, 15, 45–46, 55, 64; intimate life vs., 32; literary, 23, 45; mass media and, 121, 132; perpetuation of, 45; potential of to challenge and change norms, 79; from transgressive fiction, 78–79; as way for books to garner headlines, 113–14; willingness to trade in, 28

Schickel, Richard, 105
Schoeman, Ferdinand David, 94
scientific revolution, 26
Scoffield, Tracey, 2, 8, 13, 106, 115
The Scotsman, 57
Scott, Sir Walter, 31
secrecy, overvaluation of, 109, 111
The Seductions of Biography (Rhiel and Suchoff), 12n10
self: immortality of, 87; as layering of playful performance, 73; narratives of, 78; as pre-eminently a character, 71; usurpers of, 87
self-abandonment, writing and, 145
self-advancement, embrace of unapologetic, 41
self-concealment, 111
self-consciousness, 153
self-contradiction, authorial, 136
self-discipline, 111
self-exposure, 35
self-fictionalizing authors, 53–54
self-referentiality, 8, 23, 30, 73
self-reflexivity, 85, 153
self-representation, 23; denigration of, 28
self-revelation, literary, 35, 44, 52–53; demand for, 78
selves: fictional, 70–76; multiple fragmented, 75; reduction of, 109
semantics, of fiction, 46
sensationalism, 55
sex/sexuality, 39, 68, 84, 92n5, 108, 110, 148; Freud and, 39; psychoanalysis and, 39; taboos around, 39; and transgression, 40
sexual explicitness, 44–45, 49, 72
sexual infidelity, 110, 113n9
The Sexual Life of Catherine M. (Millet), 45
sexual revolution, 43
Sexton, Anne, 42
Shakespeare, William, 52
shame: combating of, 111; culture of, 111
Shechner, Mark, 73, 104, 130–31
Shelley, Mary, 59

Shorter, Edward: *The Making of the Modern Family*, 27n8
Shostak, Deborah, 131n2
Shriver, Lionel: *A Perfectly Good Family*, 134
Shuger, Debora, 26n7
Sidney, Sir Philip: *Astrophil and Stella*, 23
"Sir Dominick Ferrand" (James), 33n10
Smart, Elizabeth, 132; as abandoned and ignored by literary culture, 60; *A Bonus*, 54; *By Grand Central Station I Sat Down and Wept*, 16, 48–49, 53–60, 62–66, 75, 86, 97; and autobiography, 58–59; and confessional culture, 50–60; desire for control over text's reception, 59; as embracing and challenging biographical readings, 54; and irreducibility of metaphorical reality, 69; and language, 64–66; as modern-day Tithonus, 59; re-emergence and repatriation of, 60; relationship of with Barker, 53–55, 57, 59, 62, 66, 97; relationship of with narrator, 64; return of to Canada, 59; romantic experiences of, 48
social norms, 33; role of literature in combating, 106–8; transgression of, 151
Socrates, 22
Something I've Been Meaning to Tell You (Munro), 123, 136
Sophocles: *Oedipus Rex*, 22
Spenser, Edmund: *The Faerie Queene*, 23
Spillane, Mickey, 40–41; self-promotion, 40
Staël, Madame de, 26–27
star system, Hollywood, 31, 35, 41
Steedman, Carolyn, 28
Stein, Gertrude, 35
Sterne, Laurence: *Tristram Shandy*, 29, 100
Stone, Lawrence: *The Family, Sex and Marriage in England*, 27n8
Stonehill, Brian, 101
Stott, Catherine, 54–55
succès de scandale, 31, 72

Suchoff, David, 12n10
A Summer Bird-Cage (Drabble), 104
Summers, Alison, 121
Sunflower (West), 39
surreptitious publication, 136
suspension of disbelief, 8
suspicion, hermeneutics of, 39, 55, 76
Sutton-Smith, Brian, 76
Suvorin, Alexei, 151n1
"Swimming Lessons" (Mistry), 139

talk shows, 42, 121
Taylor, Charles, 152
telegraph, 31
telephoto lenses, 41
television, 10, 42, 51; reality, 45; and spectacles of personal confrontation, 105
The Telling of Lies (Findley), 135
Tennyson, Alfred Lord, 31
"The Tent" (Atwood), 117
text: author of as construction of, 65; fictionality of, 8–9; and mediation of readers' desire, 62; paratexts and, 6–7, 51; primary role of author in production of, 51; production and reception of, 19; promotion of authors alongside, 40; referentiality of, 7, 18, 20, 45, 50, 114, 120, 143; truthfulness and inventions of, 14, 21
"That Was Then" (Kureishi), 2, 3–4, 13, 84
Theft (Carey), 121
third-party commentary, 44
Thornton, Sarah L., 114
Those Barren Leaves (Huxley), 37
Through a Glass Darkly (Bergman), 100
The Tiger's Daughter (Mukherjee), 83
"To Anne Donellan" (Richardson), 29
Todd, Richard, 92n4
Tooby, John, 66–67, 69–70
Toronto Star, 59
Touching (Davis), 134n5
"Tradition and the Individual Talent" (Eliot), 36

transgression: aesthetic, 110; artistic, celebration of, 113; autobiographical, 13, 79, 113; and biographical desire, 81; biographical reading as, 67; cachet of fiction as, 105, 137; creation of space for, 137; hermeneutic habits of readers, 122; multiple, of fiction, 14; potential ethical, 55; preoccupation with, 31; referential, 21; rhetoric of necessary, 114; short history of, 20–46; social, 18
trespass: adulterous, 137; authorial, 14; autobiographical fiction and, 152
Tristram Shandy (Sterne), 29, 100
Tropic of Cancer (Miller), 39–41
truth-claims, disparate, 67, 69–70

Ulysses (Joyce), 37
uncanny doubles, 86–89, 99
uncertainty, ethics of, 145–49
Updike, John, 40

vampirism, metaphor of, 87
verificationism, societal ambivalence around, 151
verisimilitude, 68, 128
Vogue (British), 35
Vonnegut, Kurt, 102
vulnerability, injury and, 117

W, or the Memory of Childhood (Perec), 6n5
Wachtel, Eleanor, 56–57, 58
Wakoski, Diane, 43
Warren, Dorothy, 135
Warren, Samuel D., 32–33, 36
Wasserstrom, Richard, 111, 144
Watergate, 45
Watkins, Susan, 21
Waugh, Patricia, 63n1

West, Rebecca, 72n4; *Sunflower*, 39
"What Is Real" (Munro), 1
"Who Do You Think You Are?" (Munro), 128
Wilde, Oscar, 37, 86
Williamson, Alan, 42, 42n18
Wimsatt, W. K., 36
Wolfe, Thomas, 58; *You Can't Go Home Again*, 68, 100
Wolfe, Tom: dandyism of, 58
Wolff, Tobias: *Old School*, 47–48
The Woman Warrior (Kingston), 6n5
women: and autobiography writing, 58; expansion of literary canons to include voices of, 80; license to write about their lives, 130; and shame in writing, 111
women's movement, 43
Wood, James, 147
Woolf, Virginia, 35, 39; *A Room of One's Own*, 20
Wordsworth, William, 30, 32
writing: as betrayal, 3, 128; intrinsically exploitative nature of, 4; intrinsically sexual nature of, 4; process of autobiographical, 100; and self-abandonment, 145
writing back, 122–23, 128, 129–33
Wroth, Lady Mary, 23–24, 35, 46; *The Countess of Montgomery's Urania*, 23

You Can't Go Home Again (Wolfe), 68, 100
Youth (Coetzee), 138
YouTube, 45

Zami (Lorde), 6n5
Zamorna, 90
Žižek, Slavoj, 143–44
Zuckerman Unbound (Roth), 72

www.ingramcontent.com/pod-product-compliance
Lightning Source LLC
Chambersburg PA
CBHW031628160426
43196CB00006B/319